MW01110002

THE BLOOD

GOD'S GRACE INTO RELATIONSHIP

PATRICIA MARAGH

Unless otherwise indicated, all Scripture quotations referenced in this book are from the *King James Version* 1611 Authorized Version.

Scripture quotations taken from the *Holy Bible, New Living Translation*, copyright © 1996, 2004, 2007, 2013 by Tyndale House Foundation. Used by permission of Tyndale House Publishers, Inc., Carol Stream, Illinois 60188. All rights reserved.

Scripture quotations marked (TLB) are taken from *The Living Bible* copyright © 1971. Used by permission of Tyndale House Publishers, Inc., Carol Stream, Illinois 60188. All rights reserved.

THE BLOOD
God's Grace Into Relationship
ISBN 10: 1541158393
ISBN 13: 978-1-5411-5839-9
Copyright © 2017 by Patricia Maragh

A & A Publishing
P. O. Box 2833
Broken Arrow, OK 74013

Cover and Text Design:
Bobby and Lisa Simpson
www.SimpsonProductions.net

No part of this book can be reproduced, distributed, or transmitted in any form or by any means, electronic or mechanical, without written permission from the publisher. Request for permission can be made to the publisher by writing to or emailing.

ACKNOWLEDGEMENTS

Thank God for the blood of Jesus in His grace. I truly thank Him for the power of the Holy Spirit to help us in our time of need, to teach us all things, and to help us out of our trials.

I thank my family, my husband Paul, for helping me to set aside time to accomplish this task, and to all my children: Kristen Maragh, who helped me especially in the area of technology, Raven Maragh-Lloyd who gave me literary and proofing help, and Jason's input of listening to me teaching him what I was learning and giving me his feedback.

I also would like to thank all the great men and women of God in the Kingdom who preceded me. There are too many to mention here but some I've quoted throughout the book. They have helped to confirm and give understanding, in so many ways, to all that God was saying and working in me on this journey of faith in His grace.

Jesus, by His grace and the power of His Spirit, has taken me through into His rest. By my continuous hearing and practice of His Word, He promised that He will keep me in His peace. He kept His promise.

I am also grateful to A & A Publishing and his staff for helping to navigate all aspects of correcting and publishing this book.

I also would like to especially thank Pastor Howard Hatcher for his kind and heartfelt words in the forward, and to all the wonderful people who will read this book. I hope that they will be challenged to step out with their faith in God and embrace a more loving relationship with Him through Jesus Christ His Son.

His Word is truth and the truth you know will set you free. His truth learned is good, but truth acted on in relationship with Jesus is power.

God bless you.

CONTENTS

FOREWORD

As Patricia Maragh writes in her book *The Blood, God's Grace into Relationship*, "Sin dethroned God from man's heart, he lost God's glory as his covering and was forced to hide from Him. With sin and spiritual death in their hearts they were separated from God, and could no longer know and fellowship with Him intimately and continually.

Spiritual death, or separation from God, as well as physical and eternal death, entered the entire human race. This separation created emptiness and a void in the heart and soul of man."

Here is a book that is academically sound and spiritually powerful enough to take the reader from A to Z in how you gain back that fellowship with God. This study of the blood of Jesus is a manual that every believer should read and understand. Truly, a treasure chest of jewels of revelation.

"Despite man's wayward ways and rejection of God, the heavenly Father made a plan to redeem mankind from the hands of Satan and death. God made this plan even before creation. Jesus was the only way to pay for sin, so that man can be forgiven and still be alive when they sin."

Hebrews 9:26 says, "...but now once in the end of the world hath he appeared to put away sin by the sacrifice of himself."

The death of Jesus Christ on the cross and His shed blood brought all mankind new life, with a new identity" (2 Corinthians 5:17).

This is not a book that you can just read through quickly.

Each chapter takes you a step higher to understanding that our personal, powerful, and loving relationship with God comes through the blood of Jesus.

When we have the revelation of the power in that blood to change us, we will have true fellowship with a living God.

Patricia asks an important question that every believer should know the answer to. Why so much blood?

To show what the blood of Jesus freely did for us. Her list with explanations, in just the beginning of the book, is priceless. It is a deep revelation of truth that the blood provides: Access, Glory Restored, Salvation, Jesus becoming our Lord, The Great Divider (between eternal life and death), A Cleansed Conscience, Jesus on the Cross is fulfilled prophecy, Made us Kings and Priests, Gave us Communion, Our New Covenant, Jesus Became our Mediator, Peace, Sanctifies Us and so much more!

This is a complete study, done in excellence and worthy of your time and respect. It has been a long time since I have seen such a prolific study of a Bible topic on the blood. A must read. Don't miss an opportunity to graduate into the Kingdom of God.

PASTOR HOWARD HATCHER
Executive Director
The Ministers Network
Senior Pastor
International Outreach
Ministry& Training Center
Iomnetwork.org

SEEKING GREATER TRUTHS

I was born and raised in Jamaica. As a young person growing up, I was not satisfied that my spiritual life was where it could be. I yearned for more. As a young Christian, I attended Full Gospel Churches where legalism (excessive adherence to law, rules and regulations rather than personal faith in Christ) permeates their structure and modes of operation. The result was a plethora of do's and don'ts rather than emphasizing New Creation truths and a relationship with God.

I knew there was more, and I desired more. I really wanted to grow spiritually. Later on I began to teach the adult Sunday school class and, as I did my preparation, my need for more understanding became more and more evident. I began crying out to God for more truths. The Father is always open to the yearning hearts of His Children. He is so faithful. He heard and answered my cry.

The Lord led me to migrate to the United States to attend Rhema Bible College in Broken Arrow, Oklahoma. It was there that I gained God's wisdom, received greater truths, and learned to walk in the Word of God and greater faith.

After Bible School, I was led to continue volunteering and working in the church. This was a great experience as I was applying the tenets of faith and continuing to learn to walk in greater faith.

I understood that I was on a new journey with the Lord, and I continued to seek Him and hunger for greater truths. In this process of pressing into God, I experienced and encountered the Archenemy of all truth: Satan, the father of lies. The spiritual reality of the forces of the two kingdoms became apparent as the paradox of pressing into God and seeking more and greater truths also exposes one to interface with the lies of the devil and the forces of the kingdom of darkness. Satan opposed me against the truth of God's Word I so greatly desired to grasp.

Satan's attacks against me became ferocious and a great darkness descended on me. I cried out to the Lord for deliverance, but His answer was *"My grace is sufficient for you."* I then continued seeking the Lord to help me to understand and respond in faith to what was happening to me.

This time His answer given to me in the Word was found in 1 Peter 1:6, 7:

> *"Wherein ye greatly rejoice, though now for a season, if need be, ye are in heaviness through manifold temptations: That the trial of your faith, being much precious than of gold that perisheth, though it be tried with fire might be found unto praise and honor and glory at the appearing of Jesus Christ."*

The Lord helped me to discover the source of my troubles. It was that the wonderful message of faith I received was laid upon the legalistic foundation in which I had been raised in before. The result was me trying hard not to sin and harder to walk by faith in my own strength in order to be good, right and pleasing to God. This law mentality (a mindset of self-will and self-effort depending on oneself, with do's and don'ts, being right or wrong) meant I had fallen from grace.

Galatians 5:4, *"Christ is become of no effect unto you, who-soever of you are justified by the law, ye are fallen from grace."*

The law is not of faith and Romans 14:23b says "… For *whatsoever is not of faith is sin."* Legalism is not of faith and therefore creates sin-consciousness, self-righteousness and condemnation.

To help me overcome, the Lord started me on a very difficult experience, yet it was one of the most rewarding in my Christian life! As He began to teach me about His grace, He gave me this revelation, "Faith is living out of a relationship with God your Father," a topic we will examine later on.

As I continued learning to place faith in God's grace, God pointed out to me that my foundation in the blood of Jesus and the sacrifice of His Son Christ Jesus was weak. That I did not fully understand all that the blood of Jesus freely did for me to place me in relationship with God. Thus began in my life the leading of the Holy Spirit back to the source of all spiritual life: the blood of Jesus, His sacrifice and His wonderful grace to me.

The work of the Holy Spirit in, with, and through me on this very difficult journey was instrumental, as I learned to cease from independence and "doing" to choosing greater humility and dependence on God. The Holy Spirit shined His light within, eliminating the darkness which caused Jesus to be formed in me. He is helping me daily to draw nearer to God in an even closer relationship.

Galatians 4:1, *"My little children, of whom I travail in birth again until Christ be formed in you."*

There began a significant change, from fear to love, from unbelief to faith, from law to grace, from weakness to strength, from natural knowledge to revelation knowledge, from pride to humility, from darkness to light, from my own will to God's will, and from lack of trust, to trust in God.

Over time, I learned to gain greater authority over the evil one, and ultimately, God gave me greater inner peace.

Isaiah 32:17, *"And the work of righteousness shall be peace; and the effect of righteousness quietness and assurance forever."*

When Christ is formed in you, one of God's greatest blessings, His peace, becomes your most precious gift because He is the Prince of Peace.

Isaiah 9:6," *For unto us a child is born, unto us a son is given: and the government shall be upon his shoulder: and his name shall be called Wonderful, Counsellor, The mighty God, The everlasting Father, The Prince of Peace.*"

Let us go back to the cross, back to the sacrifice, back to the blood and find out what God gave us in Jesus to provide for us in the life of Christ, His eternal life. Let us journey back to a believer's only source: Jesus.

For the full benefit of this book, you are encouraged to read the Word of God for yourself. Hear and hear again until faith arises in your heart to believe God through Jesus His Son and build a solid foundation for your Christian faith in relationship with Christ. Despise not repetition; the hold on the "Will" by the enemy with Legalism is often challenging to break free from. The enemy is persistent with his lies, so be persistent with the truth until you are completely free. Also, read the given supporting Scriptures to reinforce God's truth in the Word, as you continue to build your faith and belief in God. As you read on, my prayer for you is that you will gain greater truths for yourself as a child of God, and become established in Christ Jesus as you grow in a closer relationship with God, your heavenly Father

Amen.

CHAPTER 1

SHORT HISTORY
OF THE BLOOD

G enesis, the book of beginnings, tells us of creation and of
God's intention for mankind living on the earth.

*"And God called the dry land Earth; and the gathering together
of the water called he Seas: and God saw that it was good"*
(Genesis 1:10).

*"And God said, Let us make man in our image, after our
likeness: and let them have dominion over the fish of the sea,
and over the fowl of the air, and over the cattle, and over all
the earth, and over every creeping thing that creepeth upon the
earth. So God created man in his own image, in the image of
God created he him; male and female created he them. And
God blessed them, and God said unto them, Be fruitful, and
multiply, and replenish the earth, and subdue it: and have
dominion over the fish of the sea, and over the fowl of the
air, and over every living thing that moveth upon the earth"*
(Genesis 1:26-28).

Furthermore we know:

- God is Creator and Giver of all good things (Genesis 1:21).

- God commanded man to be fruitful and multiply (Genesis
  1:22).

- God intended for man to be blessed by having dominion and partaking of all His blessings (Genesis 1:28).

- For man to be full of the life of God (Genesis 2:7) and to guard the finished work of God (Genesis 2:15).

- For man to exercise his free "will," but required to obey God's commands.

"But of the tree of the knowledge of good and evil, thou shall not eat of it: for in the day that thou eatest thereof thou shall surely die" (Genesis 2:17).

Mankind, existing in Adam and Eve, failed in every way as they sought to be god for themselves, exercising their self-will over their own lives. By choosing to create their own destiny and being wise in their own eyes, they sinned, failed God, future generations, and themselves. Adam and Eve's disobedience to God's command, which was not to eat from the tree of good and evil, caused them to forgo the blessings of God. Instead, they invoked the curse and separation from God's presence (Genesis 3:1-20; Deuteronomy 28:1-68; Proverbs 3:7).

> *Mankind, existing in Adam and Eve, failed in every way as they sought to be god for themselves...*

After they had sinned, Adam and Eve died as God said they would. They did not die a physical death immediately because they lived to be approximately 930 years old. They died spiritually, and the immediate result was becoming separated from the life-giving source of God. Mankind after Adam, who was allotted 120 years (Genesis 6:3), has since had a shorter lifespan because of their disobedience.

"The days of our years are threescore years and ten; and if by reason of strength they be fourscore years, yet is their strength labor and sorrow; for it is soon cut off, and we fly away" (Psalm 90:10).

God saw His creation in hopelessness. We were destined for eternal damnation. Every person born was destined to go to Hell without any hope of salvation. God did not waste time, and He immediately prophesied a course of action to redeem and restore mankind into a renewed relationship and fellowship with Him.

Genesis 3:15, *"And I will put enmity between thee and the woman, and between thy seed and her seed; it shall bruise thy head, and thou shalt bruise his heel."*

Related scriptures: Isaiah 53:10-12; Jeremiah 31:33, 34; Jeremiah 33:15, 16.

HISTORY OF THE BLOOD IN THE MAKING

All human beings love good things and pleasure: both of which God created for them to enjoy and both of which can only be permanently found and sustained in a relationship with God (Psalm 16:11; 23:6). The devil has offered his counterfeit of this by convincing mankind that sin brings lasting pleasure. In his book *GRACE the power of change* Dr. James Richard said, "One of the greatest lies of the devil is that sin brings lasting pleasure."[1]

This is borne out by Solomon in Ecclesiastes 1:14, 17, *"I have seen all the works that are done under the sun: and, behold, all is vanity and vexation of spirit. And I gave my heart to know widom, and to know madness and folly: I perceived that this also is vexation of spirit."*

Unfortunately, many people have believed Satan's lie. Instead of viewing sin as hopelessly destructive, they view sin as just a list of commandments or rules from God, or rules that their parents or others in authority give to keep from them the good things and pleasure they desire in life.

They mistakenly view sin as all the fun and self-fulfilling pleasures of life. But, as all soon find out, sin is only Satan's bait. When they are caught in his bait, they realize that sin only brings pain, devastation and death.

Genesis 2:17, *"But of the tree of the knowledge of good and evil, thou shalt not eat of it: for in the day that thou eatest thereof thou shalt surely die."*

Romans 6:23, *"For the wages of sin is death…"*

James 1:14, 15, *"But every man is tempted, when he is drawn away of his own lust, and enticed. Then when lust hath conceived, it bringeth forth sin: and sin, when it is finished, bringeth forth death."*

Adam and Eve sinned and death followed the whole human race. God needed to rescue mankind from his self-chosen sentence of death.

> *They mistakenly view sin as all the fun and self-fulfilling pleasures of life.*

Leviticus 17:11, *"For the life of the flesh is in the blood: and I have given it to you upon the altar to make an atonement for your souls: for it is the blood that maketh an atonement for the soul."*

Life is in the blood and in order to bring life from death innocent blood had to be shed.

"…Except a corn of wheat fall into the ground and die, it abideth alone: but if it die, it bringeth forth much fruit" (John 12:24).

The first mention of the shedding of blood was the sacrifice of an animal for the covering of Adam's nakedness and exposure that his sin created. Adam and Eve tried to cover themselves with fig leaves, but that was inadequate; so God helped them out.

Genesis 3:21, *"Unto Adam also and to his wife did the Lord God make coats of skins, and clothed them."*

This bible verse was a foreshadowing of Jesus' future sacrifice on the Cross.

The second mention of blood as a sacrifice was in Genesis 4:1-7 where Abel killed an animal as a sacrifice unto God.

God gave His instructions as to how man could stay cleansed in His presence.

Leviticus 1:2, *"Speak unto the children of Israel, and say unto them, If any man of you bring an offering unto the Lord, ye shall bring your offering of the cattle, even of the herd, and of the flock."*

Cain and Abel both knew what the sacrifice unto God required. Abel heard and obeyed, bringing the firstlings of his flock and of the fat thereof (Genesis 4:4). Cain heard and disobeyed, choosing to give not a blood sacrifice but a bloodless sacrifice of the ground, the work of his own hands (Genesis 4:5). Innocent blood of an animal is the only sacrifice that could be offered in an approach into God's presence; Obedience to this demonstrates love, faith-righteousness and belief in God.

The Cain and Abel story is a revelation of man's approach to God. Will your approach be by faith-righteousness showing a love for God, believing and obeying Him as with Abel, or will it be self-righteousness of your own ways and means, as with Cain?

The Cain and Abel story is a revelation of man's approach to God.

RESULT:

Abel approached God in (1) Faith-righteousness (2) Humility. The effects were (a) Acceptance by God (b) Union with God (Genesis 4:10) and pleasure in God's presence.

Cain's approach was (1) Works, Self-righteousness (2) Pride. The effects were (a) Rejection from God (b) Anger/ hatred and banishment from the presence of the Lord (Genesis 4:11-16).

Hebrews 11:4 *"By faith Abel offered unto God a more excellent sacrifice than Cain, by which he obtained witness that he was righteous…"*

The act of shedding blood to cover sin continued under the Old Testament system of the law with the sacrifice of innocent animals.

Leviticus Chapter 17, in the Old Testament, gives the accounts of sacrifice by shedding the blood of animals. It was the shedding of the blood of innocent and spotless animals that served as an atonement or temporary covering for sin. The animal's blood was sprinkled on the mercy seat on the Ark of the Covenant to be received by God.

Leviticus 17:11, *"For the life of the flesh is in the blood: and I have given it to you upon the altar to make an atonement for your souls: for it is the blood that maketh an atonement for the soul."*

The blood of bulls and goats covered sins and brought temporary forgiveness for one year. The High Priests would then have to offer another sacrifice year after year, because there was still a remembrance of sin (Hebrews 10:3).

The innocent animal's death in place of the sinner was a shadow of the innocent and sinless Jesus and His substitutionary sacrifice on the cross. He would come to Earth to die to save all mankind from sin and separation from God.

Hebrews 10:4, *"For it is not possible that the blood of bulls and goats should take away sins."*

Animal's blood could not substitute for the spiritual death that was in the heart of sinful mankind. The sacrifice of animals and the shedding of their blood was only a temporary measure that God used to symbolize the forthcoming sacrifice of His Son Jesus on the cross for the forgiveness of mankind's sin and for his salvation.

Sin brought death into the hearts of mankind, and only the death of an innocent and sinless human life could bring eternal life back into man's heart.

Only the blood of Jesus Christ, the sinless Son of man, could cleanse all of mankind's sin (Mark 3:28; Acts 13:38, 39; Colossians 2:13).

No human being on Earth born to man could bring salvation. All humans were born with a sinful nature.

Psalm 51:5, *"Behold, I was shapen in iniquity; and in sin did my mother conceive me."*

Some persons read this verse and have become concerned that their babies or grandchildren who died may be with sin and go to Hell. They are in heaven, because God is gracious. All children have God's grace until they are old enough, having knowledge of good and evil, and can choose. It is at this time having knowledge of good and evil that they become responsible for their own sin (Deuteronomy1:39; Isaiah 7:14-16; Romans 4:15; 7:9).

Mature mankind has a sin nature that they are responsible for, and God's only solution to mankind's dilemma was Jesus the Son of God. He was the only one who was sinless and innocent and therefore had life in His blood. He alone qualified to do the honor of removing sin and restoring mankind back into fellowship and eternal life unto God.

Hebrews 9:12, *"Neither by the blood of goats and calves, but by his own blood he entered in once into the holy place, having obtained eternal redemption for us."*

The shed blood of Jesus was mankind's only remedy.

Hebrews 9:14, *"How much more shall the blood of Christ, who through the eternal Spirit offered Himself without spot to God, purge your conscience from dead works to serve the living God?"*

Ephesians 1:7, *"In whom we have redemption through his blood, the forgiveness of sins, according to the riches of his grace;"*

Eternal redemption or the loosing from sin can only be achieved through believing on what the shed blood of Jesus Christ accomplished for you on the cross. In response, we receive His righteousness, His love in forgiveness.

John 3:16, *"For God so loved the world that he gave his only begotten Son, that whosoever believeth in him should not perish, but have everlasting life."*

John 14:6, *"Jesus, saith unto him, I am the way the truth, and the life: no man cometh unto the Father, but by me."*

Romans 5:8, *"But God commendeth his love towards us, in that while we were yet sinners, Christ died for us."*

When a person believes on Jesus and confesses Him as Lord, he or she is saved from their sin and from eternal damnation in Hell (Romans 10:9, 10; Revelation 21:8). Confession of Jesus as your personal Lord will now make you a born-again believer saved in your spirit or a Christian. As a believer, you are continuously being saved in your daily life from the plans of the devil to harm you, from natural calamities, sickness, disease, and even death; as long as you continue to have faith in God, His Word, and His Spirit, you will be saved into eternity.

CHAPTER 2

WHY THE SHEDDING OF CHRIST'S BLOOD?

Hebrews 9:12, *"Neither by the blood of goats and calves, but by his own blood he entered in once into the holy place, having obtained eternal redemption for us."*

Some people reading the Bible from the very beginning feel quite distraught that it has recorded so much killing and so much bloodshed. However, it was all for a very good purpose. God made creation good and intended mankind to have a life infinitely covered with His glory and His goodness. God intended this life to be filled with abundant peace and a satisfying love relationship with Him as their heavenly Father. As a branch cannot be sustained without the vine, so man was created in the image of God and was made to be connected to the life of God and to be sustained by Him. God's plan and desire for man was eternal life. God wanted mankind to have a life of His goodness, lived in union, oneness, and fellowship with Him, as their source.

John 15:7, *"If ye abide in me, and my words abide in you, ye shall ask what ye will, and it shall be done unto you."*

Sin dethroned God from man's heart, he lost God's glory as his covering and was forced to hide from Him.

Genesis 3:8, 9, *"And they heard the voice of the Lord God walking in the garden in the cool of the day: and Adam and his wife hid themselves from the presence of the Lord God amongst the trees of the garden. And the Lord God called unto Adam, and said unto him, "Where art thou?"*

Adam was alone in the midst of this beautiful garden and God gave him two instructions (1) To tend the garden and (2) Not to eat of the tree of good and evil. God warned Adam that he would die spiritually if he disobeyed. Later, God gave him a wife. They both disobeyed, and spiritual and physical death set in. They became separated from God, with Satan now as their master (Genesis 2:15-17; 3:5-7).

With sin and spiritual death in their hearts, mankind was separated from God and could no longer experience and fellowship with Him intimately and continuously as before. Spiritual death, or separation from God as well as physical and eternal death, entered the entire human race. Every person born after Adam was born in sin with spiritual death in their hearts (Psalm 51:5).

> **Every person born after Adam was born in sin with spiritual death in their hearts.**

Job 5:7, *"Yet man is born unto trouble, as the sparks fly upward."*

Cain proved this when he killed his brother Abel (Genesis 4:1, 8).

Separation from God created emptiness and a void in the heart and soul of man. Man has since then tried in many of his own ways to fill this emptiness without God.

1. Adam and Eve picked fig leaves to cover themselves (Genesis 3:7).

2. Esau sold his birthright, minimizing the things of God and Jacob deceived Esau of possessions to progress (Genesis 27).

3. Pharaoh was stubborn for power (Genesis Chapters 5-11).

4. The prodigal son chose riotous living and pleasure over honor, work and discipline (Luke 15:11-32).

In today's world, nothing has really changed. People are still in disobedience to God and are looking to themselves by stealing, practicing drugs, alcohol, immorality, seeking power, pleasure, status, success, fame and beauty, all to fix the void. Matt Chandler in his book *Recovering Redemption* explained that some people try to redeem themselves through *self-effort* and through *others* in relationships by seeking approval, acceptance, and worth. Still, others try to redeem themselves through the *world* of work, seeking power, money and acquiring possessions. Many people also try to redeem themselves through *religion*; they are caught up in doing works, trying to do good and obeying rules instead of faith in a loving God.[2]

> *Many people also try to redeem themselves through religion.*

Despite man's wayward ways and their rejection of God, the heavenly Father made a plan to redeem mankind from the hands of Satan and death. God made this plan even before creation (Ephesians 1:4, 5). He made Adam knowing he would fall, and that His only begotten Son would have to die to save Adam and all mankind (Genesis 3:15; Romans 16:20; Ephesians 1:3-7; 1 John 3:8).

GOD'S LEGAL AND MORAL STAND

Romans 11:29, *"For the gifts and calling of God are without repentance."* The living Bible says it this way, *"For God's gifts and his call can never be withdrawn; He will never go back on His promises."*

God is a Holy God, and He could respond only one way consistent with His perfect loving nature to Adam's disobedience: put Adam out of the Garden. This was not as a punishment but as a protection. By not allowing Adam and Eve to eat of *The Tree of Life* with a sinful heart, He was protecting them. If God had let them eat of this tree, mankind could not be redeemed or be saved. Man would have had to live forever with a sinful heart and go to Hell when they die (Genesis 3:22).

God is a God of Justice. He gave man in Adam, dominion and authority, over the Earth but man lost it to Satan. God could not just take it back for a mulligan, or a re-do. Man lost it, so only a man could redeem it. But there is a great dilemma that had to be dealt with: all of mankind had a sinful heart. Only a perfect, sinless member of mankind, or of Adam's race with flesh and blood on whom Satan had no claim, could cancel Satan's legal rights over sinful mankind.

Where could God find such a man when the entire human race was born in sin?

God is a spirit. He himself could not redeem mankind, so He turned to His only Son, Jesus, who came down to Earth as a man, perfectly obeyed the Law of Moses and died shedding His blood to atone and pay mankind's debt for sin. As the Son of man, He alone was without sin and therefore able to absorb and forgive mankind's sin.

2 Corinthians 5:21, *"For he hath made him to be sin for us, who knew no sin; that we might be made the righteousness of God in him."*

With God's righteousness in Jesus, God's Spirit could now flow into man's heart and bring eternal life back to mankind (Luke 5:21- 24).

When Jesus' innocent blood was shed, Satan was now charged with an injustice (Matthew 12:7). God now had the legal right to intervene and reclaim His creation, mankind, which Adam had lost to Satan. The life in Jesus' blood was the only thing that can overcome death in mankind hearts.

Leviticus 17:11, *"For the life of the flesh is in the blood: and I have given it to you upon the altar to make atonement for your souls; for it is the blood that maketh an atonement for the soul."*

Jesus was the only way to permanently pay for sin and offer cleansing in forgiveness, so that when man does sin he can still be alive.

Hebrews 9:26 say, *"...but now once in the end of the world hath he appeared to put away sin by the sacrifice of himself."*

The death of Jesus Christ on the Cross and His shed blood brought all mankind new life with a new identity (2 Corinthians 5:17). God covered Adam and Eve's nakedness when He killed an animal, shedding its blood, and using the skin to cover their bodies. This was the first mention in the Bible of shedding of blood for covering. It was a forerunner pointing to the things yet to come on the cross.

> *The life in Jesus' blood was the only thing that can overcome death.*

Genesis 3:21 states, *"Unto Adam also and to his wife did the Lord God make coats of skins, and clothed them."*

The sacrifice of animals had to be done every year, and the animal's blood brought life and forgiveness for one year, but it still left a remembrance of sin.

Hebrews 10:3 *"But in those sacrifices there is a remembrance again made of sins every year."*

Secondly, the blood of bulls and goats was not a complete work to cover sin. Animal's blood could not atone for future sins, offering forgiveness. Only the blood of Christ could cleanse all sins (Mark 3:28; Colossians 2:13).

Jesus laid down His life by dying on the cross so mankind's sin could be forgiven and a new life from God could enter into man's heart. They must, however, choose to receive Him by faith in His grace and believe on what Jesus has done on the cross for mankind.

John 3:16 *"For God so loved the world, that he gave his only begotten Son, that whosoever believeth in him should not perish, but have everlasting life."*

Scriptures on Jesus' crucifixion will also help you to understand more.

- Crucifixion as prophesied (Psalm 22; Isaiah 53:1-12).
- Fulfilled (Luke chapters 22, 23; John chapters 18, 19).

- Jesus' sacrifice was once and for all times (Hebrews 7:27; Hebrews 9:12; Hebrews 10:1-14).

By the shedding of Jesus' blood, God's purpose was accomplished. By Jesus dying once and for all to take away the sins of the world, He paid for man's sins as their Redeemer through death, so He could bring salvation to all mankind. God, through His plan, removed the separation between God and man and spiritually reconciled man back to Himself into a harmonious relationship and fellowship if they would receive Jesus.

- Romans 5:10
- Ephesians 2:16-18
- Colossians 1:20-22
- Hebrews 2:14, 15; 10:10
- 1 Peter 3:18

Why so much blood you ask? The answer is seen in what the blood of Jesus freely did for us.

1. Access

Life is in the blood. There can be no life without blood, in the natural, and it is also a supernatural truth. It took a sinless life with no death in it to counteract the death of sin. Jesus' blood opened the way to salvation, bringing many sons called believers, to glory.

Access by Satan into a believers' life is also denied by the blood (Leviticus 17:11; Isaiah 54:17; Luke 10:19; Ephesians 2:11-19).

2. Glory Restored

It was necessary that God dealt with Jesus as He would with us for our sin. Jesus became sin and died and, in exchange, He gave us His glory and righteousness, right standing or right relationship in Christ Jesus before God.

Hebrews 2:6, 7) "...*WHAT IS MAN, THAT THOU ART MINDFUL OF HIM...THOU CROWNEDST HIM*

WITH GLORY AND HONOUR…" (Ephesians 1:12; Colossians 1:27; 1 Thessalonians 2:12)

3. Our Salvation

God could not redeem man from Heaven, because He is a Spirit without blood.

- A human could not do it because he had sin in his blood.

- Animals, though having innocent blood, could only cover sin as a temporary measure, providing temporary forgiveness for one year.

- Therefore, a man with sinless and eternal blood, having the nature and claims of God, had to be found to die and shed His blood to bring eternal life to mankind.

- Jesus alone met all requirements.

4. Jesus Became Our Lord.

Born again, we become children of God. He is the Lord our shepherd. He will care for, protect, lead and guide us. Psalm 23 gives a description of our life which, as believers, we can appropriate. The Lord is my shepherd, I will lack nothing (Psalm 23; John 10:14; Romans 10: 9,10).

5. The Great Divider

The life of sin and death in mankind's blood had to be replaced by God's eternal life in order for man to be saved (John 3:16). You may ask this question, saved from what? You can be saved from sin, sickness, death and eternity in Hell. You will be saved from self-destruction, destruction from others and also from the devil. The blood of Jesus therefore became the great divider. Those who reject all what Jesus has done on the cross will suffer calamities without much of God's help here on Earth and later eternal damnation (Revelation 21:8). Those who choose relationship with Christ and continue to work out the salvation of their soul, growing and maturing in the things of God, will become more and like Christ as they prepare for Heaven The blood of Jesus also divides the author of evil from the author of good (John 10:10). (Deuteronomy 30:19,20; Galatians 1:4; 2 Timothy 1:9,10; Hebrews 4:12; Revelation 20:10-15).

6. Cleansed Conscience
Jesus' blood was the only one that qualified to once and for all cleanse man and his conscience from their sin, leaving him with no sense of sin and restored into relationship with God.

Hebrews 10:2 "*For then would they not have ceased to be offered? because that the worshippers once purged should have had no more conscience of sins*" (Romans 8:1, 2; Hebrews 8:12; Hebrews 9:14; 10:2).

7. Jesus Going to The cross Fulfilled Prophecy
If Jesus didn't do it then it could not have been done. If Joseph, Mary's husband, had disobeyed God, if King Herod had succeeded to kill Jesus as a baby, if Jesus had yielded to the temptation to give up at Gethsemane, all mankind would have an eternal destiny in Hell. But the ability to set mankind free gave Jesus great joy to continue on and endure the cross, in the sacrifice of Himself. Jesus persevered and succeeded in putting away the power of sin over mankind and fulfilled prophecy (Psalm 22; Hebrews 9:26; Hebrews 12:2).

8. Made Us Kings and Priests
As you watch *The Passion of the Christ,* there are so many beatings, weeping, pain, and blood, but as a believer, we see the beauty of Jesus as our substitute. He was dying our death on the cross, suffering in the natural, so we can receive continual cleansing to sustain a supernatural, eternal life, seated with Christ in heavenly places. We can rejoice and be very thankful. He took our place, bled and died for us, so that we can live abundantly in the freedom of forgiveness, reigning as kings, queens and priests (Revelation 1:4-6).

9. Communion

The blood of Jesus was so significant that a memorial of Communion was established by God in the Church for the remembrance of His sacrifice (1 Corinthians 11:24, 25).

10. New Covenant

Jesus' blood brought in the New Covenant of Grace in believing, instead of doing in one's own efforts. This is a new and better way with better promises of believing God's love and all He did for us on the cross (Matthew 26:28, Hebrews 8:6- 13).

11. Jesus Became Our Mediator

Christ, the mediator of the New Testament, is now the new voice in the earth, full of grace and truth; Our High priest mediating between God and man (John 1:17; Hebrews 9:15, 12:24).

12. Peace

God made peace with man through the blood of the cross (Romans 5:1; Colossians 1:20).

13. Sanctifies

The blood sanctifies, sets us apart as holy, blameless, innocent, without rebuke (John 17:17-19; Romans 12:1-2; 1 Corinthians 6:11; Colossians 1:22; Hebrews 13:12).

14. Righteousness

Jesus took our sins and gave us His gift of righteousness, His love shed abroad in our hearts, with a new commandment to love so we can live above sin (John 13:34; 2 Corinthians 5:21).

15. Holy Spirit

Jesus ascended and sent one like Himself in the Holy Spirit to Help us live and mature into Christ-likeness as sons and daughters of God (John 14: 16,17).

16. Overcomers

Jesus made us overcomers: Every trial or obstacle we face in life, we can overcome and be victorious. We can live in health, prosperity and protection "...and they overcame him (Satan) by the blood of the lamb and by the word of their testimony" (Romans 8:37; Revelation 12:11).

17. Masters over Satan

Jesus made us masters over Satan, who is now our slave to do what we command him through the blood of Jesus and in the name of Jesus. (Luke 10:18, 19; 11:20; Philippians 2:9-11)

What an amazing God of love, having done an amazing work of grace to set mankind free from Satan and sin.

Look in awe at the greatness of His thoughts towards you, the length and depth of love for you to send His only Son to die for you. Think of the millions of animals that had to die, under the law just to keep sin covered until God could find a virgin to bring Jesus into the world to live and die for your sin. Think of Jesus. He knew He was born to die just for you, yet He lived knowing of His pending death and went to the cross anyway with joy because He knew what would be accomplished for you and me.

God loved you and was passionate for you enough to send Jesus to set you free. Jesus did a great service to mankind. Let us all be mindful of it and return His love, and in gratitude, expressing our passion for Christ as much He did for us; let us receive His love in forgiveness, and keep growing spiritually from faith to faith and from glory to glory in His grace and His love.

CHAPTER 3

THE BLOOD OF JESUS GAVE US THE FULL GOSPEL

The blood of Jesus gave us the full gospel.

1 Corinthians15:1–4, *"Moreover, brethren, I declare unto you the gospel which I preached unto you, which also ye have received, and wherein ye stand; By which also ye are saved, if ye keep in memory what I preached unto you, unless ye have believed in vain. For I delivered unto you first of all which I also received, how that Christ died for our sins according to the scriptures; And that he was buried, and that he rose again the third day according to the scriptures:"*

The Greek word "Evangelion" from which we get, "evangelism," means good tidings or good news. The good news of the Kingdom of God is that salvation is secured through Jesus Christ: in His birth, miracle life, death, burial, resurrection, and ascension. The reality of His grace must be received by faith. Salvation is available for all to be delivered from spiritual death unto eternal life. The Gospel is for full and free deliverance from a fallen world with Satan, sin, the law and all its consequences of guilt, condemnation, sickness, and death destroyed. This freedom can be had on the basis of simple faith in Jesus Christ.

Ephesians 2:8, 9 *"For by grace are ye saved through faith; and that not of yourselves: it is the gift of God: Not of works, lest any man should boast."*

The GOSPEL HAS FOUR POWERFUL POINTS:

(1) The virgin birth

(2) The miracle life of Christ

(3) Crucifixion and burial

(4) Resurrection and ascension

The Gospel based on the Blood had a purpose:

1 John 3:8b: *"…For this purpose the son of God was manifested, that He might destroy the works of the devil"*

John 20:31, *"But these are written, that ye might believe that Jesus is the Christ, the Son of God; and that believing ye might have life through his name."*

John 17:26, *"And I have declared unto them thy name, and will declare it; that the love wherewith thou hast loved me may be in them, and I in them."*

The purpose of the gospel is Jesus coming to Earth to show the love of the Father by defeating our enemy Satan, giving us power to believe on God through Jesus His Son so that once again we can enter into relationship and fellowship with God our heavenly Father.

Whenever the Gospel is shared for salvation, these four points and what they accomplished should be included to accomplish the purpose of the gospel to give relationship and everlasting life. Every religion against Christianity has objections with one or more of these four truths and falls short of God's glory.

The Virgin Birth:

- Also referred to as the incarnation (John 1:14).
- Prophecy given of virgin birth:
  (Isaiah 7:14, 9:6; 11:1-5)

- Prophecy fulfilled (Luke 1:27-38).
- The Birth (Luke 2: 6-18).

Significance:

- This truth of the virgin birth is essential to Christianity's claim that Jesus is the Son of God (Isaiah 7:14; Matthew 1:23).
- It is evidence of His supernatural origin, conceived by the Holy Spirit (Luke 1:35; I Timothy 3:16).
- He was born God and Savior, eternal and sinless (Matthew 2:11; Luke 1:46, 47). The wise men were divinely guided to worship Him. Only God is to be worshipped.
- Incarnation is the measuring stick for truth.

    I John 4:2, 3, *"Hereby know ye the Spirit of God: Every spirit that confesseth that Jesus Christ come in the flesh is of God: And every spirit that confesseth not that Jesus Christ is come in the flesh is not of God and this is that spirit of antichrist…"*

    The Miracle Life of Christ (Luke Chapters 2-9)

- His mission was stated in Luke 4:18, 19

    "The Spirit of the Lord is upon me, Because he hath anointed me to preach the gospel to the poor; He hath sent me to heal the broken hearted, to preach deliverance to the captives, and recovering of sight to the blind, to set at liberty them that are bruised, to preach the acceptable year of the Lord."

    Jesus accomplished everything He set out to do as He went about preaching, teaching, and healing all those in need. By the power of the Holy Spirit, He opened blind eyes, healed deaf ears, cast out devils, and forgave sins (Matthew 9:2-6; Mark 6:6, 7; Luke 9:6).

Significance:

- Jesus' miraculous life was lived in relationship and complete obedience to the Father, with whom He was so united that He remained sinless. This qualified Him to die for the sins of mankind.

- Because He lived as a man, He could be touched with the feelings of our infirmities. He could understand our human frailties.

  Hebrews 4:15, *"For we have not an High priest which cannot be touched with the feeling of our infirmities; but was in all points tempted like as we are, yet without sin."*

- He confirmed His claims to be the Son of God who can forgive sins. Only God can forgive sins (Luke 5:20, 21).

- He raised His dead friend Lazarus, in John 11:43. Only God's power can supernaturally raise the dead and have power over devils.

- Jesus spoke the Word with great authority and displayed great power over the elements when He rebuked the wind and waves (Matthew 7:28, 29; Mark 1:22; 4:39).

Crucifixion and Burial (Luke 23:32-56)

- Jesus was born to die; He was born to sacrifice Himself in order to save sinners. Jesus was God's plan of redemption for mankind, to redeem them from Satan, sin, law and death. Jesus gave man Salvation or *"Sozo,"* which includes forgiveness of sins, healing, deliverance, protection, provision, and peace and much more. Everything you will ever need on earth to succeed was provided in Jesus, by His Word, and by His Spirit in the finished work of the cross.

The Gospel can be ministered to two main groups:

1. **Gospel to the unsaved: which begins with 'Christ died for me by His grace'**

- God loves me and offers a wonderful plan for my life (John 3:16; Jeremiah 29:11). The unsaved is told (a) man is sinful and separated from God (Romans 6:23) (b) Jesus is God's only provision for man's sin (John 14:6; Romans 5:8, 10; 10:9-10; Ephesians 2:8, 9;) (c) The man who accepts Jesus as presented in the gospel, is saved cleansed of his sins, made righteous, acceptable to God able to walk in relationship in His grace (1 Corinthians 1:30; 2 Corinthians 5:21; Colossians 2:6).

2. **Gospel to the saved: which begins with 'I am born again therefore'**

- Now I am dead in Christ and alive unto God (Romans 6:2-11; Galatians 2:20, Colossians 3:3, 4). For believers, this is the process of renewing the mind in the process of sanctification, transformation, and maturing in Christ. It is our path back to God to have increased relationship, fellowship and the benefits of eternal life in Christ not only here on Earth but also to eternity.

- Glorification by God's Spirit within and future glorification of living with God in Heaven (1 Corinthians 15:52, 53; 1 Thessalonians 4:16, 17).

Significance of the Cross:

- Jesus died for the remission of sins (Acts 2:38).

- God's justice demands that man must pay the penalty for sin, which is death (Romans 6:23). Jesus paid the debt that we owed, and those who believe on Jesus no longer owe this debt of God's justice except to believe God, repent, forsake sin, and receive His complete forgiveness as well as to reject every lie of Satan that you are not righteous and is still responsible for your sin. In return for such great a salvation, we owe Jesus our love, as we seek closer fellowship and relationship, and desire to keep His commandments (Matthew 22:36-40; John 13: 34; Romans 13:8). It is the union of love, relationship, and dependence on Jesus by which you will be kept free from any fear of the devil, even in the midst of trouble (1 John 4:18).

- When Jesus said, *"It is finished"* He meant that whatever separated Man from God and whatever man owed God for sin was wiped away and forever forgotten (Hebrews 8:12; 9:26b). All works and ordinances of the law, which strengthened and covered sin, were fulfilled and ended (Colossians 2:13- 15). Jesus fulfilled the law, and replaced the Old Testament law with Himself. (Romans 3:19-26) Now our faith is to be in Jesus, who is God's grace to us.

  Romans 10:4, "For *Christ is the end of the law for righteousness to everyone that believeth."*

- Christ on the Cross defeated the powers of Satan and death (Colossians 2:15; Hebrews 2:14).

- Jesus bought back eternal life, which Adam lost, and all spiritual blessings in heavenly places, including man's body as His temple (Ephesians 1:3; I Corinthians 3:16).

- Man can be made a New Creation with a new heart if they believe on Jesus (John 3:16; 2 Corinthians 5:17).

- Healing and deliverance was provided by His stripes and His blood (Isaiah 53:4, 5).

- Jesus came to Earth as a man with complete faith in God His Father. He walked on water as a man, and redeemed mankind as a man. As Jesus is so are we in this world. We too can, by faith, do the works of Jesus and even greater works if we really believe (John 14:12).

4. Resurrection:

(Luke Chapter 24; 1 Corinthians 15: 3, 4, 14 17; Acts 13:29-39)

Everything in Christianity rests on the resurrection. It is because of this truth that Jesus lives, why He can provide salvation and eternal life. The resurrection distinguishes Christianity from all religions, which care only about the spirit. Christianity however utilizes a resurrected spirit and body for its propagation. God needed Jesus' resurrected body to preach the gospel (Luke 24:13-32; Romans 10:9, 10; Colossians 1:18). In the same way, Jesus now needs our new creation or spiritually resurrected bodies to preach the gospel (Mark 16:15). The bodies of the leaders of every religion who said they received revelations about redemption are still in their graves. Jesus arose.

Everything in Christianity rests on the resurrection.

Significance:

- The resurrection is further proof of the divinity of Jesus as Son of God (Romans 1:4).

- His authority over death and the grave (1 Corinthians 15:55-57) *"O death, where is thy sting? O grave, where is thy victory?"*

- His authority over Satan and Hell (Luke 10:18, 19).

- Jesus is the source of our faith (Mark 11:24; Acts 3:16).

- Jesus was raised for our justification and righteousness (Romans 4:25; 2 Corinthians 5:21).

- Jesus said unto her, *"I am the resurrection, and the life: he that believeth in me, though he were dead, yet shall he live; And whosoever liveth and believeth in me shall never die…"* (John 11: 25, 26).

- Ensures our complete redemption unto glorification. (1 Thessalonians 4:14-17).

- Romans 1:4 and 1 Peter 1:21 tells us that believing in the resurrection power of Jesus will cause our faith to be in God. Faith in relationship with God will cause believers to pursue holiness, so that the power and glory of Jesus can be theirs as they seek to live and minister for Him.

The Ascension (Luke 24: 46-53; Hebrews 4:14; 12:2). After the resurrection, Jesus appeared to His disciples and many others over a 40-day period. He walked among men and women, demonstrating His desire for personal relationship and close fellowship with people. Relationship is the main point that differentiates Christianity from all religions, which follows rules and regulations.

Significance:

- The ascension marks the completion of the work Jesus' Father gave Him to do on Earth (John 17:4).

- Jesus' ascension ensured the coming of the Holy Spirit who would live within man's heart: "...*the Lord dwelleth not in temples made with hands. "Nevertheless I tell you the truth; It is expedient for you that I go away: for if I go not away, the Comforter will not come unto you..."* (Acts 17:24; John 16:7).

- Jesus is now touched with the feeling of our infirmities. (Hebrews 4:15).

- Jesus became our Shepherd and head of the Church (Psalm 23; Ephesians 1:22).

- As mediator of the New Covenant, He is seated at the right hand of God the Father and has raised us up to sit and reign with Him (Romans 5:17; Ephesians 2:6; Hebrews 9:15).

- Jesus is carrying out His present day ministry of making intercession for us (Romans 8:34).

- He gave gifts unto men (1 Corinthians 12; Ephesians 4:8).

- External and ceremonial worship gave way to spiritual worship, now that our bodies are the temple of God (John 4:23; 1 Corinthians 6:19, 20).

- His ascension proves that when we believe on Jesus spiritually we are raised and seated with Him in heavenly places qualified to receive all spiritual blessings (Ephesians 1:3).

- Jesus brought grace and truth to provide salvation, bringing people from death to life with a changed nature. His birth, death, crucifixion, burial, resurrection and ascension represent the finished work of the cross to purchase mankind's redemption or freedom in a fallen world from Satan.

Gospel In Jesus Brings Salvation Romans 1:16 says, *"For I am not ashamed of the Gospel of Christ: for it is the power of God unto salvation to everyone that believeth…"*

This is good news.

The Gospel is God's good news. This good news is the power of God unto salvation. The gospel saves us from Hell and every form of sickness and death here on Earth. Your responsibility is to hear and believe in your heart, speak it from your mouth and respond by acting on your faith, to receive (John 1:12; Romans 10:9, 10). You do not have to work for your salvation. It is a gift, receive it by faith, it will be your best gift ever, when you receive Him as your personal Savior.

Because of your faith in the blood of Jesus and the finished work of the cross, you are saved, justified, made righteous, and as the "just," you should now live by faith.

Romans 1:17, *"For therein is the righteousness of God revealed from faith to faith: as it is written, The just shall live by faith."* (Habakkuk 2:4; Galatians 1:13; Hebrews 10:38).

As you face life daily, look back at these four points of the Gospel, and by faith if you believe, receive and declare, and thank God you are saved or born-again. You are now qualified to receive God's complete blessings. If you are in need, then proceed to find His Word and speak it to release power to meet your need. Read, meditate on it, believe it by faith, act on what you

You are now qualified to receive God's complete blessings.

believe, and receive your need as met. Rejoice in what Christ has done for you. If you need healing, thank God for your relationship through the blood then look up healing Scriptures, read, and meditate His truth to yourself, and let His joy in choosing to die for you release the blessing of healing in your life. Let His shed blood give you something to rejoice about and bring you strength.

Nehemiah 8:10, *"…for the joy of the Lord is your strength."*

If you are saved and is at a hard place now and believe there is nothing good to rejoice about, take your mind back to the four points of the Gospel message and receive Jesus not only as Savior but now as Lord. Begin to give thanks for all God has done for you as He brought Jesus to Earth for your salvation. Also, give thanks for all previous victories in your life.

Similarly, when you are in praise and worship at church, reflect on what Christ did for you in the gospel message, and you will always have something to shout, rejoice, and be thankful about. Even in trials and troubles, we can rejoice that Jesus has done it all and, by our faith in Him the blessings we desire now will manifest from the spiritual realm into our natural lives.

Seek to abide in a close relationship with Christ by faith and continue to work out the salvation of your soul, as you grow and mature in the things of God and daily become more like Christ.

Philippians 2:12b, *"… Work out your own salvation with fear and trembling."*

Isaiah 12: 2, 3, *"Behold, God is my salvation; I will trust, and not be afraid: for the LORD JEHOVAH is my strength and my song; he also is become my salvation. Therefore, with joy shall ye draw water out of the wells of salvation."*

We have a well of salvation (John 4:14), and with the bucket of faith will always have something to draw from the well and to rejoice about, because of the gospel of our Lord Jesus Christ.

"Therefore with joy shall ye draw water out of the wells of salvation. There are wells of healing, deliverance, prosperity, protection, peace, and provision and much more to draw from. So by faith draw and become a partaker of all God's blessings to you secured by Jesus' blood

That is why Philippians 4:4 says,

"Rejoice in the Lord alway; and again I say, Rejoice."

So rejoice! Salvation has come receive it by faith.

Romans 10:9, 10, *"That if thou shalt confess with thy mouth the Lord Jesus, and shalt believe in thine heart that God hath raised him from the dead, thou shalt be saved. For with the heart man believeth unto righteousness; and with the mouth confession is made unto salvation."*

Prayer of Salvation:

Dear heavenly Father,

Thank You for loving me enough to send Jesus to die for my sins. You raised Him from the dead for my justification, so that I can be forgiven and receive eternal life. I now give You my life, and I receive Your new life in my heart. I receive Your forgiveness, and I am clean. I confess Jesus as my Savior and Lord. I am Your child, a new creation in Christ Jesus. I yield my life to You, because You are the one now in charge of me as my Father. The old me is gone, and the new me with a new spirit has come. Thank You Father for saving me by Your grace. Please help me to depend on You and Your Word as I let You live in and through me each day.

Prayer for restoration:

Dear Heavenly Father,

I come to you believing in my heart that Jesus is my Savior and Lord and that He died and rose again for my salvation. I believe that I am saved, but I have walked away, because I trusted in myself to live the Christian life more than I did You. Please forgive me. I give up on myself and all my works today and choose to depend on you through the Holy Spirit in me to live as a child of God. I receive your grace as I return into fellowship and ask you to keep me in your grace. In Jesus' Name. Amen.

If you have sincerely prayed one of these prayers and believed in your heart, then you are saved or restored into relationship and fellowship with God. Receive it as done by faith and begin to express thankfulness to God for His goodness and His grace and share your good news with someone else.

CHAPTER 4

ACCESS BY THE BLOOD OF JESUS

Romans 5:1, 2, *"Therefore being justified by faith, we have peace with God through our Lord Jesus Christ: By whom also we have access by faith into this grace wherein we stand, and rejoice in hope of the glory of God."*

In our modern computerized world, one can access the most sensitive information by putting in the correct data, password, or information. The password makes the information accessible. Access is: *The means or opportunity to approach or enter a place, to make accessible.* Believing God, by faith in the blood of Jesus and the power it produces for salvation, is the only access into the kingdom of God and Heaven.

Ephesians 2:18, *"For through him we both have access by one Spirit unto the Father"*

Hebrews 9:12, *"Neither by the blood of goats and calves, but by his own blood he entered in once into the holy place, having obtained eternal redemption for us"*

Why Is Access Necessary?

Through Adam, mankind sinned and became separated from God with no hope of reconciliation and access to the Father unless the price for sin was paid. The price was death.

Romans 6:23. *"For the wages of sin is death; but the gift of God is eternal life through Jesus Christ our Lord."*

Not anyone or anything could die to pay this debt; only a sinless man could absorb mankind's sin. All of mankind was born in sin and shaped in iniquity. All mankind was disqualified from God's presence because of his sinful nature.

God had to send His only Son, born of a virgin as that sinless man, to die on the Cross and shed His innocent blood to free mankind from sin. The blood of Jesus destroyed the effects of sin and the power of Satan, who is the master of sin.

Mark 15:37-39, *"And Jesus cried with a loud voice, and gave up the ghost. And the veil of the temple was rent in twain from the top to the bottom. And when the centurion, which stood over against him, saw that he so cried out, and gave up the ghost, he said, Truly this man was the Son of God."*

1 John 3:8b, *"...For this purpose the Son of God was manifested, that he might destroy the works of the devil."*

Jesus shed His blood as the price, which redeemed, purchased, and freed us, so that we can once again freely enter into God's presence. This act of love in dying for us not only allowed us to be able to enter into God's presence but also allowed us to enter into an intimate relationship with Him. In this relationship, His heart is for us to prosper and be in good health (3 John 2). Yet despite having done all of this for us to be prosperous and be in good health, many Christians are still poor, in lack, sick, unprotected and bound by the devil.

Believers, get in God's Word and get in faith. Access by faith is the key to fulfilling God's greatest desire for you, which is to be in an intimate relationship with Him so that He can bless you. Religion or legalism which is acting in self-will, will keep you from accessing God and having a relationship with Him. The blood of Jesus gives freedom of access into God's presence, so that we can boldly approach Him as our righteousness and rest in His peace and love, enjoying a harmonious relationship with Him as our Father.

"*In whom we have redemption through his blood, the forgiveness of sins, according to the riches of his grace.*" (Ephesians 1:7). In Christ Jesus you have access by His blood into freedom, the forgiveness of sins by the riches of His grace. Get to know Him and His heart of love for you. Listen to Him and believe Him when He speaks to you. Give Him all the praise and all the glory for His goodness to you as your Savior and only access to God.

Jesus the Sacrificial Lamb: The Only Access

Sacrifice is the act of giving up something of value for the sake of something of greater value or importance.

John 15:13, "*Greater love hath no man than this, that a man lay down his life for his friends.*"

Jesus sacrificed His life as a ransom to bring many sons to glory. Sons here refer to all people who believe on Jesus.

Hebrews 2:10, "*For it became him, for whom are all things, and by whom are all things, in bringing many sons unto glory, to make the captain of their salvation perfect through sufferings.*"

Instead of punishing us with death for our sins, as we deserve, Christ took our sins Himself in His body on the Cross and became our sacrifice. He died on our behalf and became sin, so that we can be forgiven, born-again, cleansed of all sins, justified, and made righteous and acceptable unto God.

Ephesians 1:6, "*To the praise of the glory of his grace, wherein he hath made us accepted in the beloved.*"

Jesus had Purpose in His Sacrifice to Give Access:

- To save the people by offering Jesus as the forgiveness for sins. (Matthew 1:21; Hebrews 9:26).
- To give His life as a ransom for many, providing salvation (Matthew 20:28).

- To make us new creation beings (2 Corinthians 5:17).

- To make us His workmanship, who are made unto wisdom, righteousness, sanctification, and redemption (1 Corinthians 1:30; Ephesians 2:10).

- To bring us to God as our Father for relationship and spiritual maturity (1 Peter 2:2; 1Peter 3:18).

- To destroy the works of the enemy and make us free (Hebrews 2: 14, 15, 1John 3:8)

- To prepare us by the power of the Holy Spirit to be with God in eternity (John 14:3).

Access to God Must Be By Faith; Faith Pleases God.

Hebrews 11: 6, *"But without faith it is impossible to please him: for he that cometh to God must believe that he is, and that he is a rewarder of them that diligently seek him."*

Faith believes God and His word are truth. We must believe God and His Gospel in the birth, crucifixion, resurrection, and ascension of Jesus. Believe on Jesus and His work on the cross and you will be saved for heaven and to live in the Kingdom here on Earth.

All mankind was born deficient, separated from God and in need of fixing. 'Saved' simply means that we needed to be fixed in our hearts and restored unto God.

Let's look at two brothers who sought to access God's presence, how they feared, and what the consequences of their actions were.

God's Requirement.

Leviticus 1:2, *"Speak unto the children of Israel, and say unto them, If any man of you bring an offering unto the Lord, ye shall bring your offering of the cattle, even of the herd, and of the flock."* Cain, lacking faith, went before God with a bloodless sacrifice. He gave of the work of his own hands and of his own efforts. He chose to act in pride, self-will or self-righteousness by doing things his own way. Cain went against God's requirements and God rejected his sacrifice (Genesis 4:3). Rather than repenting, Cain became angry, a normal reaction from a person operating in pride. Any person coming to God for salvation, inheritance, or blessings must believe and act in faith on God's Word. This, therefore, requires humility.

Cain was faithless, prideful, lacked humility and therefore access was denied to him. Cain's reply to God was,

> Genesis 4: 13 -16, "… *My punishment is greater than I can bear. Behold, thou hast driven me out this day from the face of the earth; and from thy face shall I be hid; and I shall be a fugitive and a vagabond in the earth; and it shall come to pass, that everyone that findeth me shall slay me. And the Lord said unto him, Therefore whosoever slayeth Cain, vengeance shall be taken on him sevenfold. And the Lord set a mark upon Cain, lest any finding him should kill him. And Cain went out from the presence of the Lord, and dwelt in the land of Nod, on the east of Eden.*"

Abel, on the other hand, acted in faith according to God's commands. He brought an animal from his flock, whose blood was shed, in presenting the sacrifice. Abel responded to God in righteousness, doing things the right way, God's way. He offered unto God a more excellent sacrifice than Cain, by which he obtained witness that he was righteous; God, testifying of his gift, accepted his sacrifice.

> Genesis 4:4, *"And Abel, he also brought of the firstlings of his flock and of the fat thereof. And the Lord had respect unto Abel and to his offering."*

There are people of many religions who seek to access God by means other than the blood of Jesus, but they are deceived. No performance of good works, good deeds, religious incantations, traditions, special doctrine on abstinence from blood, special day of worship, your denomination, special Baptism, other special revelations received, holy look in dress or hairstyle can give salvation or access into God's presence only the blood of Jesus.

Abel's sacrifice was by faith. He believed God's Word and acted on it. Faith requires a desire for relationship with God and humility enough to believe that Jesus alone is the way to access this relationship with God.

John 14:6. *"Jesus said unto him, I am the way, the truth, and the life: no man cometh unto the Father, but by me."*

John 8:24 (Jesus speaking), *"I said therefore unto you, that ye shall die in your sins: for if ye believe not that I am he, ye shall die in your sins."*

Romans 5: 8, 9 say, *"But God commendeth his love towards us, in that, while we were yet sinners, Christ died for us. Much more then, being now justified by his blood, we shall be saved from wrath through Him."*

Acts 4:12 states, *"Neither is there salvation in any other: for there is none other name under heaven given among men, whereby we must be saved."*

Access by the Blood into the Kingdom and the Family of God

John 3:3. *"Jesus answered and said unto him, Verily, verily, I say unto thee, Except a man be born again, he cannot see the kingdom of God."*

One must believe on the crucified and resurrected Christ, whose blood was shed for us to become sons and daughters of God of the kingdom, both in the family of God here on earth and into heaven our final home. John 1:12, *"But as many as received him, to them gave he power to become the sons of God, even to them that believe on his name."*

Access by the Blood into Relationship.

We have access into relationship because the blood of Jesus has forgiven us of all our sins. His blood justified us by cleansing us, making us just as if we never sinned, removed all guilt and declared us innocent. The innocent blood of Jesus not only declared us innocent, but it made us righteous, approved, and acceptable to

God. God, also by the innocence and righteousness of Jesus, made us free to once again enter into intimate relationship with Him, so that we can experience His presence and eventually grow and mature to become like Him.

1 John 3: 1, 2, *"Behold, what manner of love the Father hath bestowed upon us, that we should be called the sons of God: therefore the world knoweth us not, because it knew him not. Beloved, now are we the sons of God, and it doth not yet appear what we shall be: but we know that, when he shall appear, we shall be like him; for we shall see him as he is."*

1 John 4:19, *"We love him, because He first loved us."*

God loves us so much that He died for us, and His greatest desire is for us to draw near to Him, seek to know Him, and to fellowship with Him in the Word and in prayer and to experience His presence when you believe Him, praise and worship Him for who He is to you, you will begin to draw close to your God and heavenly Father. God loves you with an everlasting love.

Jeremiah 31:3, *"The Lord hath appeared of old unto me, saying, Yea, I have loved thee with an everlasting love: therefore with lovingkindness have I drawn thee."*

Faith in Jesus gives us access into relationship with God.

Romans 5:1, 2. *"Therefore being justified by faith, we have peace with God through our Lord Jesus Christ: By whom also we have access by faith into this grace wherein we stand, and rejoice in hope of the glory of God."*

We have Relationship with God

- Matthew 6:9: *"Our Father which art in heaven, Hallowed be thy name."*

- John 14:20: *"… ye shall know that I am in my Father and ye in me, and I in you."*

- John 15:5: *As branches we are connected to Christ the vine*

- Acts 16:28: *"For in him we live move and have our being."*

- Colossians 3:3, 4: *Our life is hidden with Christ; Christ is our life.*

- Ephesians 2:6: *We are seated in heavenly places in Christ*

"And he said unto me. It is done. I am Alpha and Omega, the beginning and the end. I will give unto him that is athirst of the fountain of the water of life freely. He that overcometh shall inherit all things; and I will be his God, and he shall be my son" (Revelation 21:6, 7)

Access into Spiritual Inheritances and Blessings:

A. The love of God (John 3:16; Romans 5:5; 1 John 4:7-11).

B. Redemption or freedom through the blood (Ephesians 1:7) freed from sin, Satan, the law, and from death.

C. Forgiveness of all sin, cleansed (Mark 3:28; Acts 13:38, 39; 1 John 1:7).

D. Righteousness: Access into right standing or love and acceptance with God. We are righteous when we believe on Jesus that God's grace restored us into a love relationship with Him (Romans 4:3-5; 1 Corinthians 1:30; 2 Corinthians 5:21; Ephesians 1:6; Titus 3: 4, 5). Righteousness brings union, acceptance and compatibility so we are bold in God's presence, able to enjoy a harmonious relationship and resting in His presence.

"Now there was leaning on Jesus' bosom one of his disciples whom Jesus loved (John 13:23).

E. To possess the Anointing: God's power in the Holy Spirit is deposited within helping to keep us in Jesus:

I John 2:27, *"But the anointing which ye have received of him abideth in you, and ye need not that any man teach you: but as the same anointing teacheth you all things, and is truth, and is no lie, and even as it hath taught you, ye shall abide in him."*

F. Access to have Peace with God: Separation from God because of sin has now ended and reconciliation is now possible (2 Corinthians 5:18). We have no need to be afraid of God or afraid to fellowship closely. The veil has been torn and access has been granted. You need to know that He isn't angry with you, and He has no desire to punish you because He already punished Jesus in your stead (Luke 1:76-79; Romans 5:1; Ephesians 2:17, 18; Colossians 1:20, 21).

G. A purged conscience: You should have no more conscience of sin, because you have been purged from sin and dead works to serve the living God. There should be no more sense of sin or guilt from wrongdoing, and failure because Jesus has become your righteousness, the one who made a way of escape in forgiveness. He is your ability to be and do right (Hebrews 9:14; 10:2).

H. Boldness to come into God's presence: Confident instead of feeling insecure (Ephesians 3:12; I Timothy 3:13; 1 John 4:17).

I. Authority to defend in faith against anything or anyone that threatens your harmonious relationship: Freedom from Satan's dominion (Luke 10:19; Colossians 1:13, 14).

J. All Spiritual Blessings: Whatever you need, you have it deposited in your human spirit through Christ Jesus, which is to be drawn out into your natural life situation by faith.

With salvation we have access to healing, provision, protection, and deliverance and many more blessings.

Ephesians 1:3, *"Blessed be the God and Father our Lord Jesus Christ, who hath blessed us with all spiritual blessings in heavenly places in Christ."*

K. A deposit of the fruit of the Spirit of God in us:

Galatians 5:22-23, *"But the fruit of the Spirit is love, joy, peace, longsuffering, gentleness, goodness, faith, Meekness, temperance; against such there is no law."*

L. We have the Holy Spirit living in us, as our helper: (John 14:16, 17).

M. We have eternal life here on Earth and later in Heaven when God is given access into your heart:
(John 3:16, 5:24; 1 Thessalonians 4:16, 17).

Access Can Be Hindered By:

- **Unbelief**: Refusing to believe and accept God through Jesus and His sacrifice for mankind's sin. The unbelieving must accept that they cannot save themselves and they must believe on Jesus. The believer must cease their unbelief from self-will, a law mentality of doubting and trying to live life in their own strength, trying to solve their own problems. The cure for unbelief is humility. Humble yourself, fast and pray for Him to show you your mistake and to help you to accept that you are less than God; that He is greater. Confess Him as Lord and be saved in your spirit and out of all life's trials (Psalm 34:6; Romans 10: 9,10).

- **Legalism**: Religion with self-will, a mentality of works and a focus on rules, law, regulations and sin. The result is sin-consciousness. This person may be saved but still have a conscience stained with sin. They are still operating with a law mentality of doing religious deeds, rather than being and resting in the grace of God's presence. The illustration to this is the story of Martha who asked Jesus for her sister Mary to help and do chores instead of resting in Jesus' presence (Luke 10:38). Many religions seek their own path to God but not through Jesus. For example, the Muslims and the Jehovah Witnesses are heavily focused on working for their salvation. Legalism robs the unbeliever of salvation and the believer of peace in and with God. Because of a lack of understanding of God's grace, the believer lacks intimacy, and when they are wrong they are in fear of God's wrath. The devil meanwhile is accusing and bringing condemnation while lying that it is coming from God. The cure for this 'works and performance' mindset suffering with condemnation is to give up on self-will, which is independence of God, and instead trust His grace through Jesus and the finished work on the cross. You are righteous not by works but by the blood of Jesus. Trusting God's grace requires dependence on Him, which will bring His power and ability to work on your behalf, doing for you all what you cannot do for yourself.

Many religions seek their own path to God but not through Jesus.

- **Believing You Committed the Unpardonable Sin also Hinders Access.**

Some believers, who have sinned, mistakenly believe that God will never forgive them. They read Hebrews 6:4-6 and Hebrews 10:26-31 and think they are unforgiveable. The truth is there is no sin greater than God's grace! Because of the blood of Jesus, sin cannot prevent access into the presence of God (Hebrews 4:16; 10:22, 23).

Hebrews 6:4-6; 10:26-31 pertains to a person born again, filled with the Holy Spirit, but deliberately choosing to reject Jesus, his only source to God. These scriptures do not apply to a believer, who is repentant, as the conviction he is feeling means that he is being drawn by the Holy Spirit to God. The person's involvement, either being in church or speaking to a minister about his situation, demonstrates God is still at work in his life, drawing him and is willing to forgive (John 6:44).

- **Un-forgiveness:**

Un-forgiveness, invites the presence of demonic activity, which hinders access into fellowship with God (Matthew 6:14, 15; 18:23-35).

- **A defiled conscience:**

  The role of the conscience is to set order to all of your experiences for accountability, peace of heart, and rest in your soul. The state of the believer's conscience can hinder access into the presence of God for fellowship.

  Titus 1:15 says, *"Unto the pure all things are pure: but unto them that are defiled and unbelieving is nothing pure; but even their mind and conscience is defiled."* A person with a defiled conscience is in sin- consciousness, suffers with condemnation and shrinks from God.

  It is God, in His Son Jesus, that gives us the riches of His grace. Let us, by the blood of Jesus, access the riches of His glory and the surpassing greatness of His power. Let us not neglect to partake of the inheritances and blessings He gave us to establish us in His grace. God did it all for us when He redeemed us through the blood of Jesus. He gave us everything that pertains to life and godliness (2 Peter 1:3). He made us righteous, freed from all guilt and shame, control by the self-will and restored into right relationship with God and into His presence. God loves us so much that He even gave us a measure of faith so we can access His grace and His perpetual love for us to be saved. As we depend on Him, He gives us all of His blessings, so receive by faith.

Access can be denied:

- To the enemy working against you as you stand in faith and by pleading and applying the blood of Jesus upon persons or situations concerning you, for divine protection and deliverance (Exodus Chapter 12).

- To God for rejecting Jesus: (John 3:16-18; 8:24; Revelation 21:8).

The way has been made by the blood of Jesus. There is nothing of hindrance between you and God. So come boldly unto the throne of grace that you may obtain mercy and grace to find help in the time of need (Hebrews 4:16).

Access has been granted. The table is set with salvation in Jesus and all of God's goodness and His blessings. Let us, by faith in God's grace, access and freely partake in all that has been freely given to us.

You have gained access: enter in, believe, receive, be saved and be blessed.

CHAPTER 5

GOD MADE
A COVENANT OF BLOOD
WITH JESUS

Hebrews 8:10 *"For this is the covenant that I will make with the house of Israel after those days, saith the Lord; I will put my laws into their mind, and write them in their hearts: and I will be to them a God, and they shall be to me a people"*

A blood covenant is an unshakable and unbreakable agreement between two people cut on the exchange of blood. It has commitments and pledges, the exchange of promises, gifts, authority, protection, and even one's own life before the covenant can be broken. The basis of such a covenant is a deep commitment to relationship, caring, and protecting each other.

There are eight covenants given in eight different dispensations showing God's will and care for His people.

1. Edenic: Innocence. From creation to the fall of man (Genesis 2: 5-17)

2. Adamic: Conscience. From the fall to the flood (Genesis Chapters 3-8)

3. Noahic: Human Government. From the flood to the call of Abraham (Genesis Chapters 9-12)

4. Abrahamic: Promise, from Abraham to the Law of Moses (Genesis 12:1-3; Chapter 17)
5. Mosaic: Law, Given at Mt Sinai to Jesus Christ (Exodus 20: 1-20)
6. Grace: Beginning of the early Church in Acts to second coming of Jesus (Jeremiah 31: 31-34; John 13:34)
7. Millennial: Second coming of Jesus till the end of millennial reign(future) (Revelation Chapters 19,20)
8. Universal Kingdom: God's everlasting kingdom from the end of Millennial reign to eternity. (Revelation Chapters 21,22)

We are currently in the dispensation of Grace and this and all Covenants, with the exception of the last one, are all temporary divine administrations of God towards His people (Matthew 11:13; Galatians 3:19). God sought to build a nation for Himself with the first promise given to Abraham.

Genesis 12:2, *"And I will make of thee a great nation, and I will bless thee, and make thy name great; and thou shalt be a blessing."*

The covenant agreement to seal that promise was given in Genesis chapter 15:17, 18. This was a type and shadow of the shedding of Jesus' blood, as God made the way to come to man through Jesus Christ (Luke chapter 23). Circumcision was the chosen sign by which God made this agreement in the Old Covenant and blood was shed in this process (Genesis chapter 17:11; Acts 7:8). The people of the Old Testament looked unto God and called upon Him as their Covenant God and as their provider, caregiver and protector, especially in times of trouble. The covenant caused God to remember His chosen nation Israel, even when they rejected Him for idols. The covenant also causes God to listen to His prophets when they pray and interceded for deliverance of His people in trouble. For example Abraham, who interceded for Lot in Sodom and Gomorrah (Genesis 17:1, 7; Genesis 18:20-33).

A second example is of David depending on his covenant God as he faced His enemy Goliath. He approached him in the strength of his knowledge and security in divine protection from His covenant God. David said, "*Who is this uncircumcised Philistine?*" David knew Goliath was outside the covenant and therefore outside God's power to absolutely help, protect, and deliver Goliath. David trusted the God of his covenant and valiantly fought Goliath, killed and beheaded Him (I Samuel 17:20-47). David and other Old Testament saints learned about the covenant from their forefather Abraham and used it to their advantage.

In Genesis chapter 15, God cut (made) a covenant of blood with Abraham and, even though he was old and childless, gave him a sign pointing to the promise of a son, from which he would be the Father of many nations. In verses 6-8, Abraham believed God and responded to obey God. God counted his love in his obedience for righteousness. When you love God enough to believe and obey him God calls that righteousness. Abraham asked God the question for clarification "*...whereby shall I know that I shall inherit it?*" Genesis 15 Verses 9-18 describes how the Covenant was cut in blood to seal the agreement between God and Abraham. God honored His promise and gave Abraham a son, a son whom God then commanded him to sacrifice. The question is how Abraham could be the father of many nations if the only son of his loins is dead?

> *When you love God enough to believe and obey him God calls that righteousness.*

Abraham believed God because God's Covenant with him communicated to him God's irrefutable, unbreakable promise, never to be broken. He believed God loved him and would deliver, or resurrect Isaac (Genesis 22:5). God did deliver, when He provided Abraham with a lamb for the sacrifice.

A. A blood covenant is God's commitment guaranteeing His faithfulness.

B. A blood covenant seals God's sincere and unending goodness and mercy.

C. The covenant with Abraham joined them in union, acceptance, and a covenant love relationship.

D. The sacrifice of his son Isaac was a pre-enactment of what God was going to do in offering His own Son Jesus, on the cross, His Son who would bring to Earth God's grace, mercy and truth. Jesus brought a New Covenant to us as believers (Luke 9:35; John 1:17; Hebrews 8:6-13).

Jesus lived under, fully obeyed, and fulfilled the Old Covenant of the Law, the Ten Commandments, and all its ordinances when He lived on Earth. The death, burial and resurrection of the sinless Christ, cancelled the law that was working against us. When Jesus nailed it to the cross and said, "It is finished." He was talking about Him fulfilling and ending the law and ushering in His grace (Isaiah 28:16, 18; Matthew 5:17, 18; Colossians 2:14, 15).

THE NEW COVENANT OF GRACE

Hebrews Chapters 8 -13

By all His Covenants, God has always set standards to regulate His people. We saw this was the case with the Covenant of Promise to Abraham, and the Covenant of the Law, with the Ten Commandments given to Moses.

Jesus fulfilled and ended the Old Covenant of law, and made a New Covenant with the church, us at present. God made an agreement with Jesus for the shedding of His sinless blood on the Cross providing salvation, in the redemption or freedom from Satan, sin, death, and the law. Jesus came to mankind bringing a New Covenant which cannot be broken because of the eternal availability of God's love in forgiveness, and the presence of His Holy Spirit to help us. His blood which made us righteous and acceptable to God causes mankind now to have a secure foundation of entering a relationship with God, which in Christ Jesus can never be broken.

Hebrews 13:5 *"… I will never leave thee nor forsake thee."*

John 14:16, *"And I will pray the Father, and he shall give you another Comforter, that he may abide with you forever."*

God made a New Covenant available to all mankind to be received if they believe on His Son Jesus Christ (Ephesians 2:10-22). The church in this age no longer has to relate to God by the Ten Commandments of working or performing to be right in order to please God or to avoid punishment. Relating to God this old way is having a wrong relationship with God. No matter how hard you try, work, and perform, your actions will always be insufficient. Constantly failing the perfect requirements of obedience to the law. This will give a sense of never being able to measure up, having a sense of insecurity, unworthiness, and insufficiency. Under the New Covenant of grace we live in, God's love is the standard by which we live, and there is no height, nor depth to prevent Him from reaching you with His love. As we turn to Him, all our thoughts, words, actions, and performance are to be governed by His love. His love gave us grace in Jesus and our love and dependence on Jesus cancels self-will, self-effort law or legalism.

As we turn to Him, all our thoughts, words, actions, and performance are to be governed by His love.

John 13:34, *"A new commandment I give unto you, That ye also love one another; as I have love you, that ye also love one another"*

Romans 13:8, 9, *"Owe no man anything, but to love one another: for he that loveth another hath fulfilled the law. For this, THOU SHALT NOT COMMIT ADULTERY, THOU SHALT NOT KILL, THOU SHALT NOT STEAL…and if there be any other commandment, it is briefly comprehended (summed up) in this saying, namely, THOU SHALT LOVE THY NEIGHBOUR AS THYSELF."*

God is love and the only direct connection to a living breathing part of the God-Head we have on this Earth daily is God the Holy-Spirit who is deposited in the hearts of believers when born- again. Now you are to be dead to self and self- will and alive unto God's will being led by the Holy Ghost.

Romans 5:5 *"And hope maketh not ashamed; because the love of God is shed abroad in our hearts by the Holy Ghost which is given to us."*

Romans 8:14 *"For as many as are led by the Spirit of God, they are the sons of God."*

When we believe on God by faith for a promise, through all that Jesus accomplished on the cross and onwards, your faith activates the Holy Spirit to go to work on your behalf to fulfill it and bring it to pass. Because of Jesus' great love for us and our hope in God, we will never be ashamed, or have to work for God's love or blessings because He is always for us. We are in the age of the Holy Spirit as we depend on God through Him, and hold in our hearts the substance of Jesus; He the Holy Spirit will testify and make Jesus real to us to meet our needs.

In your Christian walk, let Jesus be real to you. Stop looking at the shadows of the Old Testament as the way to walk and relate to God. Law keeps you tied to the Old- man and self-will. Know that:
• The Old Testament gave us patterns and examples to learn from so learn from them. (1Corinthians chapter 10)

- The gospels of Matthew to John show us how Jesus on the cross began, fulfilled and established the New Covenant. This is still Old Testament under the law, but showing transition, so read carefully within context.

- Acts gives an account of the early church, journeying on as God's New Covenant people. Here we see the church in the power of Christ but also sorting out its foundational beliefs seeking to end law and establish grace. (Acts chapter 15)

- The Pauline Epistles from Romans continued to firmly established God's grace and contain all the terms, agreements, and inheritances, of the New Covenant for all believers.
- Revelation shows the present and future end of believers God's covenant people, and unbelievers who reject Jesus.

WHAT ARE SOME OF THE
BENEFITS OF THE NEW COVENANT?

- Christ's shed blood ended the Old Covenant of the Law which demanded strict obedience or punishment. He instead gave a New Commandment of Love in His grace (John 13:34; Hebrews 13:20, 21). After Jesus ended the law on the cross, a new way is opened for grace covenant relationship to deal with His people, to restore the blessings Adam lost, and guarantee His unfailing love just as He had with Adam and Abraham's generation.

- God and man have made a union, of one spirit (1Corinthians 3:23; 6:17). He took your sin and gave you His righteousness so you can be restored in a love relationship with God (2 Corinthians 5:21). Because love never fails, we can take the promises of a loving Father as 'yes' and 'Amen!' (and worship Him in them!)

- The Old Covenant gave us external sacrifices, but under this New Covenant, the guiltless Christ sacrificed Himself, that we could die to "self." By the power of Jesus' blood, the Holy Spirit will cause to die in us, everything Christ died on the cross for. We are to be dead to sin, self-will and all its attachments and be alive in the newness of life to God's will, by the power of the Holy Spirit.

- On His ascension, Jesus became our mediator, advocate, and intercessor before God. We were not left comfortless (Romans 8:26; Hebrews 12:24; I John 2:1).

- Christ has made us able ministers of the New Covenant because we are led by the Holy Spirit. In dependence on the Holy Spirit the miracle life of Christ can also be ours as we live our daily lives and minister (Romans 8:14; 2 Corinthians 3:6).

- We enter New Covenant relationship by faith in the blood of Jesus, not works. Self- effort was replaced by the power of the Holy Spirit as our helper. God is now directly involved in our lives by His Spirit not only to save us but also to lead us on in the Christian journey (Romans 8:9-11).

- The Old Covenant had external rules to govern, but in the New Covenant, God came to live within us by the Spirit of Jesus Christ bringing internal standards to a new heart. Now as we are led by the Holy Spirit, God sees not only actions, but also the motives of our hearts, and we become accountable to God for both; not to rules or to the demands and regulations given by denominations for holiness purposes anymore (Jeremiah 31:31-34; 1 John 3:15,16).

- We have been given power of attorney, authority to use the name of Jesus, power in the blood of Jesus, and the Word of Jesus as weapons to enforce the Satan's defeat and to maintain the victory which Christ won for us (Luke 10: 18,19 ; Philippians 2:9-11; 1 John 1:7).

- We are given a better covenant with better promises. Jesus bore the wages of sin, which is death and, all our sicknesses and diseases. Now we don't have to remain sick, but can only believe, and speak or confess every promise Christ fulfilled for us, act on what we believe by faith and receive our healing (Isaiah 53:4, 5). We have a better covenant because of our faith in Jesus which brings God on the scene to us every time.

Galatians 3:26- 29 tells us in verse 29, *"And if ye be Christ', then are ye Abraham's seed, and heirs according to the promise."*

The original Covenant given in Genesis 12:2 was intended for the whole world. Now all who believe on Jesus can become partakers of the same Covenant blessings as Abraham.

Now what are the blessings? We see them in Deuteronomy 28 1-14 and all through the Gospels and New Testament.

We are partakers by faith in Jesus who shed His blood to give us access into the grace of God in salvation, inheritance and all spiritual blessings. Anywhere you find God's promise as a blessing in the New Testament or an example in the Old Testament, it can be yours.

Galatians 3:13, 14, "*Christ hath redeemed us from the curse of the law, being made a curse for us: for it is written, Cursed is everyone that hangeth on a tree: That the blessings of Abraham might come on the gentiles through Jesus Christ: that we might receive the promise of the Spirit through faith.*"

Take whatever is coming against you negatively, recognize it, and identify it with the Word in Deuteronomy 28 as a curse and speak the opposite Word of your redemption blessings. For example: sickness in cancer (Deuteronomy 28:21, 35, 61).

Matthew 15:13) "*…Every plant, which my heavenly Father hath not planted, shall be rooted up.*"

Isaiah 53:5 "*But he was wounded for our transgressions, he was bruised for our iniquities: the chastisement of our peace was upon him; and with his stripes we are healed.*"

Read the Word, meditate the Word, speak the Word of blessing, believe the Word, act on the Word by faith, rejoice and receive its manifestation from the life of God.

The New Covenant does not depend on your ability to keep it in order to be qualified to receive. It depends on Jesus' ability to keep it, and He kept it and therefore qualified you to receive (Colossians 1:13-14). He did and is still doing it on your behalf as intercessor and advocate as you stand in faith. Just like Abraham and David, you have a covenant with Almighty God. Just like Abraham, you can become fully persuaded that what God has promised you, He is able also to perform and bring it to pass. Just like David, you can stand on your covenant and whip any uncircumcised circumstance that stands in your way: no matter how big it looks. 3

You overcome by simply putting your faith in God's grace. Give it over to Him, believe, hear, do as He says acting in faith, rejoice and receive. God's Covenant of Love gives us assurance that our faith in God's love will cast out all fear as we trust in God.

I John 4:18, "...*there is no fear in love; but perfect love casteth out fear...*"

We enter New Covenant by faith in the blood of Jesus, not works. This humility before God ends self-will and legalism. There is nothing you will have to "do" to get God to love and bless except humble yourself, yield to His love in the Word, and the voice of the Holy Spirit, believe, act on your faith and receive.

Romans 4:16-22, tells us that Abraham was fully persuaded, but fully persuaded by what? It was by the covenant that God made with him with blood. Abraham was fully convinced of God's love, care, and faithfulness to do as He said in Genesis 12:2. Because of The Covenant cut between God and Jesus' blood, we as believers can also be persuaded, be fully assured of God's love, His faithfulness, care, and commitment, never doubting God, because:

- We became one family with God as our heavenly Father who joined us in union relationship with Him, as one in the spirit. In Him, we live and move and have our being. (Acts17: 28).

- Ephesians 1:3 tells us that we are already blessed with all spiritual blessings in heavenly places, and we will receive our blessings when we by faith confess as ours the promises Jesus fulfilled for us. Say the same thing the written Word says, the same thing that Jesus- the living Word- spoke about us and to us, and be assured of God's blessings to you.

- We have been given ordinances of Baptism and Communion as remembrances that the promises and blessings of our covenant are true, sure, and worth remembering because they are eternal (1 Corinthians 11:23). Under the New Covenant of Grace, with better promises, God has given you the same guarantee by His grace. He will do for you all that you cannot do for yourself. He will bless and faithfully care for you if by faith you believe on Him. He will never bring wrath or judgment on His believing children, Whatever God's response is to you, look for His grace because somewhere in all that is happening even in the darkest of times, there is His goodness and mercy at work to see you through (Psalm 23:6; John 3:36; Romans 5:9; 1Thessalonians 5:9; Hebrews 12:1-15).

John 1:17. *"For the Law was given by Moses, but grace and truth came by Jesus Christ."*

Grace is God's power and ability in His love, to show goodness and mercy, to help you both in the spiritual and in the natural realms, where we are unable to help ourselves.

Ephesians 2:8, *"For by grace are ye saved through faith, and that not of yourselves, it is the gift of God"*

Salvation is in Jesus Christ Alone. He alone went to the cross, did it all to save us from sin and death.

Romans 1:16, "For *I am not ashamed of the gospel of Christ: for it is the power of God unto salvation to everyone that believeth: to the Jew first, and also to the Greek."*

The blood of Jesus ushered in the New Covenant of Grace with new and better promises, greater promises is His love, His forgiveness in the power of His Word and His Spirit to deliver. The Holy Spirit within us will keep us in God' will and help us to be transformed and always growing in the likeness and image of our heavenly Father. Jesus is God's grace to the world. He came to Earth bringing God's power in the Holy Spirit and truth in His Word for us to live victoriously under His New Covenant.

The law, which is God's spoken Word in the Old Testament, was truth and was good to point out and contain sin, but it was not God's living word and was harsh and demanded death. Everything the law touched in judgment died, man and beasts alike as it kept people tied to the Old man and to self-will, sin and death. Jesus the living Word however, brought not only truth in the Word of God that pointed out sin, but He also brought life in God's love, and compassion, grace and mercy in forgiveness that wiped out death when one sins. God sent Jesus, to show His love to the whole world. Mankind would not die when they sinned but could now repent and be cleansed of sin and receive the power of the Holy Spirit to keep him in God's will and from practicing sin.

We are saved or born-again in our spirit, at the point of believing in Jesus. It was the love and compassion of God that caused Him to send His only Son to die for our sins (John 3:16). We are continuously and daily being saved in our soul and body, and kept in life by God's grace. We are saved by His power of healing from sickness, protection from death, prosperity from lack, and deliverance from oppression, love from fear. The soul (mind with the imagination, will and emotions) overtime is being saved by being renewed and transformed as we read the Word of God and become doers, continually practicing the Word. The grace of God abides in the power of Jesus through faith in the written Word and through the faith in the spoken Word of the Holy Spirit.

The grace of God abides in the power of Jesus through faith in the written Word and through the faith in the spoken Word of the Holy Spirit.

Complete dependence on God's grace both for salvation and for daily living is the only way to submit to God and have continued victory in the Christian life.

Romans 5:17 says *"... death reigned by one; much more they which receive abundance of grace and the gift of righteousness shall reign in life by one, Jesus Christ."*

Death ruled like a king because Adam sinned. But what Jesus Christ has done on the cross was greater as He caused us to overcome death and to be accepted by God as His children. Now we can live, rule and reign like kings with eternal life. Now Jesus Christ our Lord is the King of us His King's

Revelation 1:6 *"And hath made us kings and priests unto God and his Father..."* This Speaks of Success for us!

Colossians 2:6, *"As ye have therefore received Christ Jesus the Lord, (grace through faith) so walk ye in Him."*

This implies that there is another way Christians could choose to walk. That way is the way of the enemy by the law and self- will. Those having no faith in God doing life their way, exhibiting self-righteousness, restlessness, striving, difficulty, struggle, frustration, self- effort and defeat will experience the law of sin and death.

Romans 8:2, *"For the law of the Spirit of life in Christ Jesus hath made me free from the law of sin and death."*

The Spirit of Life is the life of God in you, it is Faith in His love to depend on the Holy Spirit to help you to do God's will. Righteousness through faith releases grace, which brings peace, joy, rest, victory, and am overcoming life. Jesus, God's grace brought life wherever He went through His love, compassion and power.

Matthew 14:14, *"And Jesus went forth, and saw a great multitude, and was moved with compassion toward them, and he healed their sick."*

Matthew 15: 32 -39, Jesus had compassion on the weary and hungry multitudes and fed the five thousand.

Matthew 20:34, *"So Jesus had compassion on them, and touched their eyes: and immediately their eyes received sight, and they followed him"*

Luke 7:11-15, Jesus had compassion on a widow's only son who died and raised him back to life. John G Lake puts it this way, "Compassion reaches further than law, further than demands of judges. Compassion reaches the heart of life, to the secret of our being." [4]

The law or Ten Commandments and ordinances by themselves bred superiority and self-righteousness, self- will and death. Grace on the other hand promotes love, compassion, humility, God's will and life. That is why the new commandment in the New Testament of grace is love; loving God and others fulfill God's law. This is why the promises are better, the yoke is now easy and the burden light.

THE COVENANT OF GRACE:

John 13:34, "*A new commandment I give unto you, That ye love one another: as I have loved you, that ye also love one another.*"

We need faith in God's grace for our salvation (Romans 4:16; 5:1, 2; Ephesians 2:8; Titus 3:5). We also need faith in God's grace to live our daily Christian life (Matthew 11:28-30; Colossians 2:6; 1 John 2:6, 5:4).

Let's look at some tenets of the Law/ legalism versus Grace/ Power in love: Applied.

- Law refers to a system of rules including the Ten Commandments, ordinances and all other regulations set by the Church, giving man a standard to judge their performance/ behavior as right or wrong, good or bad. There is a strong dependence on self-will and man's ideas of what's right or wrong, also man's own effort or man's ability trying to keep the law in order to be holy and acceptable to God.

This walk of the law in the life of a Christian is in one's own ability and strength and self-will. One of always 'doing', trying to be good to please God. I refer to this as 'law mentality' having a lifestyle based on the law, which keeps you in bondage to self- independence and sin. It brings sin consciousness and the result is condemnation and fear. Law mentality keeps you in bondage as it hinders you from receiving from your full redemption, the freedom which Christ has purchased with His blood.

The law lasted from Moses to Jesus Christ. Now Christ has come and died on the cross all law mentality must cease when in relationship with Jesus Christ (John 14:16, 17; Romans 10:4; Galatians 3:19; Hebrews 10:9, 10; 1 Peter 1:13).

GOD MADE A COVENANT OF BLOOD WITH JESUS

✓ Grace came with Jesus and rests in the finished work of the cross to the ascension. Grace believes Jesus did it all. The work is already done only to be received by faith, believed and rejoiced in for Jesus to continue working on your behalf to meet your current needs. This walk by grace is trust in God's ability as we live and move and have our being "in Christ." It is your believing by faith in and trusting God's love to save and keep you that will bring your desire in times of need (Galatians 3:13, 14; Philippians 2:13; 1 Peter 1:5).

- Law has a belief system of "doing before being," believing God demands righteousness by what you do. "I will give this or do this for God by the way I live or what I do, in strict obedience of self-discipline, or holiness, trying hard to avoid sin". This is self-righteousness, trusting in your own ability, or self-will to be right in God for Him to accept you.

  ✓ Grace is the belief system of "being before doing." Trusting God's will in what He did for you. The righteousness of God is faith in His love. Believing who God made you "in Christ." Be forgiven, be loved, be righteous, be redeemed, be holy, be wise, be complete, be filled, be led by the Holy Ghost, be God's workmanship, all being before doing. Agree with God in who He says you are and stand in faith as the redeemed. Now with God's confidence you can face any mountain and speak in faith for it to be removed (Mark 11:22-24).

- Law Terms that are used to describe law-mentality and self-will are: fleshly, carnal, self-righteousness (being right by your performance), selfishness, self-focus, self- confidence, self- assurance, self-aggrandizement, self- dependence, self- effort, self- performance, and self- protection, a harsh, critical, judgmental and legalistic spirit quick to punish. Law mentality as a way of life, living by the flesh, will fail or always have you needing more as the flesh can never be satisfied.

Haggai 1:5, 6, "...*Consider your ways. Ye have sown much, and bring in little, ye eat, but ye have not enough, ye drink, but ye are not filled with drink, ye clothe you, but there is none warm, and he that earneth wages to put into a bag with holes.*"

Isaiah 14:12, 13, *How art thou fallen from heaven, O Lucifer, son of the morning...For thou hast said in thine heart, I will ascend into heaven, I will exalt my throne above the stars of God: I will sit also upon the mount of the congregation, in the sides of the north.*"

✓ Grace -Terms used to describe God's grace in God's will are: gracious, compassionate, righteousness by faith, walk in the spirit, yielded, humble, love relationship, presence of God, dependence on the Holy Spirit, and trusting in God. Grace admits that we are powerless to save ourselves and, as imperfect beings, our perfection is in God's love. As we allow Him to live in and through us, we will relinquish self-will and be saturated in His love and His will and become satisfied with Jesus.

John 5:14, 15 "*And this is the confidence that we have in him, that if we ask anything according to his will, he heareth us: And if we know that he hear us, whatsoever we ask, we know that we have the petitions that we desired of him.*"

- Law, Believers are saved by grace through faith. But through ignorance or pride, they resort to or choose to walk out their Christian life by law and self-will with works or self-effort to be saved, or to accomplish their life's goals. "Self" often feels good when things are going alright, but will fall to pieces when things are bad and later crash in despair.

✓ Grace - 1 Peter 1:5, "*Who are kept by the power of God, through faith unto salvation...*"

- Law ignores the power of the Holy Spirit living within to help you grow and live for Christ. Always struggling and trying or striving harder. One often fails, to believe God by taking His Word as true, and to walk in faith trusting God (Romans 7:15-21).

✓ Grace is living smarter, living by Jesus' power:

Romans 8:14, *"For as many as are led by the Spirit of God, they are the sons of God."*

1 Thessalonians 5:24, *"Faithful is he that calleth you, who also will do it."*

- Law minded persons do not really know the power of God for them and very often depend on others who they believe are in a closer relationship with God to pray for them.

  ✓ Grace. Because righteousness is by faith, we are reconciled into God's love and into relationship through the Holy Spirit. Who is our connector. As you walk on the Christian journey, keep drawing near to God through the Holy Spirit and He will draw near to you. In the relationship, trust will develop to receive from God for yourself (Hebrews 10:22; James 4:8).

- Law focuses on self-will, and what one often sees in "self" is weakness, insecurities, unworthiness, failure, sin, or sin-consciousness or pride. This often creates distance between you and God with the feeling you do not have the power to connect to Him or to overcome in order to live a victorious Christian life. Therefore, living in the flesh from the external cause's one to "give in" to a life of sinning and repenting or internally succumb to guilt, condemnation, feelings of insecurities, unworthiness, shame, depression and defeat. Give yourself up to God!

  ✓ Grace is living from the internal from the Spirit, by God's Word, where there is Love, joy, peace, patience, gentleness, goodness, faith, meekness, and self-control (Galatians 5:22). Righteousness; peace, and joy in the Holy

Ghost. Power love and a sound mind. We become doers of the Word, overcomers and conquerors because God's love causes us to rejoice in His greatness within us, and knowing His love never fails we believe and receive of Him. (Romans 8:37; 14:17; James 1:22-25; 2 Timothy 1:7).

- Law mindedness still holding on to self-will not ready to surrender fully to Jesus is always thinking the devil, or people are the source of all their trouble. One engages in constant spiritual warfare with Satan- binding and rebuking and casting down. Binding and loosing in this way is not of faith but in fear and gives the Devil way too much attention multiplying demonic activity in your life or strife with other people. Faithlessness is sin and that is why legalism attracts demonic activity to your life.

- Romans 14:23, "...*Whatever is not of faith is sin*

  ✓ Grace, whatever the problem is, turn to God's will first, whether in the Word, praying, fasting, or praying in the Spirit. Take what Jesus says in the Word, by the Spirit, or by another trusted believer: receive it by faith, as a done deal. Enforce Satan's defeat over your situation by binding Him in faith, then immediately turn your attention to God and His Word believe and speak what God said to you. Agree with God's Word in all things, act in faith on His Word and stay rejoicing until the victory is won (Matthew 18:18).

- Law mentality often brings feelings that one is imperfect and does not measure up to God's standards. This causes doubts that He will not hear or answer your prayers. Often one judges oneself and others harshly, feeling as though if one is not perfect, he or she is not worthy or acceptable to God or anyone else. Helplessness in the thinking of this person's behavior is "since I cannot always be good I might as well be bad." Carnal or criminal behavior is often the result.

✓ Grace says Jesus is your righteousness. You are the righteousness of God in Christ, worthy and accepted in the beloved, why? It is because of the blood of Jesus alone. Satan has tricked you into looking at yourself and your performance, as the way to determine your worth or righteousness. Reject Satan's lies, and his use of the law against you, and live by God's grace, "looking unto Jesus the author and finisher of our faith." (2 Corinthians 3: 17-18; Hebrews 12:2)

- Law, Keeps you tied to the Old man and self-will, always looking at yourself how you're doing spiritually and otherwise. Excessive introspection, looking at yourself, puts you back under the law with a right versus wrong mentality. The devil will then always keep pointing at you that you are wrong, and in need of judgment and punishment. The consequences which follow are accusations, sin- consciousness, guilt, fear, condemnation, unworthiness, discouragement, and ultimately depression. Let us as believers not side with the Devil who is always pointing fingers to self.

✓ Grace looks unto Jesus at all times, keeping your eyes on Him. Keeping your eyes on Jesus means letting your thoughts, words, attitudes, and actions be directed by the Word of God and the Holy Spirit. If you are right you rejoice with your eyes on Jesus, and if you are wrong you rejoice in the precious blood of Jesus that provided forgiveness with cleansing, and receive it by faith then:

"Rejoice in the Lord alway, and again I say rejoice" (Philippians 4:4) (Micah 7:8-10; 1John 1:7).

- Law sees sin as simply a given set of rules and regulations, to be strictly obeyed while others see them as a list of the fun pleasurable things that God is keeping from them. No one can keep the law, therefore this view keeps people falling back into sin again and again for more pleasure, also

because flesh cannot obey the law perfectly, failure and self
-condemnation is imminent.

✓ Grace sees faith in the person of our Lord and Savior
Jesus Christ and His love as the standard. When you show
your love for Jesus, by having faith in Him, His grace in the
power of His Holy Spirit comes and helps, keeps, sustains
you above sin and He also will, lead and guide you into
obeying God (Philippians 2:13).

- Law often has a wrong concept of God, seeing Him as
distanced, insensitive, angry, demanding, distanced, stingy
or mean, condemning, harsh, A Joy- killer, controlling,
inaccessible, a hard- taskmaster, full of judgment, and
punishment.

✓ Grace sees God through Jesus' eyes: full of love, mercy,
compassion, gentleness, kindness, He is accessible, and
a good Father. God gives you freedom to make choices
and wants you to enjoy life, but within the boundaries of
His love, in order to avoid bad consequences. In spite of
whatever you do in life He is accepting, loving, intimate,
and forgiving.

- Law or legalism keeps the old-man alive through self-will;
as you continually keep struggling with the same old attitudes and mindsets you had before you became born-again
with seemingly little hope to overcome. (Romans 6:11-14).

✓Grace gives up on oneself. Yielding to God in complete
surrender of our hearts over to Jesus. A divine exchange
takes place when we receive God's love and His gift of
righteousness: sin in exchange for His love (Romans 6:17,
18).

- Because of an incomplete surrender of the legalistic heart
to God, there will be wrestling and a struggling to hear
God speak to you. Why? Because this heart is divided and
will most times be asking, is it God or is it me? Is it me or is
it the devil. Legalism tells you that you have already failed

God in this your imperfect and inconclusive response in hearing God. Therefore as you continue to wrestle with indecision trying in your own strength to get it right in order to obey God. The devil moves in with accusations, confusion, guilt and condemnation. This was one of the most challenging aspects of this journey. But thanks be to God who causes us to triumph in Christ Jesus.

✓ Grace gives it all up to God. This struggle was about yielding the self-will to the Holy Spirit. Give up that instruction you thought you heard to God. Confess who you are in Christ, made in His righteousness, the very righteousness of God in Christ Jesus, born of His incorruptible seed. Confess that the Holy Spirit dwells in you, you have the mind of Christ and He will lead you into all truth. Now go pray in the Holy Ghost (This will be addressed in a later Chapter) and ask God to confirm His truth of what you think He said to you, and be expectant to hear in the spirit of peace with the aim of exalting Jesus and the Kingdom of God. Never yield to condemnation or resort to looking at yourself or your perceived failure in hearing or obeying God. Trust in God, the Holy Spirit will help you to obey God (Philippians 2:13; Colossians 3:15; Hebrews 8:10-11; 13:21).

• Law minded people are often those who are afraid of grace, that grace is a license to sin. This is a man- engineered thought, and is a lie from the devil to keep Christians under the Law. It keeps their human will tied to Satan, listening to him, acting in their own efforts, and in the flesh to get to God by works or to solve their own personal problems or the problems of the church in self-effort. Often the results is failure or strife and as mentioned in (Galatians 5:19-21, 1 Timothy 1:9, 10).

✓ God's grace is not a license to sin but God's power given in forgiveness, for a person to repent of sin, and receive His grace in the power of the Holy Spirit to be kept unto God and from sin or from practicing sin. One needs grace to keep them from sin and if, or after, they sin they can still go to God for His grace in mercy.

"Who are kept by the power of God through faith unto salvation ready to be revealed in the last time (1 Peter 1:5).

"Let us therefore come boldly unto the throne of grace, that, we may obtain mercy, and find grace to help in time of need" (Hebrews 4:16).

(Luke 7:46-47; Romans 6:14; 2 Corinthians 5:14, 15; 1 Timothy 6; Titus 2:11, 12; 1 John 3:3-9)

- Law mentality gets weary, tired and gives ultimatums which justifies giving up or controlling others. This failure to fully trust God is the very source of giving up on the calling and the things of God as well in difficult relationships. Divorce and break up of many Christian families is the tragic result (Galatians 6:9, 10).

✓ Grace trusts God's will, and His righteousness, in every person and every situation for His solution (Proverbs 3:5,6; Romans 14:4; 5:17).

I am always reminded of this. We are children of God and a good parent does not neglect or cast away the child when, in learning to walk they fall down, we should not do the same to the adults in our lives, when they fall or fail. God likewise without rebuke picks us up brushes us off, and helps us to continue to walk on. Trust His covenant of grace in every life connected to yours.

Always run to God! Trust His will and not your own. God's Covenant is a covenant of grace, establishing you and keeping you and others always in His love.

Romans 8:35, *"Who shall separate us from the love of Christ? shall tribulation, or distress, or persecution, or famine, or nakedness, or peril or sword?*

His Covenant love for us is unbreakable. Always trust in His love and His care.

CONFESSIONS-:

1. The blood of Jesus has shed the love of God abroad in my heart. I receive His Covenant love and I rejoice in so great a salvation. His perfect love in my heart casts out all fear sanctifies me wholly spirit, soul and body and preserves me blameless before my Father, filled with love, joy, peace, longsuffering, gentleness, Goodness, faith, meekness and temperance. In Him I live move and have my being. I live in His strength. Jesus loves me, and I receive His love, deep within my heart, because I receive His sacrifice in the blood of Jesus. I rest in His great love for me as I live in His Grace and rejoice, for the Joy of the Lord is my strength (Nehemiah 8:10b; Acts 17:28; Romans 5:5;1; Galatians 5:22; Thessalonians 5:23)

2. Jesus loves me. His love is shed abroad in my heart. I belong to Jesus I rest in Him. I rest in His grace and let Him rule and reign in and through my heart, as I trust in Him.

   Proverbs 3:5, 6 *"...trust in the Lord with all thine heart; and lean not unto thine own understanding: In all thy ways acknowledge him, and he shall direct thy paths."*

3. Father I need deliverance. As the children of Israel under their covenant rested in you with blood on their door posts, I now rest in the blood of Jesus and I rest in His Anointing. I am your Covenant child; deliver me from_____ in Jesus' name. Spirit of _____ (sickness, worry, fear) come out in Jesus name. I believe, rejoice and receive. Amen

4. I thank you for the anointing within to raise a standard and drive out every darkness and every evil from me and put me over. I rest in your grace I believe and receive your deliverance in Jesus' name Amen.

CHAPTER 6

MADE RIGHTEOUS TO LIVE IN RIGHTEOUSNESS

2 Corinthians 5:21, "For he hath made him to be sin for us, who knew no sin; that we might be made the righteousness of God in him."

Romans 5:17, "For if by one man's offence death reigned by one; much more they which receive abundance of grace and of the gift of righteousness shall reign in life by one, Jesus Christ."

The definition of righteousness from the Greek translation is: Purity of heart and morally correct behavior in life. It is the purity of heart, being free from sin, that gives us the ability to see things God's way and with faith in His love believe that we can stand righteously in the presence of God as loved, worthy, acceptable, and free from fear, guilt, and condemnation.

"Righteousness is the rightness of God. The rightness of God in your spirit, the rightness of God in your soul, the rightness of God in your body, the rightness of God in your affairs, in your home, in your business , everywhere."[5]

Adam's sin brought sin on the whole human race. God, by His grace, sent Jesus to die on the cross. On the cross, Jesus became sin by absorbing all the sins of everyone in the whole world into Himself. God seeing sin in His Son turned His back on Him, when

Jesus said My God, My God, why hast thou forsaken me? Jesus was forsaken that we could be accepted.

Ephesians 1:6 *"To the praise of the glory of his grace, wherein he hath made us accepted in the beloved."*

Jesus took our sins to the grave when He was buried. He paid the penalty for our sins to satisfy the demands of the Law which says, *"The wages of sin is death"* (Romans 6:23). With the born-again experience, all your sins are forgiven, all guilt removed, and in exchange, God gave you Jesus' righteousness: His right relationship or right standing with God, His Father. Jesus had a perfect relationship of approval and acceptance with God, and we do too through the blood of Jesus. We have been made right with God.

"According as he hath chosen us in him before the foundation of the world, that we should be holy and without blame before Him in love" (Ephesians 1:4).

We have been drawn into a love relationship with God through Jesus His Son. "…That the love wherewith thou hast loved me may be in them, and I in them" (John 17:26b)

Believe that you are in union with God, in one spirit with Him, and this union relationship is righteousness by faith. Righteousness is being positioned with the gift of acceptance, restored love, and belonging, given from God to everyone who is born- again.

God accepted Jesus, and we are "in Christ"; therefore He loves and accepts us too when our faith is in Jesus. The gift of being positioned in righteousness must be acknowledged and accepted by faith; otherwise a person will start a pattern of working to earn right relationship with God. This is works, self-will, self- righteousness, legalism or a law mentality, which says, "If I do a task that pleases God, I am ok with God." This is a lie from the enemy. When salvation is accepted by faith, it is faith- righteousness in the heart, which believes that God's love is received and the yoke of sin is destroyed.

You are now righteous and are put back in right standing or restored relationship with God your heavenly Father. God now sees you as loved, acceptable, chosen, valuable, righteous, worthy and free from all guilt and condemnation which separated you from Him. He also placed the Holy Spirit within to help you obey Him as you are led from the heart, and not rules of the law. Now when you believe God by faith, your actions can be counted as righteousness just as our forefather Abraham.

The gift of being positioned in righteousness must be acknowledged and accepted by faith.

In Christ Jesus, a believer is forgiven, made pure, holy, innocent, righteous, and redeemed. It is having the faith to believe in this truth of God's love and forgiveness in repentance why no accusation or condemnation should succeed against a believer. Jesus is truth and Satan cannot successfully counter truth. He tried before and was kicked out of heaven (John 14:6; Ephesians 4:21; Colossians 1:22).

We have power in the blood of Jesus and His Word to kick Satan out of our life and situations.

Romans 8; 1, 2 *"There is therefore now no condemnation to them which are in Christ Jesus, who walk not after the flesh, but after the Spirit. For the law of the spirit of life in Christ Jesus hath made me free from the law of sin and death."*

What is the law of the spirit of life in Christ Jesus? It is righteousness, faith in God's love (John 13:34; Romans 4:5; 13:8-10; James 2:8). When we love God by faith we believe and obey Him and when we mess up the gateway of love is forgiveness; forgiveness with repentance gives salvation and causes all the blessings of God to flow. Love in obeying God by faith and true repentance or received forgiveness, will set you free from the enemy and his law of sin and death, which may be lack, sickness, condemnation, demonic oppression and so on. The role of the believer is to love God and others and to live by God's truth, in faith-righteousness. This means turning to God first, hearing and obeying Him, repenting genuinely and quickly with your heart towards God to receive His grace. If you do this, no condemnation can ever come to you.

If condemnation still comes after you have repented, either you are still in self-will or self-effort neglecting God's grace or the devil is attacking and lying to you that you are not righteous or not for given. Reject his lies. Cast your cares to God, to end self-effort and cast Satan's attacks down choosing Christ word on your righteousness (1 Corinthians 1:30; 2 Corinthians 10:4-5; Philippians 4:8).

> *If condemnation still comes after you have repented, the devil is attacking and lying to you.*

Examples of your righteousness before God:

The enemy accuses you, "Your nose is crooked and you are ugly."

Righteousness says, "I reject you Satan because God says (Psalm 107:2; 139:14-17)."

The enemy says, "You are unworthy, because you did not behave well or you did something wrong." Then, turn to: (2 Corinthians 5:21; Ephesians 1:6; Philippians 2:13; Hebrews 9:14; 10:2).

The enemy says, "You are a bad person." Turn to: (1 Corinthians 1:30; Colossians 1:22; 1 Peter 2:9).

When there are accusations or condemnation from the enemy, first claim your position of union relationship based on the blood and then speak out:

Jesus bore all accusations and condemnation for me and opened not His mouth. "I stand in His silence and I command every mouth opened against me speaking unrighteousness to be stopped because no weapon formed against me can prosper. I am pure, holy, innocent and righteous by the blood of Jesus, which made me free" (Isaiah 53:7) (Romans 5:17; Philippians 4:8; Colossians 1:22; 1 John 4:4).

A righteous person sees himself and everything about him and others as God sees in through His blood and in His Word. Righteousness is very important because it answers the question, "What is my relationship to God like, and how do I see myself and others?" Am I a believer, established in right relationship with God and His Word by grace through faith knowing I am loved by God? Am I believer but still religious doing works, striving and trying to feel connected to God by my own efforts? Am I an unbeliever who has no relationship with God and is in sin or unrighteousness? Also, do I see others through the eyes of faith or condemnation?

Am I a believer, but still trying to feel connected to God by my own efforts?

When the gift of righteousness is accepted by faith, a loving relationship is restored between God and yourself. He is your loving Father and you become established in a loving relationship with Him as His loving child completely dependent on Him for your care and your works or actions are only a response to His Word and His Spirit. When the gift of righteousness is neglected, that person has chosen to work for God's love, meaning they do works and good deeds to please and to be accepted by Him.

For example, one can believe she should not wear pants, only skirts, or not wear make-up or jewelry to be holy. This is feeling that one must always do good or do everything right and holy-looking before God will accept you. These people might also say, "I can't miss church one Sunday without feeling guilty, I must worship on a particular day, be baptized in the name of Jesus only, follow doctrine or denomination rules by the letter of a book or God will not be pleased." These are "Works:" performance or self-righteousness. This will also manifest in your daily life, as trying to solve life's problems on your own, in your own way, or in your own strength. This is all self-will, law mentality (legalism) and opens the door to the devil's attacks in your life, bringing sickness, guilt, fear and failure and death.

"Ye which rejoice in a thing of nought, which say, Have we not taken to us horns by our own strength? But, behold I will raise up against you a nation O house of Israel..." (Amos 6:13,14)

IT IS IMPORTANT TO
MAKE TWO DISTINCTIONS HERE:

(1) You must separate (a) God's love for you from (b) your efforts of trying to gain His love or to please Him for acceptance. God loves you and accepts you in Jesus Christ! He loved you enough to die for you, even when you were a sinner. His love is unconditional, not dependent on your performance (Romans 5:8, Romans 8:31-38). Separate the real you, in your human spirit, from your actions; whether you are good or bad, as a believer, God still loves you. Just like a parent's love for his child is not diminished when they are bad, fellowship may decline, but love never will, so it is even more so with God, your heavenly Father. He will continuously seek to bring you back into righteousness or right relationship with Him. The correct approach in response to God's love and acceptance is to believe you are loved and accepted by faith. Whatever the situation good or bad, choose right relationship and respond to Him by faith, and trust Him in return to help you to make the wrong right in order to live pleasing Him (Hebrews 13:21).

I John 4:19, *"We love him, because he first loved us."*

If your actions displease God, He still loves you. He still will not abandon you, but He will cause the Holy Spirit to teach and lead you back into truth, repentance, righteousness, and fellowship. Turn to Him and trust Him to do it; do not try to work your way back to God with works (John 14:26; John 16:8, 13; Philippians 2:13).

(2) You must also separate (a) who you are from (b) what you do. If you are born- again, you are righteous, Period. Your works, actions, performances - good or bad- does not affect your right relationship with God. Your fellowship will be affected, but you are loved, valuable, accepted, and worthy just because Jesus died for you. His blood alone made you righteous.

If you sin or miss the mark, you are a righteous person who has sinned , or has done an unrighteous act, and whose fellowship has been hindered. Since you know you have done wrong, as the Holy

Spirit is convicting you of righteousness, first acknowledge your righteousness, go to God and confess the wrong, receive His forgiveness by faith, and receive His grace to turn from the sin. Now forget it and move on in Christ, rejoicing in His goodness and trusting His grace to keep you cleansed with forgiveness (Romans 5:1; Philippians 2:13; Hebrews 4:16; I John 1:9).

If the devil is trying to chump up a charge of wrongdoing or unrighteousness against you, even though in your awareness you did nothing wrong. He is attacking your righteousness for you to question your position of love and acceptance towards God. Reject him by confessing your redemption from Him and that your righteousness before God is by the blood of Jesus and not your performance (Psalm 107:2; 1 Corinthians 6:11; 2 Corinthians 5:21; Ephesians 1:7)

This explains 1 John 1:7:

"But if we walk in the light, as he is in the light, we have fellowship one with another, (God and man) and the blood of Jesus Christ his Son cleanseth us from all sin."

Jesus is the light of the world, because you walk in the light of His word and His Spirit you have fellowship with God and His blood is cleansing you now and continually from all sin.

Neglecting to believe and confess your righteousness:

- Leads to legalism and works of self-will, or trying to earn acceptance (Galatians 3)

- Leads to performance of one's own efforts which ultimately leads to failure, instead of trusting God's grace, through faith, to overcome and succeed (Ephesians 2:8).

- Leads to one's performance, operating by the law to never feel like it measures up to God's standard, because the yoke of sin and sin-consciousness is still alive. When failure comes, guilt and condemnation follows (Romans 7).

- Leads to being unsure of your identity, as to who you are, and your correct relationship with God. This insecurity causes you to be exposed to the lies of the devil, telling you who he, the devil, says you are influencing you to forget what God has said to you to and about whom you are "in Christ". The result will be carnality increasing in your life as you yield to the devils lies.

- Will cause you to feel distanced from God in relationship, shrinking from Him, especially when one sin thinking you are unworthy and that He is angry and wants to judge and punish you.

- Leads to accusations and condemnation from the enemy; fear will constantly be a part of your life. You will become a legalistic person, focused on self and doing works, impatient with self and others, judgmental, critical, and easily angered fearful and lacks peace.

How Does Righteousness Apply to Your Everyday Life?

1. When you accept by faith that you have been made righteous, you accept God's grace in Jesus and all He has already done for you in the Gospel. You know that God loves you, accepts you, and that you are worthy and valuable to Him. You can rest in the loving arms of your Father and can look to and depend on Him at all times for salvation, healing, deliverance, protection, peace, and provision. Christ's righteousness qualifies you to position yourself in a love relationship to believe and receive from God.

2. God made you righteous by His grace through Jesus Christ, just as He made water into wine. It happened at His Word. When you believe on Jesus Christ His righteousness in you gives you right standing or right relationship with God. He now expects you to put faith in what He did and walk in righteousness by the power of His Spirit.

Colossians 2:6, *"As ye have therefore received Christ Jesus the Lord, so walk ye in him."*

3. You received the righteousness of God in Christ, so walk out your salvation (Christian life), seeing yourself for who you are

in Christ, as righteous, a saint, redeemed, holy and free. His Word said so, believe it! Rest in His righteousness and perfection, and see yourself as acceptable to God only because of the blood of Jesus and not your performance.

4. God's grace (God's ability in Jesus) can only work through righteousness. Grace can only reign with power and strength in you if you know and accept that you are righteous. Grace in righteousness releases the power of Holy Spirit to work on your behalf. Law the opposite, leads to works/selfishness, flesh, self-life, absence of Holy Sprit's power and eventually death.

Romans 5:21, *"That as sin hath reigned unto death, even so might grace reign through righteousness unto eternal life by Jesus Christ our Lord."*

5. Knowing that you are a righteous child of God will settle your identity and show His acceptance for you. It will give you security, confidence, and a healthy self-esteem in God. When you read the Word and see yourself as God sees you, then you will have stability and assurance forever (Isaiah 32:17, 18).

6. You will see yourself in Christ and choose to live in the newness of life as a new creation, which is in God-consciousness and not sin-consciousness. Righteousness will always keep your faith turned toward God your Father in loving dependence. If you sin, acknowledge you're still the righteous child of God in need of forgiveness. When you receive forgiveness, by faith, the Spirit of God will go to work by Jesus' blood and cleanse you of all unrighteousness. Let God be your first focus and response in all situations.

7. Because you are righteous (have right standing/ right relationship with God), you will live the Christian life as a righteous person who is doing the right thing and living God's way. Rest in faith towards God first, and then do only what He directs by the Word and Holy Spirit.

James 2:17, *"Even so Faith, if it hath not works, is dead, being alone."*

By faith you bless and curse not (Luke 6:28; Romans 14:4), cast all your cares instead of worrying (1 Peter 5:7). Instead of being critical, trust God in your life and with the life of others (Romans 5:17) Righteousness, with right thinking, according to God's word in your mind frees you from worry and fear.

"Father, I trust your righteousness and your abundant grace in the life of _____to make things right for them. I release them to you and thank you in advance for what you will do In Jesus name Amen" (Romans 5:17). No need to worry about our loved ones instead we are to pray, trusting in God.

8.   Righteousness causes grace to flow from God to us and from us to others, rather than un-forgiveness, judgment, condemnation, harshness and threats of punishment.

9.   Righteousness will cause you to live in rest and peace, not in the burden of the self-life which lacks faith. When In the performance-mode, you will always be working, trying, striving to succeed, and always seeking approval from people. All these things put you back under the law of self-will and under Satan's power. Substitute 'trying' for yourself with 'trusting' in Jesus.

10. Righteousness makes it possible for you to open your heart and receive God's unconditional love, which will free you unto greater fellowship, greater faith and intimacy with God (Colossians 1:20, 21).

11. The opposite of righteousness is sin and condemnation. Righteousness frees you from the power of sin-consciousness and condemnation from the enemy and other people. (Romans 3:21-25).

12. Righteousness, faith in God's love, frees you from the power of Satan. Righteousness declares you loved, justified, not guilty but innocent before God freed to receive all of God's blessings. Satan lied on, accused, and condemned Jesus, an innocent man. Because you are in Christ, He absorbed all accusation and condemnation for you. If you believe God's truth as to who you are in Christ, none of Satan's lies, accusations and condemnation can stick to

you, because Jesus bore it and made you righteous (Isaiah 53:7; Romans 8:1,2; 1 Corinthians 6:11).

13. Righteousness which is receiving God's love, innocence, and right-relationship will result in you, by faith in God's grace, do right or taking the right action, which in turn, brings peace (Isaiah 32:17, 18; Romans 5:1; Colossians 1:20-22).

14. You will reign in life, be victorious, because of the gift of righteousness and God's abundant grace (Romans 5:17).

15. Freedom in conscience and in the mind: Righteousness, right standing and repentance in daily life, frees the conscience and mind from guilt of sin and sin-consciousness that comes as a result of sin, or the lies, accusations and condemnation, that the enemy speaks to you about yourself and others. When you see yourself as God says in His Word, you will reject the lies of the enemy and prevent the development of fear, intimidation, unworthiness, guilt condemnation, depression and oppression.

16. Righteousness gives boldness: When you know you are righteous (right, acceptable and loved in God's eyes) because of the blood of Jesus, it gives you boldness and freedom to enter into God's presence. Similarly, because you know you are righteous and justified before God (innocent, just as if you never sinned) you can stand in authority against the enemy. Without righteousness or right relationship with God, you are weak before God, weak in yourself, and weak against the enemy.

17. Righteousness causes one to see God in His true nature as loving, kind, just, good and faithful; not, wrathful, judgmental, and harsh as portrayed by the law of the Old Testament where Love of the Father in the face of Jesus was not yet revealed as was done in the New Testament.

18. Righteousness leads us to holiness and an abundant life (John 17: 3; Romans 6:11-18), not law mentality, which says; "If I look, behave and speak holy, my holiness will make me righteous and acceptable with the Father." Righteousness leads to holy living NOT holy living leads to righteousness.

19. Righteousness gives freedom from the power of sin. Righteousness destroys the dominion of sin (Romans 6:11), thereby destroying the power of the enemy to enslave you. Righteousness is what the Holy Spirit uses to bring conviction to help you resist temptation; or, if you have already sinned, the Holy Spirit urges you to repent and return to the path of righteousness (John 16:8-10; Hebrews 4:16).

20. Righteousness increases capacity for faith towards God. Righteousness is a restored love relationship and fellowship with God which breeds faith and trust. When you know God loves you because of Jesus' righteousness and know that He is pleased with you because He is pleased with Jesus, faith will increase in fellowship and in your ability to receive from God (1 John 1: 7-9, 3:21, 22).

21. Righteousness keeps you seated in heavenly places in Christ (Ephesians 2:6). The enemy's job is to constantly try to unseat and get you to believe you are unrighteous or try to pull you down to walk in the flesh or self-will which is unrighteousness or sin.

22. James 5:16b, *"... The effectual fervent prayer of a righteous man availeth much."* Righteousness gives assurance that God hears you when you pray. A believer standing in righteousness and assurance of right relationship with God knows God hears and answers their prayers (1 John 5:14, 15).

Grace is God's power working in your life through His Spirit to show goodness and mercy.

Live in God's grace through righteousness, instead of law and self-effort with condemnation. Grace is God's power working in your life through His Spirit to show goodness and mercy. The opposite of grace is the law, self-will or flesh, so reject it (Psalm 23:6; Romans 8:1, 2; Galatians 3:1, 4).

(Philippians 3:3-10), *"For we are the circumcision, which worship God in the spirit, and rejoice in Christ Jesus, and have no confidence in the flesh. Though I might also have confidence in the flesh. If any other man thinketh that he hath whereof he might trust in the flesh, I more...*"

Paul in this scripture described how he trusted in himself and the system of the law to do what he thought was right. The flesh refers to man's ability and self-achievement within man's world system. We are operating under the law and in the flesh when we try to change ourselves or others. We are also under the law when we perform, becoming what we think we should be by our own strength, efforts, and ways without God's help (Psalm 27).

God gave the law to Moses in the Ten Commandments. They were a system of rules and regulations for people to follow so that they could show love for God and man. The law gave mankind a standard of conduct and was a means of showing man where he went wrong or sinned. Law depended on man's power to keep changing and trying to do better. The law demanded perfection in behavior, but it gave no means or ability to help man to behave or change (Romans 3:19-22)To live by the law is to live in the flesh, meaning in your own strength and your own power, trying to succeed in pleasing God and succeeding in life by your own thinking. Because man left to himself is selfish and is always looking out for number one, the law will always work selfishness of the flesh and produce death. God had instituted the law for a period of time to keep man from sin until Jesus could come. (Romans 10:4; Galatians 3:19).

Jesus came, died, forgave our sins, and made our spirit perfect and righteous when He chose to live inside of us at the born-again experience. We could now be directed from within by the Holy Spirit. Our soul and body were redeemed but unchanged (not saved). God told us what to do about our soul and body in (Romans 12:1, 2; 2 Corinthians 6:16, 17). Having now established yourself in God by faith — righteousness, God expects you to continue your everyday life in faith by feeding your righteous spirit with the Word of God and get strong on the inside. Your righteous spirit within having gotten strong will begin to dominate and to direct your soul and body into a righteous lifestyle. We must believe God's truth about us and live our lives in faith doing the right thing through God's grace, rather than through your own self-effort or legalism.

Through Grace, we are born again and positioned in right relationship with God by the gift of righteousness. More grace flows in the baptism/power of the Holy Spirit, and as we grow, our capacity of faith in God's grace increases with power to live a successful Christian life and to give God's love and grace to others. Give God all the Glory!

John 1:17 says, *"For the law was given by Moses, but grace and truth came by Jesus Christ."*

Man, in himself, has no ability to keep the law, but when he is born-again and puts faith in what Jesus did for him, trusting God's righteousness, grace flows from his heart to follow after God. This means that Jesus is the source of all your power and strength for a successful life. If you try to keep The Ten Commandments and other regulations of the Old Testament, without the Holy Spirit or try living by the flesh, you will fail. In the flesh there will always be weakness, because it lacks God's power and ability to help you to succeed (John 15:5).

Satan often tricks people into thinking that they can do life without or ahead of God. He tricked Eve in the Garden of Eden, and he has been tricking people ever since.

When you look at what you do towards God or for yourself (works, good actions, performance without faith) as the way to be right with God that puts you back under the law, because you will not always get it right. When you are wrong, the enemy uses the law to accuse you of wrongdoing, sin and failure. He then judges you as flawed, inferior and unworthy. This knowledge of weakness and sin-consciousness will lead to condemnation, fear, discouragement, lack of motivation, and depression. This is self-dependence and pride. To counter this, people take drugs to bring them back up; as they try to get a false high feeling that all is well. This will all lead to destruction and death.

On the other hand, when you put your faith in Jesus and you have faith-righteousness and dependence on Him, even in your weaknesses and flaws, He will come to you in His strength and power of His Spirit to show the way out or give immediate deliverance and lift you up.

> *He will come to you in His strength and power to show the way out.*

2 Corinthians 12:9 *"...My grace is sufficient for thee: for my strength is made perfect in weakness..."*

Humble yourself unto God; He will give you real life.

1 John 5:12 says, *"He that hath the Son, hath life."*

When you believe by faith the truth of God, His Word, who He says you are, what He says you have in His promises, and what He says you can do, then you have a righteous heart that will allow you to be empowered by the Holy Spirit with the resurrection power of Jesus to overcome.

Ephesians 1:19, 20 says, *"And what is the exceeding greatness of his power to us-ward who believe, according to the working of his mighty power, Which he wrought in Christ, when he raised him from the dead, and set him at his own right hand in the heavenly places."*

A righteous heart believes what God says, even if at first it's only by mental assent. Keep speaking the Word over yourself until the heart begins to believe it. Once the heart believes what God says, then pray, because you believe. Act on His word, worship and let His Grace, His power, and His ability begin to flow to bring the change that is needed to bring life to you (Mark 11:24).

Walk In Righteousness

A. Walk in righteousness before God by putting faith in His Grace. This is faith- righteousness: put faith in God's love in what Jesus has accomplished for you at the cross through His shed blood. You are made righteous (1 Corinthians 1:30). Speak this often until your heart believes. "God loves me, God loves me. His love is shed abroad in my heart, and I love Him because He first loved me. His perfect love in my heart believes He will take care of this situation and therefore I cast out all fear. I am the righteousness of God in Christ Jesus, and I am delivered."

Stand before God in faith at all times, never in works or self-will or effort.

Hebrews 11:6, *"But without faith it is impossible to please him: for he that cometh to God must believe that he is, and that he is a rewarder of them that diligently seek him."*

B. Let God be God in your life. It takes humility for you to ask of God. Allow Him to minister to you and wait for Him to do it. Never exalt yourself on the throne of your life by taking pride in doing things by yourself or trusting in your ability only. Instead, trust His grace, power, and ability to precede yours and lead you to bring to pass whatever you need in your life.

Colossians 2:6, *"As you have therefore received Christ Jesus the Lord, so walk ye in him."*

Acknowledge that you are righteous; you were "made" righteous. This truth never changes when you sin, so assure your heart always with this truth.

If you have sinned, receive forgiveness and grace to overcome; then, move on (I John 1:9; Hebrews 4:16; 10:2).

If you have a problem or lack in finances, go to the Lord of all Grace and, pray, *"Lord Jesus, I no longer want to be anxious about this problem. I hand it over to you and ask for your grace to deliver me. I leave it in your care. You are in charge, and I thank you for taking care of it, because of what you word says in Philippians 4:19."*

Speak the Word concerning finances, begin to rejoice, and give thanks in advance; worship God as your provider. Then, listen for

---

instructions or watch for His response to you (it may be a response like working overtime on your job or giving of your financial resources). Obey Him and you will overcome.

If you have a bad habit (e.g. smoking), grace says *"Lord, I am trying to stop smoking, but it is hard and I cannot stop on my own. I place my trust in you because I am righteous and I am trusting your grace and the power of your blood to deliver me. Thank you, Father, for deliverance in Jesus' name."*

With your trust in God speaking the word of deliverance in Colossians 1:13, resist the flesh and be led by the Holy Spirit; it may be to resist the enemy and the urge to buy more cigarettes.

When temptation comes to make you fall back into the bad habit, use Hebrews 4:16:

"Let us therefore come boldly unto the throne of grace that we may obtain mercy, and find grace to help in time of need."

Father, I just messed up again, I run to your throne of grace and by faith I trust in your power to help and deliver me. Thank you for doing it for me. Help me again to avail myself to your strength to overcome. Amen

Run to the throne of grace and ask for His help and His grace to resist the temptation. Every time you slip, stay in faith and continue to thank Him for His grace and His strength to overcome. Worship Him as your deliverer and if you are sincere about giving up that habit you will by His grace be free.

Live in thanksgiving, praise, and worship to God for His goodness, grace, and His faithfulness as He helps and keeps you to walk in righteousness before God. Staleness and heaviness that comes to you will flee in truth, righteousness and rejoicing (Isaiah 35:10).

Run to the throne of grace and ask for His help and His grace to resist the temptation.

CONFESSIONS: Confess righteousness scriptures often they will assure your heart before God.

1. Jesus purchased me by His precious blood and through His blood I am redeemed out of the hand of the devil and made free. I know this is the truth, that the Son has made me free and I am free indeed therefore I REJOICE!! And I will continue to rejoice until freedom is mine (Psalm 107:2; John 8: 32, 36; Ephesians 1:7; Philippians 4:4).

2. I am the righteousness of God in Christ Jesus. I am totally forgiven and cleansed from all guilt. The blood of Jesus cleanses me from all sin and dead works. I am innocent, accepted in the beloved, approved, chosen, and favored in Christ Jesus to serve the living God (2 Corinthians 5:21; Ephesians 1:4,6; Hebrews 9:14, 10:2)

3. 2 Corinthians 5:21, *"For he hath made him to be sin; for us who knew no sin; that we might be made the righteousness of God in him."*

4. Romans 8:2, *"There is therefore now no condemnation to them which are in Christ Jesus, who walk not after the flesh, but after the Spirit. For the law of the Spirit of life in Christ Jesus hath made me free from the law of sin and death."*

5. I reject the lie that my righteousness comes from my goodness or how well I perform. The blood of Jesus deposited God's perfect love in my heart and constantly draws me into fellowship and intimacy. My faith in God's love and His care for me frees me from all fear, especially the fear of being inadequate in my performance and the fear of failure in pleasing God (Psalm 23; Romans 5:5; 1 John 4: 18).

6. God loves Jesus, Jesus lives in my heart and I am in Christ. Since God loves me equally as Jesus, I receive the blood of Jesus as my forgiveness and cleansing. I receive His righteousness as my own, as I receive His love. Jesus loves and accepts me and I rest in His love (John 17:23, Ephesians 1:4, 6).

7. The account and debt the old man owed God has been settled. Jesus paid it for me with His blood. The old man is dead unto sin and the new me is in righteousness and alive in Christ. I am justified by the blood of Jesus; I am declared not guilty but innocent and acquitted. Therefore I REJOICE, I REJOICE!! Because Jesus made me free from the guilt of sin and I have peace (Romans 5:1, 9; 6:11, 8:1, 2; 1 Peter 3;18).

8. Because of the blood of Jesus, I reject all law mentality, self- will and effort. My old man is dead and I reject all self-consciousness from the devil. I am completely forgiven, and I trust in Jesus and the power of the Holy Spirit to be free from the devil and the flesh with self-effort, self-righteousness, exceptionally high and false standards, false-responsibility (things of or from other people that are none of my business) I release them to God and trust His grace to deliver them).

9. I choose to depend on God and trust His Word as being right and His grace and power in the Holy Spirit to see me or others through this difficulty (Romans 5:17).

10. I reject every lie of any pain or sickness or pressure in my body because of Jesus' Word that by His stripes I am healed (Isaiah 53:4, 5).

11. I believe God's Word by faith in His grace, and I have rightness with God, rightness of God in my spirit, rightness of God in my soul, rightness of God in my body, rightness of God in my affairs, in my home, in my business, everywhere. I *am* the righteousness of God in Christ Jesus. I trust only His righteousness and His abundant grace in every situation in my life, and all is well (2 Kings 4:8-26).

12. The blood of Jesus sanctifies me, sets me apart from sin and unto God my Father. I am sanctified pure, holy, innocent, righteous and free. Therefore I worship and praise God

with my whole heart (1 Corinthians 1:30; Colossians 1:22; Hebrews 10:10).

13. I walk in the light that I am righteous and I have fellowship with God through Jesus His Son and His blood cleanses me now and continually from all sin. Therefore I REJOICE!! My heart is clean and I am free to love and serve God in spirit and in truth (1John 1: 7; 9; Romans 6:4, 17, 18).

CHAPTER 7

UNION WITH GOD

John 14:20, *"At that day ye shall know that I am in my Father, and ye in me, and I in you."*

This verse is speaking of oneness with God the Father Himself. Jesus prayed that we, as believers, would be in union and oneness with God, as He was with God His Father. The religious Jews only saw Him from a distance as "God" their Creator and provider. Earlier in John 10:30 Jesus declared, *"I and my Father are one."* In the next verse the Jews took up stones again to stone Him for committing blasphemy, saying He as a man, was making Himself God. They could not understand His claim to be close, much less being one with God, because they served a God who was far off and not personal to them. The Israelites, under Moses' leadership, were the same way.

Exodus 20:19, *"And they said unto Moses, speak thou with us, and we will hear; but let not God speak with us, lest we die."* The opposite is true for Jesus. He said in John 17: 22, 23:

> *"And the glory which thou gavest me I have given them; that they may be one, even as we are one: I in them, and thou in me, that they may be made perfect in one; and that the world may know that thou hast sent me, and hast loved them, as thou hast loved me."*

Jesus was personal with God His Father and personal with His people, as He purchased salvation for all who would believe and gave them His glory (Psalm 8:5; John 1:14; 2 Corinthians 4:6; Hebrews 1:3).

Jesus was the brightness of God's glory and God gave us His glory in the presence of His Holy Spirit who lives within a believer's human spirit. We became one with God in spirit when we enter a relationship with Jesus.

1 Corinthians 6:17, *"But he that is joined unto the Lord is one spirit."*

Jesus was one with the Father in relationship, in Spirit, and in character. He was one in His attributes, His will and purpose, His motives, His desires, and one in agreement with His eternal destiny. God's desire for us is to be one with Him in the same relationship through Jesus. Before Jesus left to go to His Father, He gave us a promise:

John 14: 16, 17, *"And I will pray the Father, and he shall give you another Comforter, that he may abide with you forever: Even the Spirit of truth; whom the world cannot receive, because it seeth him not, neither knoweth him; but ye know him; for he dwelleth with you, and shall be in you."*

The Holy Spirit was given to help and guide us to understand God as our Father through Jesus, and to help us mature to be Christ-like, therefore bringing God's presence to us. The Holy Spirit also helps us to be one with our Father God as Jesus was one with God. A segment of His role is to teach us all things, bring all things to our remembrance, testify of Jesus, guide us into all truth and show us all things to come. He also helps us to pray and fill us with God's power (John 14:26; 15:26; 16:13; Acts 1:8; Romans 8:26). The presence of the Holy Spirit in us created union, oneness, unity with God and made relationship possible. This unity creates the atmosphere for

> *The Holy Spirit was given to help and guide us to understand God as our Father through Jesus, and to help us mature to be Christ-like.*

intimacy to develop between God and man. Relationship, intimacy and unity with Himself are God's greatest desire for mankind. He intends for all the glory He has placed in the human spirit to draw us close to our Father as we worship God for who He is. Also to manifest Him on the outside, in our soul and bodies, making us victorious overcomers in our life and to share His blessings with those around us.

> Proverbs 20: 27, *"The spirit of man is the candle of the Lord, searching all the inward parts of the belly."*

The spirit is the lamp of the Lord and the Holy Spirit who dwells in our human spirit gives out God's light. His personality is within us, and His presence is with us to teach, lead and deliver. Galatians 5:22, 23, *"... The fruit of the Spirit is love, joy, peace, longsuffering, gentleness, goodness, faith, meekness, temperance (self-control) ..."*

The fruit of the Spirit is Love. All the others mentioned from joy to temperance are as seeds within that fruit of love. When they are planted in the heart, practiced, and nurtured, these seeds bring forth and demonstrate more love, the very character of God. Because God is love, union with Jesus and Christ-likeness brings more of God's love, character and presence to us. Read the Word, worship, and meditate on Jesus, communicate with Him in prayer, confess and become a doer of the Word, believing you're in union with God. As you do these things you will see yourself as a partaker of His divine nature, in divine union with God and not as a sinner saved by grace. You and God are in harmony: one heart and one spirit. A lamp gives light, and Jesus is the light of the world (John 8:12). The light of His Spirit in you will shine forth, so that His personality and power in the Holy Spirit will shine in and through you and all believers for the world to see Jesus. As you stand in faith, allowing the power of Christ to flow through you,

Because God is love, union with Jesus and Christ-likeness brings more of God's love and presence to us.

minister in His grace to bring health, healing and deliverance to those in need.

Our responsibility is to maintain and nurture our union relationship, so His Spirit can develop and flow through us to bring the presence of God into every situation we face. In order to do so, speak and minister God's Word from this place of union, oneness with God, so that Christ in you will indeed be the hope of your glory (Colossians 1:27).

Union places you in Christ to meet all your needs; speak who you are in the human spirit, the real you.

- Forgiveness of all sins (Ephesians 1:7).
- Cleansed from all unrighteousness (1 John 1:9).
- Healed in your body (Psalm 103:3).
- Restoration in your soul (Psalm 23:3).
- Mended your broken heart (Colossians 2: 2).
- Delivered from the powers of darkness (Colossians 1:13).
- Given His Peace (Isaiah 32:17, 53:5).
- Provision (Philippians 4: 19).
- Experience the presence of God (John 14:21)
- Power with rivers of living water, flowing to bring blessings to the world (John 7:38).
- You are a new creation in Christ Jesus (2 Corinthians 5:17).
- You are forgiven of all your sins (Mark 3:28; Ephesians 1:7; Hebrews 10:2).
- Made righteous and acceptable to God (2 Corinthians 5:21; Ephesians 1:6).
- Redeemed, by the blood of Jesus (Revelation 5:9).
- Raised up and seated in heavenly places (Ephesians 1:3).
- Freed from Satan, freed from his condemnation (Romans 8:1, 2; 1 Peter 2:9).

- Led by the Holy Spirit (Romans 8:14).

- I am a child of God, adopted by my heavenly Father (Romans 8:15, 16; Ephesians 1:5)

- I am born of God and the evil one touches me not (Ephesians 1:13 ; 1 John5:18b-20).

- I am complete in God, and secure (Colossians 2:9, 10; Proverbs 3:19-26).

- I have been bought for a price, and I belong to God (1 Corinthians 6:19, 20).

- I have access to God through the Holy Spirit (Ephesians 2:17, 18).

- I am free from fear and given power, love and a sound mind (2 Timothy 1:7).

- I am established, sealed by the Holy Spirit in Christ (2 Corinthians 1:21, 22).

- I am kept by His grace. Nothing can separate me from His love (1 Peter 1:5; Romans 8:35-39).

- You can read Ephesians Chapters 1 to 3 and find about 30 others which tells you "who you are in Christ", beginning in verse 1: "I am a saint", verse 2, "I have grace and peace from the Lord Jesus Christ."

- Any other the Holy Spirit quickens to you, as you continue to expand these for yourself.

Who you are "in Christ" gives you identity. When you identify with whom Christ made you because of the blood of Jesus, you will be empowered by the Holy Spirit to stand confidently, knowing that you are in God's strength and you would then begin your Christian life walking in the Spirit.

Galatians 5:16, *"This I say then, Walk in the Spirit, and ye shall not fulfil the lust of the flesh."*

Identify yourself with God through Jesus and believe you are who He says you are. You will never feel alone, worthless,

THE BLOOD

insignificant, or insecure again in your life. Parents, Pastors and teachers, never teach rules of conduct (law) before establishing identity in Christ (grace). This will be perceived as legalism and control causing condemnation, insecurity, and rebellion. Parents, tell your child "God loves you, and I love you (identity); that is why I have to set these boundaries (rules) for your protection." Demanding obedience to rules and regulations without relationship brings rebellion, but union relationship with God the Father establishes identity first and produces faith to yield to God, which in relationship brings rest and peace. Matthew 11:29, *"Take my yoke [union relationship of love] upon you, and learn of me; for I am meek and lowly in heart: and you shall find rest unto your souls."*

Significance:

- Union relationship brings assurance and security. This is the right atmosphere to stimulate faith and to hear clearly, believe, and yield to God (1 John 2:5-6).

- Union causes you to see yourself as God sees you, "sanctified by God's power, infilled with His Spirit, created with and in Jesus Christ. One nature, character, and substance.[6]

- Union relationship is aligning yourself with the Spirit and the heart of God. In His presence, you draw all of who He is: grace, goodness and mercy.

- One in Spirit: God inhabits us in our praises and delivers us as we worship (Psalm 22:3-5).

- Over time we will have experiences with God in union relationship. We too can experience God's presence and do what we see Jesus does; just as He did with God. Abiding in Christ, we can now minister from a place of oneness in confidence, believing we can ask what we will and it will be done (John 14:10; 15:7, 8).

- As we take up the yoke of union love relationship, and learn of God, we will be in unity with God and with fellow believers as Jesus was with God and His disciples (Matthew 11:29, John 13:34-35).

- Union creates unity with God and man. Legalism, man's ways to be right, seeks uniformity; let us, speaking the same language, build a tower, let us all be circumcised. God chose oneness and unity not uniformity (Genesis 11:4; Acts chapter 11).

BE RAISED UP

Believe by faith that you and God are one in relationship and seek to develop close fellowship. Be in divine harmony, as with Moses, who in oneness with God, divided the Red Sea (Exodus 14:15, 16).

We are one with God in Christ, and must move on from the cross, seeing only what Jesus did for us and be raised up to be seated with God in Christ in Heavenly places, prepared to rule and reign as kings and Priests. We must be prepared to bring God to the people as Kings, and share God's spiritual riches and treasures as priests (Revelation 1:6).

Believe you are raised up with power and authority.

Luke 10:19, *"Behold, I give you power to tread on serpents and scorpions, and over all the power of the enemy: and nothing shall by any means hurt you."*

In union relationship, exercise your power and authority over the devil and all circumstances of life. John 15:5b, "Without *me you can do nothing.*" no longer applies to you and me, because we are not without Him. You are "In Him." All things are possible, and you can do all things through Christ who strengthens you (Matthew 19:26; Philippians 4:13).

Union stimulates faith and brings the power of Christ through us to meet our needs and that of others.

Authority Scriptures: Matthew 18:18, Mark 16:17, 18, Romans 5:17, 2 Corinthians 10:4,5, Ephesians 1:19-21, 2:6, 3:16-20, 6:10-16,Philippians 2:9,10, Colossians 2:15, Hebrews 2:14-15, James 4:7, 1 Peter 2:9, 5:8, Revelation 1:6.

Let our hearts yearn for the newness of life, and the resurrection power available in Christ. Let our hearts yearn for a new awakening of revival power in our hearts to combat the evils the devil brings against us and in this present world.

As we come up higher in oneness and union with God in power and authority, let us see ourselves in Him as risen and full of resurrection power and eternal life, ready to rule and reign.

Union stimulates faith and brings the power of Christ through us to meet our needs and that of others.

"Let the throne life, the throne love, the throne power, and the throne spirit and the Holy Ghost… possess you, and you will be a new man in Christ Jesus." [7]

Let us rise up and refuse to be earth-bound anymore, so that we can become true children and ambassadors of our Father God.

Union with God "Being one with God"

Confessions:

1 John 4:15, *"Whosoever shall confess that Jesus is the Son of God, God dwelleth in him, and he in God.*

Confession:
Christ is in me and I am in Him. I have everything I need. I am protected; anything coming against me must pass through God and Jesus. I am safe in Christ. In Christ, I have the best identity and greatest self-worth in His grace. His power gives me the ability to live the Christian life. I belong to the greatest Father ever!

John 15: 5, *"I am in the vine, you are in the branches; he that abideth in me, and I in him, the same bringeth forth much fruit: for without me, you can do nothing."*

Confession:
Jesus is the Vine and I am the branch. I am in union with God, and I am in oneness with Him. I was in Christ when He died on the Cross. My old man is truly dead just as Jesus was dead,

because I was in Him when He died. He rose and I rose in Him in righteousness. Now His life flows from Him, the Vine, into me so that I can bear fruit. As I dwell in Christ, Christ dwells in me. I am one with Him and I draw all I need from Him. He is my source to bear the fruit of love.

Galatians 3:27, *"For as many of you as have been baptized into Christ have put on Christ."*

Confession:

I am a child of God, and I have clothed myself with Christ's life and character. My new beliefs are (a) I am dead to sin because the old me was in Christ when He died on the cross (b) The old me with his sin nature was buried in the grave with Christ. I am dead to sin. When Christ arose, and I believed on Him I was washed, justified, made innocent and righteous, reconciled into a love relationship with my Father.

Confession:

I am in Christ. I am in union with Christ. I am one with Christ and, because of this I have clothed myself with Christ. I am a child of God by faith in Christ Jesus (Galatians 3:26). His nature and His qualities are inside me, and in my spirit. I choose to let the spirit of Christ in me flow out into my soul and body, making renewed in the spirit of my mind making me the child of God I need to be as I grow up in Christ.

Romans 6:5,6, *"For if we have been planted together in the likeness of his death, we shall be also in the likeness of his resurrection. Knowing this, that our old Man is crucified with him, that the body of sin might be destroyed, that henceforth we should not serve sin."*

Living Bible – *"For you have become a part of him, and so you died with him on the Cross when he died, and now you share his new life, and shall rise as he did."*

Confession:

My old self was crucified on the cross with Christ, dead; it is no more in me. I am in Christ. I am a new creation freed from sin; I have no more remembrance of sin. Christ did this for me on the cross over 2,000 years ago. This is true therefore I believe it. I am one in Christ, dead to sin, and alive unto Christ who is the righteousness of God. I am secure. I am His very own son, or daughter in Christ. I receive my new identity in Christ and choose to live it.

Colossians 3:3,"*For ye are dead, and your life is hid with Christ in God.*"

Confession:

I died to the world, sin, Satan, and the law (self-effort, trying to die to sin by myself, is self-righteousness). The real me has the Holy Spirit in my spirit, hidden together with God. I do not have to try to be dead to sin. The Word says that I am dead and I believe it. I am hidden, protected with Christ in God, and therefore, I am in Christ and choose to live from my spirit where God dwells with His goodness, peace, strength. My trusting in God brings His goodness to my soul, mind, will and emotions. Imperfect me trusts a perfect God, of perfect love, and I can never fail. Because love never fails, nothing is impossible with my God living through me.

Ephesians 1:3, "*Blessed be the God and father of our Lord Jesus Christ, who hath blessed us with all spiritual blessings in heavenly places in Christ.*"

Confession:

I am in Christ; my life is dependent on Him because of my union with Him He has given me access to all spiritual blessings in the heavenly realm. I am blessed and everything God has, He has given to me (Romans14:17; Galatians 5:22; 1 Timothy 1:7). I believe it, I claim it as mine, and I receive it in me in Jesus Name.

1 Peter 1:23, "*Being born again, not of corruptible seed, but of incorruptible, by the word of God, which liveth and abideth forever.*"

Confession:

I am God's child, born of the incorruptible seed of the Word of God, which lives and abides forever. I cannot be minimized, ostracized, criticized or condemned into failure. With the Word of God, I will arise in Christ and abide forever. I overcome by the blood of the lamb.

1 Corinthians 6:17, *"But he that is joined unto the lord is one spirit.*

Confession:
I am one spirit with my heavenly Father, I have union relationship. By His righteousness I am washed, justified, sanctified and redeemed. Thank You Father for the sacrifice of Your Son and His shed blood which makes me pure, holy and innocent why? So that I can come boldly into your presence, to receive your love and mercy to be saved and continually being saved daily. I am so thankful Father that you joyfully receive me only because Jesus is my Lord and Savior. I receive your great love as shed abroad in my heart. I rejoice, I rejoice Jesus love me and His perfect love for me frees me from all fear.

Confession:
I am one spirit with the Father: the shed blood of Jesus draws me into oneness and love just becuase He is my Savior. I come to you gladly and cry Abba Father. Thank you for loving and receiving me, not because of my actions, works or performance but by your great love. Jesus loves me, and I receive His love freely as I rest in grace, His righteousness, love and peace.

Stay in union relationship with God through the blood of Jesus Christ. Grow in fellowship and closer relationship standing in the Word of "who you are made in Christ." Having done all of this, stand in faith, and keep growing in unity with Christ. Be raised up with authority and power, seated in heavenly places. Now you are armed with union love. Sit, enthroned in His grace, believe Jesus has done it all by His grace, respond and receive of every promise that He has given you in His Word. Be blessed, always continually growing in unity with God and man.

CHAPTER 8

REDEMPTION

Ephesians 1:7, *"In whom we have redemption through his blood, the forgiveness of sins, according to the riches of his grace. "*

Redemption is the loosing away by paying a price. To be redeemed means that you were in bondage, but have been delivered and made free, because the price necessary for your freedom has been paid.

Sin, by our forefather Adam, brought mankind into bondage to Satan. The price for sin is death. Jesus, by dying on the cross, paid that price for the remission of sins for the whole world. Anyone can have redemption from sin when they choose Jesus and the forgiveness offered through God's grace in the blood of Jesus.

Titus 2:14, *" Who gave himself for us, that he might redeem us from all iniquity, and purify unto himself a peculiar people, zealous of good works."*

How is Redemption Achieved?

Colossians 1:14, *"In whom we have redemption through his blood, even the forgiveness of sins:"*

To obtain redemption, Jesus once and for all times died on the cross, paying the wages of sin and death, which God's justice demanded (Romans 6:23). In exchange God provided forgiveness and freedom in Christ Jesus. Jesus is our substitute. He died as us, taking all of mankind's sins past, present, and future sins for all time until eternity, because He will not die again for sin (Romans 6: 9, 10; Hebrews 9:25-28; 10: 10-14).

Jesus was the Son of God whose death broke the dominion, power, and authority of sin over all mankind. It was through the crucifixion and the shedding of Jesus' blood that mankind's sins were paid for and forgiveness in redemption was given. Jesus' sacrifice for our sins was completed when He rose from the grave, ascended and conquered the authority of Satan and his dominion of sin over us. He opened the way for us to be justified, cleansed, made innocent and righteous or acceptable to God; free and blessed.

Redemption or freedom comes to the person who, by faith, believes on and receives Jesus as their Savior and Lord and is delivered from darkness to light (2 Corinthians 6:14; Colossians 1:13; 1 Thessalonians 5:5). The person who neglects or rejects this redemption cannot be saved or be redeemed and will suffer separation from God in Hell forever (Luke 16:19-31; Revelation 21:8)

Start your belief in God and your Christian walk from a starting position of faith in God's grace and the finished work of the cross.

Start your belief in God and your Christian walk from a starting position of faith in God's grace and the finished work of the cross, leading you to a place of death to self and surrender to the lordship of Jesus for your life. Then continue your lifelong Christian journey the same way you started, grace through faith, depending on the Holy Spirit to teach you how to grow and transform to be like Jesus both in identity and character. Jesus surrendered His will to the Father in the Garden of Gethsemane when He said, "Nevertheless not as I will, but as thou wilt" (Matthew 26:36-75; Ephesians 2:8; Colossians 2:6).

Redeemed From What And From Whom?
From the power of the old-self.

Once the gospel is preached and a person decides in their heart to repent and receive cleansing through forgiveness of sins, the Spirit of Jesus moves within the heart and into their human spirit. They are now dead to sin in their spirit, and made free to follow Jesus, as their new Lord and master.

The thoughts and memory of sin however, may still reside in the soul (mind and imagination, will, and emotions) and the desires of the body. When the memory of sin surface as thoughts, pictures or feelings they must be rejected and cast them down as you remind yourself that you are a new creation dead to sin. Move forward with God as you seek to be renewed and be transformed (Romans 12:1, 2; 2 Corinthians 10:4:5; 1 Peter 4:1, 2).

1 Peter 1:18b, "*Redeemed… from your vain conversation received by tradition from your fathers.*"

Romans 6: 4, 6, "*Therefore we are buried with him by baptism into death: that like as Christ was raised up from the dead by the glory of the Father, even so we also should walk in newness of life. Knowing, this that our old man is crucified with him, that the body of sin might be destroyed, that henceforth we should not serve sin.*"

Colossians 3:9, 10, "*… seeing that ye have put off the old man with his deeds; And have put on the new man, which is renewed in knowledge after the image of him that created him.*"

A person speaking and believing Romans 10: 9,10 has confessed Jesus as Lord, which means he has submitted his life to God through Jesus, for Him to be in charge. Christianity is a relationship based on exchanged lives, Jesus's life to the new believer and the believer's to Jesus. Redemption from the power of the old-self, frees you to yield to Jesus, to belong to Him as you are no longer left on your own to live as you were used to (1 Corinthians 6: 19, 20).

Redeemed from Satan

Jesus purchased the whole world with His blood, delivered us from the bondage of slavery to Satan, and allowed us the ability to choose Christ (Romans 6:16).

You are loosed and redeemed UNTO JESUS, free to depend on the power of the Holy Spirit to keep you unto God, and given all the necessary power to enforce the enemy's defeat. He, the Holy Spirit, will help you to be sober and stand watch; 1 Peter 5: 8,9, submit to God, by walking in the light of His Word to resist the devil(James 4:7) and to help you by faith to overcome. As overcomers, you will always rejoice in what the blood of Jesus accomplished for you (Mark 11:24; 1 John 2:14; Revelation 12:10-12).

Colossians 1:13, *"Who hath delivered us from the power of darkness, and hath translated us into the kingdom of his dear Son:"*

Psalm 103:4-6, *Redeemed from all evil, and* Psalm 49:15 *from grave.*

Psalm 107:2, *"Let the redeemed of the Lord say so, whom he hath redeemed from the hand of the enemy;"*

1 John 5:18, *"We know that whosoever is born of God sinneth not; but he that is begotten of God keepeth himself, and that wicked one toucheth him not."*

God's children living from the spirit do not keep on sinning. God's own Son protects them by His Spirit, and as they live by faith in God's grace the devil cannot defeat them.

Redeemed from death

Death and all varying degrees of death in the form of sickness and disease have been separated from us.

Galatians 3:13, 14 *"Christ hath redeemed us from the curse of the law, being made a curse for us: for it is written, Cursed is everyone that hangeth on a tree: That the blessing of Abraham might come on the Gentiles through Jesus Christ; that we might receive the promise of the Spirit through faith."*

1 John 3:14, *"We know that we have passed from death unto life, because we love the brethren…"*

Hebrews 2: 14, *"Forasmuch then as the children are partakers of flesh and blood, he also himself likewise took part of the same; that through death he might destroy him that had the power of death, that is, the devil;"*

Isaiah 53:5, *"But he was wounded for our transgressions, he was bruised for our iniquities: the chastisement of our peace was upon him; and with his stripes we are healed."*

Psalm 72:14, *"He shall redeem their soul from deceit and violence."*

Psalm 103:4, *"who redeemeth thy life from destruction who crowneth thee with lovingkindness and tender mercies.*

Redeemed from sin

Christ was made sin for us, and in exchange He gave us a new heart and His righteousness, His right standing or right relationship with the Father. As a child of God you are now acceptable to God, beloved, valued, favored, qualified to receive your Father's love, forgiveness and blessings by faith (2 Corinthians 5:21).

The Holy Spirit was given as your Helper, to keep you in God's grace, and separated from sin. (John 16:6-13; Romans 6:14; 8:14, 26).

Ephesians 1:7, *"In whom we have redemption through his blood, the forgiveness of sins, according to the riches of his grace;"*

Romans 6: 2, 14, *"… How shall we, that are dead to sin, live any longer therein? V14, For sin shall not have dominion over you: for you are not under the law, but under grace."*

Romans 6:18, *"Being then made free from sin, ye became the servants of righteousness."*

Hebrews 10:2, *"For then would they not have ceased to be offered? Because that the worshippers once purged should have had no more conscience of sins."*

Redeemed from all iniquity (Psalm 130:8; Titus 2:14).

Redeemed From The Law.

We are redeemed from obeying the Ten Commandments as rules and regulations for Christian living, or any other man-made regulations deemed necessary for salvation or to maintain relationship with God. We still obey the Ten Commandments. Because it's God's Word which is good because it is truth (Psalm 119:142; Romans 7:16; 1 Timothy 1:8, 9) but the church, because of the shed blood of Jesus obeys God through a love relationship with Jesus being led by the Holy Spirit (John 13:34, 35; Romans 8:14; 13:8-10; Philippians 2:13).

As a believer you are not under the law constantly endeavoring and trying in self-will and your own strength to obey, in order to gain acceptance from God, or trying to do right to please God so that He would not be angry at you. Instead as a believer under grace, you are a person in relationship with God through Jesus and delights, depend on, rely on and trust in God for His Holy Spirit to help you to be and do right. The law relies on self- will, self-focus and self- performance and judges you with guilt, shame, accusation, condemnation and punishment when wrong or you fail.

In God's grace there is no judgment for the believer from God.

In God's grace there is no judgment for the believer from God, only His goodness and mercy, in wisdom, guidance, forgiveness, correction, and restoration (Psalm 23:6; Hosea 10:12; Galatians 6:7,8; 1 Thessalonians 5:9; Hebrews 4:16; 12:5-13).

Colossians 2:14-15, *"Blotting out the hand writing of ordinances that was against us, which was contrary to us, and took it out of the way, nailing it to the cross."*

Romans 6:14, *"For sin shall not have dominion over you: for ye are not under the law, but under grace."*

Romans 10:4, *"For Christ is the end of the law for righteousness to everyone that believeth."*

We no longer live by rules and regulations, standards and principles, always "doing" without God's power, trying to relate to God. Now we are under grace in a love relationship with a loving God, humbled in His presence and dependent on Him and as a child would depend on his father. We are led by His Holy Spirit from the heart (Romans 8:14).

Redeemed From This Present World,

"They are not of this world, even as I am not of this world (John 17:16; 1 John 2:16, 17.)

Hindrances That Keep Us from Being Free?

As mentioned in Chapter 2, page 23, and sharing more insights from Matt Chandler's Recovering redemption, I believe the main hindrances to people being free in their personal lives are: lack of knowledge, continued disobedience to God and trying everything else because of refusal to completely humble oneself and receive the Gospel. People, including believers are trying to seek redemption, to free their own selves by their own means; and they may succeed for a while, but eventually will fail, at which time many finally turn to Jesus alone.

Let's expand more fully on some of these hindrances, which postpone full redemption or true freedom.

Trusting In Themselves

Man cannot redeem himself. Yet, in order to remain in control they try self-discipline and self- help to fix one-self. They study to be smart, diet to be thin and beautiful, fix their hairstyle exquisitely: strive for status, fame, money and power. They try to become the person that will make themselves happy and content and confident and strong, exalting their independence from God.

119

Jeremiah 10:23 says, *"O Lord, I know that the way of man is not in himself: it is not in man that walketh to direct his steps."*

Independence from God and dependence on one's self-will often seems okay and good as long as things are going all right, but self-dependence will cause you to crash, in times of testing and difficulties. Stop looking at yourself for redemption, as you will never be good enough to please yourself, much less be good enough to please God on your own. You need Jesus.

Stop looking at yourself for redemption.

You cannot do well all by yourself, because at your best, you will fall short of God's expectations of you, your perfection in Jesus.

Romans 3:23, *"For all have sinned and come short of the glory of God"*

You cannot redeem yourself. You must believe by faith on Jesus Christ alone, and God's grace to be saved, both for salvation and from the negative circumstances in your life. You must accept this as truth and stop looking inward to yourself and instead throw yourself upon the Lord for His mercy. Say:

"Father, I give myself and my life situations to you, please forgive me, and please help and deliver me."

Jesus gave up His self-will to the Father and we are to do the same. Words used to describe this process are, to submit, yield, surrender, and trust. The moment you give yourself up to God, His grace and power will be present to help.

Looking to Others

Many depend on others for their redemption in acceptance and validation. We are a people who are looking to other people to fill what is missing inside. When we get it from them we are good, confident, and happy, but if not, we become insecure, self-conscious, unhappy, and empty. Your approval does not come from friends, co-workers, critics, or any-one. Their favorable opinion of you is not your highest good. Your approval comes from God. He's the only one you will stand before at judgment day. His opinion is all you need, so be satisfied with Jesus.

Believe God said you can do nothing by yourself (John 15:5). He saved you by His grace and gave you acceptance, approval, favor, and love. Your report card was given and signed in the blood of Jesus with an approval grade of A+ the day you were born-again and placed 'in Christ'. Let your satisfaction come from God and who He says you are.

Isaiah 43:4, *"Since thou was precious in my sight, thou hast been honorable, and I have loved thee: therefore will I give men for thee, and people for thy life."*

Looking to the World

People sometimes turn to stuff in the world, such as new and better things, more money, stuff for greater pleasure, and for a short period of time we convince ourselves we are somewhat better off. But we keep doing it, wanting new things, more things, better things, faster things, all to fill the gap in our souls. But Solomon says in:

> *Let your satisfaction come from God and who He says you are.*

Ecclesiastes 1:14, *"I have seen all the works that are done under the sun; and, behold, all is vanity and vexation of spirit."*

Solomon knew, because he tried it all, and all was incapable of fulfilling him.

- The problem with worldly pursuits is that when we substitute them for God in our lives, we have elevated created things above Jesus, because we have the faulty thinking that things or activities or pleasure can satisfy us, by themselves.

- We look to the world and that will give you, the 'up today and down tomorrow' effect. Feeling good today when things are good and very bad a couple days away. Or moving from one bad habit to the next, because we are trying worldly things to fill us up.

- No! Your satisfaction must come from your relationship with God through Jesus. God is responsible for your being, He is to be sought for the things and the boundaries of what can give you pleasure and peace. He is to be thanked, worshipped, and praised, for all His gifts and blessings. He is to be sought out for forgiveness when you mess up. When we look for our redemption in the Gospel and not the world we trust God to provide for us and we give Him the honor of caring for our lives as a loving Father. We also give Him gratitude and praise when He comes through for us. For all His care and goodness we will leave His presence, feeling fully satisfied with Him and with His life in and through us.

Trusting religion

Void of relationship many people turn to religion to get God's approval or to appease their conscience. Notice I said religion, not relationship that only Christianity offers (John 14:17). Religion is always external outside- in and excludes the Holy Spirit. People start "DOING" in self-effort, striving to earn a good report card or acceptance and favor from God and man.

- They are trying very hard to perform, either not to sin and displease God or doing actions trying to please Him. These people have missed out on the understanding of the Love God has for them.

- Religion causes one to never feel cleansed or forgiven, enough to measure up to God as being worthy. The result is a fear of failure and feeling unworthy before God, unworthy enough to want to stay away from Him, or trying hard to love Him by what you do in works, but still never feeling close to God.

- Religion encourages self- will, self-righteousness, works mentality, neglecting God's Grace.

- Feeling your efforts and good works will please God enough for Him to bless you or to keep Him from being angry with you.

- Causes one to be constantly repenting for sin, again and again asking forgiveness but never feeling free. This shows you are still feeling responsible for your own redemption and have not given your-self fully over in genuine repentance to be cleansed by the blood of Jesus and to be kept by the power of God's grace (Romans 10:9,10;1 John 1:9;1 Peter 1:5).

- Religion is a lie. You are either completely justified by the blood of Jesus Christ or you are not saved at all. It is only those who believe on the saving grace of Jesus to pull them out of sin that will overcome. You cannot be redeemed by religion, but must receive Jesus, believe on Him and be born-again with Him on the inside by His Spirit, in relationship with you. For the believer you received God by grace believing in Jesus should now continue your entire Christian walk the same way depend on your relationship with Him to provide or deliver you completely in all situation

John 6:40," *And this is the will of him that sent me, that everyone which seeth the Son, and believeth on him, may have everlasting life: and I will raise him up at the last day.*

God has now imparted in you His very life and nature, and now dwells in your body by His spirit. The gospel impacts us from the inside- out by the power of the Holy Spirit not outside- in as religion suggests.

"... *Christ in you, the hope of glory*" (Colossians 1:27).

(5) Spiritual warfare the wrong way

This is one hindrance I see that's keeping people bound. With undue focus on the devil, constantly binding and rebuking and casting out, with fear in their heart instead of in faith believing the Word that Satan is defeated. Constant speaking of the devils name and activities will give him too much room in your life. The Lord said this to me, "whatever you focus on will multiply in your life." So do not let demonic activity and torment increase in your life because of undue focus on the devil. Correct warfare focuses more on the Word; you bind the devil in faith and immediately turn your attention to God and His Word in faith. Loose the power of God by speaking what Jesus accomplished on the cross, choosing to exalt Jesus above the devil and all his activities." When you accept that Jesus' sacrifice is much greater than Satan, sin, failure, or the devils troubles, you will rest in God's grace and receive His Eternal Redemption and freedom when you bind and loose in faith (Matthew 18:18; 1 John 4:4).

Romans 6:22, *"But now being made free from sin, and become servants of God, ye have your fruit unto holiness, and the end everlasting life."*

Christ made us free, unto righteousness and redemption in His grace we are, FREE IN CHRIST JESUS, so walk out of Satan's trap of religion, self-will, legalism or works and be free!

The only true redemption for fallen man is in the blood of Christ Jesus. The way is for man to humble himself before His Creator, believe the Gospel, yield his whole sinful life over to God, and in exchange by faith, and receive God's eternal life. This is salvation God's way, believing, responding and receiving by faith all Jesus has done for you with no addition or subtraction (1Timothy 6:20, 21; 2 Timothy 2:16). Let your dependence on God, through the leading of the Holy Spirit; guide you into God's abundance. He alone is eternal and His eternal redemption brings eternal freedom.

CHAPTER 9

ETERNAL REDEMPTION A BELIEVER'S FREEDOM IS FOREVER

Hebrews 9:12, *"Neither by the blood of goats and calves, but by his own blood he entered in once into the holy place, having obtained eternal redemption for us."*

Eternal means lasting or existing forever, valid for all times from the point of salvation until eternity. Our redemption is covered by the entire work of God in Christ Jesus, from His incarnation to His future second coming. We have been redeemed, made free from all evil, as the power of all sin was removed in the crucified body and shed blood of Jesus Christ on the cross when He provided cleansing and forgiveness in repentance. You must believe and accept this as true; otherwise Satan will keep your soul in bondage with a consciousness of sin and its effects of control with self-will, accusation, shame, guilt, condemnation, judgment and death. He will continually plague you to keep you in the bondage and insufficiency. The enemy will cause insufficiency of love, finances, peace, intimacy and spiritual growth. But in Christ Jesus, He is your sufficiency.

Although Jesus purchased the redemption of every human being on the face of the earth, only those who believe on Jesus and in the work of the cross and choose to receive salvation grace through faith can be saved.

John 1:12, *"But as many as received him, to them gave he power to become the sons of God, even to them that believe on his name"*

Old Testament Priests used the blood of goats and bulls to cover the sins of the people. They did this continually because it was only a temporary measure. Jesus came and died on the cross and put away sin once and for all in the sacrifice of Himself (Hebrews 10:10-14).

A New Testament believer's main focus should not be trying hard not to sin in order to be a good Christian. Focusing on sin in your life creates sin- consciousness and legalism or works with the net result of guilt, instead of the righteousness of Christ in the human spirit. Religion, self-will or legalism gives a false belief that your redemption through Jesus is temporary and therefore dependent on your actions to keep right with God. Instead believe, when you're born-again, your spirit is made perfect or made holy because God lives there and He sees you perfect in your spirit. You are loved and acceptable to Him, 100% God and 100% redeemed, with an eternal not temporary redemption.

1 Corinthians 1:30 says, *"But of him are ye in Christ Jesus, who of God is made unto us wisdom, and righteousness, and sanctification, and redemption."*

This says God made you wise, acceptable, holy and free. When you do sin, you will feel guilty as the Holy Spirit is convicting you of righteousness, that which is right (John 16:10). The Holy Spirit will lead you away from guilt and sin and back to seeing yourself as the righteous new creation 'in Christ' God made you to be. He will help you get back on track and to live and behave in righteousness.

The Bible says in Romans 2:4b *"… the goodness of God leadeth thee to repentance."*

We are not our own. We belong to Jesus because His precious blood purchased us unto Himself (1 Corinthians 6: 19, 20; 2 Corinthians 6:16;).

Waste no more of your time seeking redemption on your own, from others, the world or religion. Turn fully to Jesus and do not be like many people who choose to believe on Jesus to receive their salvation but then make the mistake of believing that only their past sins are forgiven. They mistakenly believe they have partial redemption or temporary freedom, as if they are left on their own to deal with all present and future sins. The old Pentecostal believers often remark, "Put sin under the blood" or take it to the cross. No! Jesus did that for you so take the cross to your sin believe and receive forgiveness. This belief of "handling sin" is rooted in partial forgiveness and is a symptom of religion and legalism, or a law mentality of reliance on works and self-effort and not the true gospel.

The Holy Spirit will lead you away from guilt and sin and back to seeing yourself as the righteous new creation 'in Christ' God made you to be.

Religion lacks faith, and its dependence on works and self-performance is self-righteous which is sin and opens the door to the enemy to bring demonic activity into your life with confusion, accusations, fear, and condemnation, because whatever is not of faith is sin, and sin is Satan's playground (Romans 14:23b).

Therefore, to end this one must fully trust God through what Jesus accomplished on the cross. Believe, respond and receive Jesus by faith, and continually walk your Christian life of grace through faith as you rest in Him (Hebrews chapter 4).

A new believer must, by faith, believe all their sins are forgiven: past, present and future (Mark 3:28; Acts 13: 38-39; Colossians 2:13; 1 John 1:7). You know your future sins are forgiven, because Jesus died and offered forgiveness over 2,000 years ago; if you're now anywhere up to 100 years old, it means the sins you're committing now and those you will commit are future sins which were forgiven when viewed from the time and events of the cross.

Romans Chapter 6:1-11, tells us we are dead to sin and buried in Christ. We rose with Him in His resurrection, and are alive unto God. Sin has no more dominion or power over us. Why? Because Jesus became sin, took all our sins into His body, and became marred beyond recognition (Isaiah 52:14). He took all sins to the grave and Hell where they belong and after three days He rose again without them Hallelujah! He gave us His forgiveness and righteousness, and declared us justified or innocent (just as if we never sinned).

A new believer must, by faith, believe all their sins are forgiven: past, present and future.

Acts 13:39, *"And by him all that believe are justified (forgiven, pardoned, cleansed, made innocent) from all things, from which ye could not be justified of by the Law of Moses."*

Believe Jesus Took Care of Your Sin

(1) Romans 4:8, *"Blessed is the man to whom the Lord will not impute sin."* God is eternal, His forgiveness is eternal. He does not hold sins to your account, but to the account of Jesus' blood where they are paid for, cleansed, forgiven and forgotten. Your sins were not forgiven at the cross, you as a person were, you were washed, forgiven and cleansed; but your sins were paid for in full by the blood of Jesus and cast as far as the east is from the west. Sin was separated from you (Psalm 103:12).

(2) Hebrews 10:2, *"... because that the worshippers once purged should have had no more conscience of sins."*

(3) Hebrews 8:12, *"For I will be merciful to their unrighteousness, and their sins and their iniquities will I remember no more."*

(4) 2 Corinthians 5:21, "For *he hath made him to be sin, for us, who knew no sin, that we might be made the righteousness of God in Him.*

(5) Revelation 3:8 – *"… Behold, I have set before thee an open door, and no man can shut it…"*

(6) 1 John 1:9, *"If we confess our sins, he is faithful and just to forgive us our sins, and to cleanse us from all unrighteousness."*

We are forever forgiven, just as we are forever healed by the blood. All we have to do when we need forgiveness or healing is to believe Jesus has provided them, thank Him and receive by faith. By faith, declare you are forgiven, cleansed, redeemed, healed and made free. Reject every leading of the enemy to beg God or believe God didn't do a complete job of your redemption, therefore putting the responsibility back on you to free yourself. When you are unable to free yourself, as you will be, the devil subjects you to his accusation, condemnation, causing feelings of insufficiency, inadequacy and unworthiness to later bring fear and oppression. His aim is to usurp your righteous position before God and man, rob your faith and block your blessings. You have been completely redeemed and freed by God.

Redemption God's Way

Adam's sin plunged the entire human race into slavery to Satan, sin, and depravity.

Romans 5:8 say, *"But God commendeth his love towards us, in that, while we were yet sinners, Christ died for us."*

Jesus' death and His shed blood on the cross purchased our complete freedom when he forgave us of our sins.

Ephesians 1:7, *"In whom we have redemption through his blood, the forgiveness of sins, according to the riches of his grace."*

Every religion, as well as Christianity, teaches that there is a God, that there is sin, which separates man from God, and that sin must be paid for. Something must be done to pay for sin so people can be free in their conscience and get to go to Heaven. Religion, not Christianity, teaches that man must do something, an action or some performance, to earn forgiveness. Christianity however teaches the truth that your redemption is already done; Jesus did it all. Redemption in salvation is a free gift to be received; it cleanses one from sins, end separation and brings restoration fellowship and relationship with God. Man is now given eternal life, adopted into the family of God and as he continues in faith is destined for Heaven.

If you are a sinner who genuinely confessed from your heart, Romans 10:9, 10 then you are saved, redeemed and freed from Satan unto God, believe this is true. God in His love has opened the door of freedom with forgiveness; walk out in that truth free! If you are a believer and you have sinned, confess to God using 1 John 1:9, turn away from it and ask for His grace to keep you free. God is love, love forgives, and forgiveness brings freedom.

God in His love has opened the door of freedom with forgiveness.

If the devil is tormenting you with accusations of wrongdoing and sin-consciousness, cast them down as lies and speak in faith of your righteousness to him.

Christianity, therefore, is receiving God's forgiveness for your sins and simultaneously being joined unto God in a loving, dependent relationship through the Holy Spirit, who lives in your heart and fills you with Christ as Lord. The Holy Spirit in us, here on Earth, leads teaches, and empowers us, to live the Christian life by continually bringing real and genuine change from our spirit, to the soul, and body; this is a change from sin to eternal life and from the slavery of sin's bondage to freedom in Christ and peace with God.

John 10:10b, *"...I am come that they might have life, and that they might have it more abundantly."*

Redemption Is For Everyone

John 3:16, *"For God so love the world that he gave his only begotten Son, that whosoever believeth in him should not perish, but have everlasting life."*

John 14:6, *"Jesus saith unto him, I am the way, the truth, and the life: no man cometh unto the Father, but by me."*

John 6:37, *"All that the Father giveth me shall come to me; and him that cometh to me I will in no wise cast out."*

Romans 10:9, 10 *"That if thou shalt confess with thy mouth the Lord Jesus, and shalt believe in thine heart that God hath raised him from the dead, thou shalt be saved. For with the heart man believeth unto righteousness; and with the mouth confession is made unto salvation."*

2 Corinthians 5:17, *"Therefore, if any man be in Christ, he is a new creature: old things are passed away: behold all things are become new."*

If you believe you are now a new person in Christ. This is the only true redemption for fallen man is for him to humble himself before his Creator, believe the Gospel as correctly presented in the Bible, and yield his whole sinful life over to God. In exchange, receive God's eternal life. This is salvation or redemption God's way, believing, responding in faith and receiving all that Jesus has done for you on the cross.

Ephesians 2:8, *"For by grace are ye saved through faith: and that not of yourselves: it is a gift of God."*

Having received redemption grace through faith, now choose to live your present and future Christian life in loving dependence upon God in the same way you received grace through faith (Colossians 2:6).

Otherwise, the joy and peace you received at the point of salvation when the burden of sin was lifted will slowly be lost, and the Christian life soon becomes one of trying, struggling, striving, trying harder, and self-effort; this puts you back under the law of self-will and self-effort. Trust the Holy Spirit to lead and guide you into God's abundance. You have been given all spiritual blessings in heavenly places. Depend on the Lord to cause all blessings to manifest from within your spirit, flowing outwardly and causing you to prosper in every area of your life. God has done away with the power of sin over you. A new believer must walk out of sin- mindedness and all its effects, just as an ex-convict walks out of prison. Believe you've served your last day in the bondage of sin, which has no more power over you because you have forgiveness and you are forgiven, cleansed, redeemed and made free.

Trust the Holy Spirit to lead and guide you into God's abundance.

The prison door is opened, what are you still doing inside? 8

A believer does not have to sin. A believer chooses to sin. We are made the righteousness of God in Christ, sanctified and rightly related to God by the blood of Jesus. We do not keep our eyes on sin, but on Jesus by the power of the Holy Spirit so that when temptations come we do as:

Hebrews 4:16, *"Let us therefore come boldly unto the throne of grace that we may obtain mercy, and find grace to help in the time of need."*

God Himself will never be angry at you in a wrathful, judgmental way and be quick to condemn or punish you for sin. He did this to Jesus for you already. Neither will He not answer your prayers, or not help you when you call upon Him. You are forgiven.

God's judgment for sin, in this church age, is for you and I to receive the consequences of our choices (Judges Chapter 2; Romans 6:16; 2 Corinthians 9:6 Galatians 6:7, 9). When you sin and feel condemnation and judgment it is from the devil not God because God told you no condemnation can come to you (Romans 8:1,2). Yet, when you repent and call upon Him, He is faithful to hear you and help you out of your trouble every time. God is love.

When you do sin, the way out is to confess and receive the forgiveness that God has already provided (1 John 1:9). Never resort to looking at yourself and your failure, beating up on yourself, thinking you failed God, or that because you fell short, you will never measure up to the standard God requires. Trying to live your life by the law of what is right or wrong, holy or unholy is legalism, the very opposite of grace. Living with this law mentality will cause the devil to accommodate you with lies about your situation, yourself and others with accusations and judgments, constantly pointing out wrongs or imperfect behavior to bring condemnation and push you into fear, torment and depression.

> *When you do sin, the way out is to confess and receive the forgiveness that God has already provided.*

Instead, move from looking at yourself and own- effort and receive God's redemption by the blood of Jesus. You are forgiven, cleansed and made free in God's forgiveness, only by the blood of Jesus. He will never fail you because He is truth, with the power of grace to help you live that truth; so never for any reason, focus on sin or submit to thoughts of sin-consciousness from the devil because there is no condemnation to a believer (John 1:17; 1 John 5:18; Romans 8:1, 2).

As a believer you are completely redeemed and made free from the hand of the enemy, because your righteousness is of faith in the blood of Jesus, not of yourself or your own efforts. Humble yourself and receive God's forgiveness in your redemption as complete in Christ Jesus. Trust His love and have faith in His blood and all He did for you. Have faith in His character, of love and forgiveness which made you eternally and forever free unto your Father for relationship and worship!

Walk out in God's truth, because Jesus forgave you and made you free. Reject every thought, every word, every feeling, every accusation, every condemnation from self, others and the devil, manifesting with a bad low feeling or pressure on the inside. Reject every comparison, every tendency towards perfectionism and every lie to you against God's Word, all seeking to keep you from surren dering to Jesus and gaining your freedom. Whatever tactic the devil uses, let the Holy Spirit help you to recognize them and take your stand by casting them down and declaring that you are the redeemed, and you will say so! (2 Corinthians 10:4, 5; Psalm 107:2).

Walk out in God's truth, because Jesus forgave you and made you free.

Walk As the Redeemed

- Walk in God's grace, believing what Jesus has done for and in you and rest in the finished work of the cross. Cease from striving to avoid sin, or do works to please God. Cease from letting the devil push you into an awareness of your weakness and flaws and into self-condemnation. Instead, let self-effort, your sin, sin-consciousness, weakness, and flaws, pull you into the arms of Jesus for salvation or redemption, relationship, restoration and worship.

- Acknowledge and accept the atonement of Jesus' blood. Praise Him for it. Let His forgiveness cause you to lift Jesus higher in your mind and heart over yourself, any sin you may commit, and over the devil. Do not walk according to ways and the opinions of or requirements of man for your justification, but only God's Word. God ties your acceptance to Jesus. The church, however, often ties your acceptance to living holy or by your right actions. Choose God's way.

- Accept the eternal redemption that you are 100% free from sin in your spirit where God communes with you (John 4:23). Christ purchased your complete freedom for you. Your freedom didn't happen from your own understanding of temporary redemption until you sin again and have to "do" something about it. Some Pentecostal churches, if they suspect sin in a person's life, they prevent them from taking communion instead of praying for and encouraging repentance at communion, trusting the Holy Spirit to do His job. As Jesus is freedom in your spirit, so are you free in this world. Believe, respond to and receive His grace (1 John 4:17).

- Place value on the blood of Jesus and let the blood draw a line in the sand. Stay on God's side. Confess your position of righteousness, sanctification, and redemption. Exalt the name of Jesus and His truth over that sin, or condemnation, and keep the enemy defeated. Stand in Jesus and declare the enemy's defeat by not getting into the flesh, or getting into works, legalism or condemnation, which is siding with the enemy and making the problem, the devil or what he says to you, bigger than Jesus.

- Eternal redemption is for the entire Christian walk. Once saved, the believer must accept all their sins, past, present, and future, as forgiven and you have been made unto redemption, forgiven and free. When you do sin, confess and, by faith, believe you are forgiven; turn your back on that sin and ask for grace to be free. If the devil is still bringing condemnation, reject him completely and declare you are the righteousness of God in Christ by the blood of Jesus.

Prayer, *"Thank you Jesus I do not do everything right, but I know you love me. I confess I was wrong; I now receive your forgiveness, your righteousness, and your grace. I am forgiven, cleansed and redeemed and I receive it in Jesus' name. No weapon formed against me can prosper and every tongue that rises in judgment I condemn and remain free."* Amen.

- You cannot be free from a sin you are still loving or practicing, so give it up. Forgive yourself and move on in God's grace. Walk in the light, walk in faith looking unto Jesus in good times, rejoice in bad times and ask for His help to overcome.

- When you sin or fail, turn to Jesus. Do not look at yourself or your sin. Concentrating on your sin, weakness, failures and flaws will bring fear, accusations, and condemnation from the enemy, as he will try to confirm to you that you are too weak or not good enough to be a Christian. Jesus is your Savior, look to Him, the author and finisher of your faith, believe the Word as truth and that there is no condemnation that can come to you.

- Confess your sin or failure. Agree with God that according to His Word you were wrong or didn't do well. Enter the throne of grace boldly; talking to your Father and asking for the help you need to overcome. Stay in the relationship with God in front and in charge with the Holy Spirit, leading and directing you.

- Walk knowing God sees you in the spirit realm with a perfect spirit, holy, sanctified, and redeemed (1 Corinthians 1:30; Colossians 1:22). You are not valued less because of the actions of sin or failure. You are a child of God in need of forgiveness, exposed to the attacks of the enemy and in need of restoration. So repent, turn to God and walk in righteousness, walk in the light and resist any attack from the enemy by believing who God says you are by His Word.

- The freedom you actually possess is hinged on you being a doer of the Word, walking in the light and on you taking a stand against the devil. Use your authority by doing what the Scripture says,

"Submit yourselves therefore to God. Resist the devil, and he will flee from you" (James 4:7). Micah 7:8-10).

Mark 11:25, *"And when ye stand praying, forgive, if ye have ought against any: that your Father also which is in heaven may forgive you your trespasses.*

Philippians 3:13, *"Brethren, I count not myself to have apprehended: but this one thing I do, forgetting those things which are behind, and reaching forth unto those things which are before."*

Forget the negatives of the past.

I Peter 2:9, *"But ye are a chosen generation, a royal priesthood, an holy nation, a peculiar people; that ye should shew forth the praises of him who hath called you out of darkness into his marvelous light."*

You are chosen to live in the light of God's Word.

Ephesians 5:8, *"For ye were sometimes darkness, but now are ye light in the Lord: walk as children of light."*

Choose the law of life in Christ, which is faith in His love, and His righteousness. Bless always and curse not.

2 Corinthians 6:14, *"Be ye not unequally yoked together with unbelievers: for what fellowship hath righteousness with unrighteousness? and what communion hath light with darkness?"*

Philippians 4:6-8, *"Be careful for nothing; but in everything by prayer and supplication with thanksgiving let your requests be made known unto God. And the peace of God, which passeth all understanding, shall keep your hearts and minds through Christ Jesus. Finally, brethren, whatsoever things are true, whatsoever things are honest, whatsoever things are just whatsoever things are pure, whatsoever things are lovely, what-soever things are of good report; if there be any virtue, and if there be any praise, think on these things."*

Refuse to dwell on the bad situations in your life. Pray about it and ask God to work it out. Prayer will take the burden off you and rest it on God. If there is something He wants you to do, then listen, He will tell you, do it, and then you will have peace. Always go to God first, not examining your situation or performance. For once you were in darkness, but now in the Lord, you are light. Live in relationship as children of light.

I Peter 5:7, *"Casting all your care upon him; for he careth for you."*

Cast your cares, troubles, and situations on Him and leave it there. When temptation comes back to worry you say, "No, I have given that to God and He is fully able to keep what I have committed to Him." Then worship and praise God that He is working it out for your good. Worship leaves control in His hands. Grace is not passive, hear from God and do what you know you should be doing in the natural to live, for example, praising God or working (Psalm 69:30; 90:17).

Philippians 4:4, *"Rejoice in the Lord alway: and again I will say, Rejoice."*

Rejoice and praise God continually. Give Him thanks for His goodness. Your gratitude to God acknowledges your need for Him in relationship and cancels the blues. He is greater than you and more than capable of handling your cares. Meanwhile, tell the devil that despite his attacks, you are redeemed and free to worship and to rejoice and to act as if it is so.

Prayer *Father, I thank you that Jesus has paid the price for my sins. The debt has been paid in full. Satan you are no longer my master because I have been made righteous and am redeemed. I am redeemed from you Satan, from sin, from death, and from the law of self-will. I choose now to be surrendered to God's will. You Satan now have no legal right to my soul. Father, please reveal any place I have allowed the enemy a place in me and let the blood of Jesus, which has made me holy and wise, reconcile me unto Christ. So I stand in the power, love and authority of the name of Jesus and command you to stop your accusations and condemnation now. I know who I am in Christ Jesus and in Him, I am innocent and I will stand as the righteousness of God in Christ. Amen*

Confessions

- Isaiah 53:7 says, *"He was oppressed, and he was afflicted, yet he opened not his mouth: he is brought as a lamb to the slaughter, and as a sheep before her shearers is dumb, so he openeth not his mouth."*

The verse above is a very good verse to cast down the voice of the enemy in your head or from others with accusations against you. Jesus submitted His will to the Father and bore it all for us so that we can submit our will to His grace believe and receive our deliverance.

Speak out, *"Jesus bore it all in silence so every mouth opened against me in accusation and condemnation, I command to shut up and leave in Jesus name! I know I am righteous ONLY by the blood of Jesus and nothing in or of myself. Jesus made me pure, holy, innocent and righteous and no accusations against me can stand. I reject all efforts to get me to respond to acts of self-redemption because I belong to Jesus. I have right relationship in Christ, restored into His love, and free to come into His presence and trust His word. Jesus loves me God and therefore, I have no fear because God's perfect love for me cast out all fear (1 John 4:18) and I love God and I am full of His power, love, and sound mind , righteousness peace and joy in the Holy Ghost free to come into His presence and worship Him (Romans 14:17; 2 Timothy 1:7)."*

Reject every lie, for example, those that say that you are not good enough, not holy enough, perfect enough or worthy before God or man, and that you are inadequate or imperfect because of your actions. No! It is not about you or your actions; it is about what the blood has done to take care of them both (2 Corinthians 10:4, 5).

"Father, I thank you that the same resurrection power that raised Jesus from the dead dwells in me and causes the anointing in me to rise up in God's power and loose my mind, will, imagination and emotions and put me over. I am set free, from Satan's stronghold of self-will by the blood of Jesus and I worship God my Father and rejoice in the God of my salvation."

- I believe God's Word that I have been delivered from the kingdom of darkness and have been translated into the Kingdom of light. I have freedom in my spirit because God's forgiveness has made me free, and I stand still and speak that Jesus has redeemed me from the hand of the enemy and I prevail over him. Now I rejoice because whom the Son has set free is free indeed.

"Nay in all these things I am more than a conqueror, I am an overcomer and by God's abundant grace and the gift of righteousness I reign in this life by one Christ Jesus in victory and freedom from the enemy" (Romans 5:17; 8:37; Revelation 12:11).

- Now stand, rest, and wait, prevailing against the enemy in faith (not fighting back, as this engages the enemy with fear) but commanding every tongue of the enemy that rises against you in accusation and judgment or oppression in the body as condemned to silence and commanded to leave in Jesus name! Rest until the anointing within rises and loosens his grip of fear and pain. **He must know you believe you've been redeemed** (Romans 5:9; 1 Corinthians 1:30; 6:11; Hebrews 10:10; 1 John 1:9; Revelation12:11). Repeat the Word, prayers, or commands that ministered to you most when Satan tries to return. Pray again, but now do so as praise and worship and thanksgiving because it is already done. YOU ARE FREE, NOW REJOICE!

- Psalm 107:2, *"Let the redeemed of the Lord say so, whom he hath redeemed from the hand of the enemy."*

I rejoice in the blood of Jesus, I am forgiven made righteous and acceptable to God. I am loved, worthy, reconciled, favored, qualified to be in God's presence without feeling I have to earn the right. I have eternal redemption and my spirit is free and sealed with the Holy Spirit of promise. The Holy Spirit abides with me always to help me overcome in all things I trust in God and worship Him.

- The yoke of sin is broken with complete and permanent forgiveness of sin. I walk free in God's truth through the precious blood of Jesus shed for me. I receive the power of His Name and His blood. I am forgiven and I have no sense of sin, no sense of wrongdoing, no sense of failure. The blood of Jesus purges my conscience from all sin and sin -consciousness. Jesus loves me and His perfect love casts out all fear. His love never fails me.

- The Blood of Jesus has made me holy, unblameable (faultless), unreprovable (innocent) and purged of every evil work of the enemy that seeks to defile or condemn me. Father, help me to accept your grace in all you have done for me, as I reject all suggestions of the enemy to depend on my ability to be holy, good or righteous in your sight (Colossians 1:22).

- Jesus is greater than condemnation because the blood of Jesus purged my conscience of sins (1 John 3:20, 21; Hebrews 10:2; Hebrews 9:14). I exalt the name of Jesus above Satan and sin and every attack on my soul to diminish or condemn me; because greater is He that is in me, than He that is in the world (I John 4:4).

- The blood of Jesus redeemed me, made me pure, holy, innocent sanctified, separated from sin unto God that I may come boldly into His presence to worship Him.

Thank you Father that Christ has delivered me from the kingdom of darkness and translated me in the Kingdom of His dear Son, in whom I have redemption thorough His blood, even the forgiveness of sin. I am no longer a slave to Satan and he is no longer my father. Jesus is my Father and Lord, so by the blood of Jesus, I choose the Kingdom of God with righteousness, joy, and peace in the Holy Ghost. I run into Him and I am saved (John 8:44; Colossians 1:13, 14; Romans 14:17).

Lord, I rejoice in you that your precious blood has made me righteous, sanctified, redeemed, and free (I Corinthians 1:30).

I choose to WORSHIP GOD, JESUS IS MY LORD and No weapon formed against me can prosper (Isaiah 54:17).

Jesus, I honor you above every attack of the enemy. I lift the name of Jesus above accusation, condemnation, sin consciousness, and fear. I declare by faith that I am redeemed and lifted up in Christ; the enemy is under Jesus' feet. I am seated with Christ in the heavenlies and therefore Satan is under my feet. I am the redeemed of the Lord and I say so!

I am accepted in the beloved, Jesus loves me, forgave me completely, and I am highly favored and accepted. I reject Satan's lies to me that my acceptance and worth is determined by my "right" actions, of obedience through self- effort, trying hard to obey, or my performance of works. God loves and accepts me because of the blood of Jesus. I am in Christ and I have the power of the Holy Spirit to help me.

Jesus, I thank you for your love, mercy, and your grace. I choose to stand strong in your righteousness by faith. I reign in life by your righteousness and abundant grace.

Praise the name of Jesus, praise the name of Jesus, and praise His glorious name. I am eternally redeemed, delivered, healed, and I am set free in Jesus' name.

God richly bless you as you come to know and accept that you are made in Christ Jesus, unto eternal redemption and can walk as you have been made ETERNALLY FREE.

CHAPTER 10

PERSONAL RELATIONSHIP

The main purpose of Jesus' shed blood was to bring us into personal relationship with God.

Jeremiah 31:3, *"...Yea, I have loved thee with an everlasting love: therefore with lovingkindness have I drawn thee."*

1 John 4: 19**,** *"We love him, because he first loved us."*

Jesus was born and raised under the system of the law which God through Moses had instituted. Jesus lived His life fully as God intended it to be lived, without breaking the law, and therefore fulfilled the purpose of the law in Himself. Now we are to listen to and follow Jesus in relationship. (Luke 9:35). The law sent Jesus to the cross and Jesus went willingly to save man who would turn to God by believing on Him. God wanted man to recognize and acknowledge the futility of the law and its helplessness to save. *"... Christ is the end of the law for righteousness to everyone that believeth"* (Romans 10:4).

Jesus Christ terminated the law because of what the law could not do. The law could not provide righteousness or right relationship with God the Father. Jesus provided that for us, when He came to Earth died to show us the Father's love and gave us the gift of righteousness, which is God's love received by faith. When we believe on God's Son and His work on the cross, we are saved (John 1:12; Romans 3:20-22; Acts 13:39).

Christ ended the law, and all systems of belief, all rules and regulations that dictated behaviors and all commandments, rituals and principles designed to produce right relationship with God by self-will and self- effort. All these, were used in the Old Testament to tell you who God is, who you are and how you were to interact and respond to God and others. The law ended in Christ Jesus as rules to live by for relationship with God. He became the fulfillment of all types, shadows, and patterns in the Old Testament from Genesis to Malachi, as well as the gospels. The gospels must be read with the understanding that it was a period of transition from law to grace through Jesus (Matthew chapter 5) The New Testament showed us how Christ fulfilled the law so that when we believe on Jesus we have relationship with God.

For example, Israel was God's chosen people. Now, in Christ, believers are

"… a chosen generation, a royal priesthood, an holy nation, a peculiar people" (1 Peter 2:9).

God was the cloud by day and the fire by night. Now, Jesus is the light of the world (Exodus 13:21; Isaiah 60:19; John 8:12).

God gave the Israelites, manna (bread) from heaven. Now, Jesus is the bread of life (Exodus 16:4; John 6:32-35).

God gave them water when they were thirsty. Now, Jesus is the living water (Exodus 17:6; John 6:35).

God gave the Word at Mount Sinai. Now Jesus is the *living* Word (Exodus 19-20; Luke 9:35; John 1:1-4)

Jesus shed His blood, and when you believe His work on the cross you receive salvation and the gift of righteousness, having right standing or right love relationship with God. By faith, the Holy Spirit comes right in to live in your human spirit, which is often referred to as the heart. The Holy Spirit's job is to draw and unite you to the Father, to convince you're a born again child of God, and to keep you in a living union relationship. He fills you with Holy Spirit power to minister for God and also helps you to live the Christian life by changing your character, to become Christ like. Every desire in your born-again heart can be met in your relationship with Jesus Christ by the Holy Spirit.

- John 6:44, *"No man can come to me, except the Father which has sent me draw him…"*
- Romans 8:16, *"The Spirit itself beareth witness with our spirit, that we are children of God:"*
- John 14:26 *"… he shall teach you all things, and bring all things to your remembrance, whatsoever I have said unto you."*
- John 15:26, *"… I will send unto you from the Father, even the Spirit of truth… he shall testify of me."*

> **By faith, the Holy Spirit comes right in to live in your human spirit.**

In the work of the cross through Christ Jesus, God ended the law of commandments, fulfilling its requirements for us to perform perfectly good works unto God in order to be accepted and loved. When in faith, you believe on Jesus, receive His love in His forgiveness and His righteousness which makes you saved and restored into right relationship with God.

Now, you possess Him in your spirit with all His love, His provision, all the protection, all the blessings and inheritances He secured for you. This is the work of the Holy Spirit. He is your divine connection into relationship with the Father. When you are yoked to God in a love relationship by the Holy Spirit then your burden is light because Jesus is carrying them for you as you believe by faith. As children of God, we are to be totally dependent on and led by the Spirit of God. Jesus, by the Spirit of God, is your good Shepherd; He loves you and you shall not want. Be in union relationship with Jesus and His Spirit, resting in His presence and let Him glorify Himself in you His creation (Psalm 23:1; Matthew 11: 29, 30; Romans 8:14).

Do Not Excuse Yourself From Relationship

There is always one person who will believe falsely, that God couldn't love them or desire relationship with them for some reason or another. Listen to what God says in His Word to you. Romans 5:8, "...*while we were yet sinners, Christ died for us.*"

God knew everything about you. He knew that you would do the bad things you did, your every sin, weakness, flaw, bad attitude, He knew your every fault. Yet, He loved you anyway. You are valuable to God, enough for Him to send His only Son to die for you, so you can be saved from Sin, Satan, death, and Hell and to be changed within from weakness to His strength and as you are continually being changed into Christ-likeness.

God knows everything about you and He still loves you. The hairs on your head are numbered by Him (Psalm 139:1-17). The presence of the Holy Spirit in you causes Him to be present with you in everything and in every situation you face. This is the good news of the Gospel: It includes all. God is in you and with you helping, guiding, protecting, delivering, healing and upholding you. You are never far from His presence in your life; and all you have to do is call on Him, as a child to their Father and He will hear and answer. If you are born-again, whatever your situation, He is ready to help you. Verse 17 of Psalms 139 says His thoughts towards you are precious. He loves you and respects you as His creation. We therefore should honor our Father and respect ourselves enough to believe that what He says to us about Jesus, and what He says about us is the truth and by faith receive it.

> *The presence of the Holy Spirit in you causes Him to be present with you in everything and in every situation you face.*

Jeremiah 29:11 tells us, He knows the thoughts and plans He has for you ...plans to prosper you, not to harm you, plans to give you hope and a future. Believe God, and draw near to Him, and He will draw near to you (Psalm 73:28; Ephesians 2:12, 13; James 4:8). Because God loves you so much, never undervalue yourself in His sight or devalue your need to run to Him anytime.

Receive His love and seek to reciprocate. He values your love and waits for it.

Draw Near To God And Build
a Closer Relationship with Him.

Daily fellowship with the Father is necessary to succeed as a victorious Christian.

1. Be born again by accepting Jesus as Lord and you are cleansed with the forgiveness of your sins. Payment was by the blood of Jesus to give you eternal life (John 1:12; John 3:16; John 4:14; 1 John 5:11-13). If you are already born again, accept by faith that all sins are forgiven; and you are justified (just as if you had never sinned). Because you have been justified, you have been made innocent, righteous, and acceptable, and restored into relationship with God, through Jesus your Lord.

2. Failure to accept by faith that you are righteous will cause you to exercise your self-will seek your own righteousness by works because you have a wrong picture of God, as perceived in the Old Testament: distanced, hard, angry, and quick to punish. This wrong picture leads to a wrong relationship which results in fear, guilt, and condemnation coming on you. Your righteousness is to be of faith in Jesus, not works of self-effort. Righteousness, or right love relationship with God is now possible without the law (Romans 1:17; Romans 3:21-22; Romans 4:5; Romans 5:17, 10:3; 2 Corinthians 5:18, 19; Colossians 1:20).

3. Know and accept that God is your loving Father and has only His goodness towards you. This will give you confidence to freely come to Him knowing He only wants to bless you (Hebrews 4:16). Remember, even when God gives correction or discipline, He still loves you, and believes there is better for you. Correction is

only seen as judgment to those who still want to love and live in their sin (Hebrews chapter 12).

4. You must know He loves you. God is love and I Corinthians 13:4-8, shows what His love is like. When you know the Father loves you and is at peace with you then you, in turn, will want to meet with Him and spend time with Him.

(a) I know God loves me because: (John 3:16; 15:14,15; Romans 8:31-33; Ephesians 1:6; Colossians 2:13-15; Hebrews 8:12; 12:5,6; II Peter 1:3; I John 1;7,9; 4:9,10,19). These verses will explain His love clearly.

(b) Because God is love and His unconditional love is shed abroad in your heart you can abide in His love and can always love others unconditionally by separating the person from their mistakes while trusting God for their restoration. We are to always put our faith in the blood of Jesus to get whatever we need, even to meet our relationship needs. By faith in the blood, we can forgive. No matter what the person is doing wrong, we can still love them (love the person, hate the sin) while trusting God for the needed change in their lives. So we can say,

"Thank you Lord that your unconditional love is shed abroad in my heart. I rejoice in your love and I choose to love _____ (person) unconditionally and I trust you with their life. I now release them to you and I ask that you cause them to hunger and thirst after righteousness and that your righteousness and your abundant grace will make all things well for_____ in their life. I trust you Father as I now I give to you this situation____ and I let Go and choose to let you God meet their need, in Jesus name Amen (Proverbs 3:5,6; Matthew 5:6; Romans 5:5, 17).

5. Go to God and set aside undisturbed time to spend time with Him (Matthew 6:6). Abide in Jesus to continually

improve your relationship (John 15:1-8). Find the best time of the day for you. The Bible says, *"…early will I seek thee: my soul thirsteth for thee…"* (Psalm 63:1). Keep a journal and record your impressions from God, your prayers to Him and His answers. You will be amazed over time to see how much He is involved in leading and helping you daily in your life.

6. Be consistent with your devotion time; go to Him regularly at the time you have set aside. If you become too busy to spend quality time with God, just as the Word says, you will begin to wither and die (John 15:6). Seek to have regular and consistent fellowship because it cannot be stored up. Just like manna in the wilderness, it must be gathered fresh every day. So, by faith, wake up a little earlier, set your alarm, ask the Holy Spirit to wake you up or to help you set some time aside before the day ends, to help you to build the relationship you desire. Avoid becoming legalistic by setting a specific duration or time to end. Remember it's about relationship, not how hard or how long you pray. Furthermore the Holy Spirit knows your schedule, so let Him lead you to the end, which is usually a time of rejoicing in God for fellowship and for His goodness in meeting with you.

7. If you falter or miss sometimes, just get back in and ask the Holy Spirit to continue to help you. Do not entertain any discouragement or condemnation by beating up on yourself or give up because you were not perfect in your devotion times. Remember His mercies are new every morning.

8. Approach and relate to God according to faith in His grace and His finished work on the cross; don't try to relate to Him by the law or self-will acting in your own strength and effort. Look at the story of Jacob as he wrestled with God: (Genesis Chapters 32, 33)

Jacob was a trickster and a cheat. He deceived his brother Esau and robbed him of his birthright. Now the time came for him to face his brother. Jacob in self-will tried to control the situation in his own strength as he strategized how to meet Esau. He separated his family for protection and sent gifts ahead for Esau. But God confronted Jacob and asked him what his name was. God wanted him to confront himself and to realize that he needed to come clean and change. God wrestled with Jacob until he was broken before Him; his hip joint went out of socket, and thereafter Jacob limped and learned to lean on God and to depend on Him to help in meeting Esau. Jacob stepped over into God's grace. He contended with God, and made a demand on Him for greater relationship and blessing. God helped him, blessed him, and changed his name to Israel. We must first go to God for His grace and help, not falling back into law of doing and trying to fix things for ourselves without God. We would avoid God having to wrestle with us to change us from self-will to God's will.

Hebrews 4:16, *"Let us therefore; come boldly unto the throne of Grace that we may obtain mercy and find grace to help in the time of need."*

This story of Jacob is one that mirrors the journey which led to the writing of this book. God will not leave us the same that way we come to Him. He wrestles with us to change us into His image. Sometimes when the enemy brings dark or painful times to us God allows it (Job chapters 1-3; 2 Corinthians 12:9). Sometimes God has to work in the dark, in trials and trouble to increase relationship as in those times we have little option but to run to Him for help to turn our darkness to light so we can see and later shine in His light. He responds by leading and guiding us out of our trouble, as He restores, and supervises our spiritual growth, by stretching and developing our faith into greater dependence on Him. So yield and embrace God's grace both in good times and in bad times because He is your best help.

9. Give yourself over to God in praise, thanksgiving and adoration.

Psalm 100:4 says *"Enter into his gates with thanksgiving, and into his courts with praise: be thankful unto him, and bless his name."*

You may listen to praise and worship songs, but sing in your own voice, let your ears hear your own voice praising God to build your spirit up. Choose the posture the Holy Spirit is leading you into. This may be sitting, laying prostrate (Flat) on your face, kneeling, a bowed head, or standing. Praise God by how you're led by the Holy Spirit.

You may pick one attribute of God at a time, for example faithfulness, deliverer or healer. Find Scriptures and speak them to Him. Remind Him how thankful you are that He is faithful to you. Or speak scriptures on "who you are in Christ." He loves to hear that you know and appreciate His workmanship in you (Ephesians 2:10).

10. Seek to become more and more aware of the Holy Spirit. Listen to Him, He lives in you. He may have something to say to you, such as a word of encouragement, a correction, or a word of direction. Whatever it is, believe He will speak to you. He is God, so agree with Him and say and do just what He speaks to you.

11. Matthew 6:11 *"Give us this day our daily bread…"* Give God your petitions, supplications, responsibilities, and all your needs to be successful in your daily life.

12. Listen and raise your expectations to hear Him. He may drop a word in your heart, or a scripture. Look it up, read and meditate on it, He may have further instructions for you on that topic you're meditating on or the situation you gave to Him. Stay in the relationship and fellowship, stay in the process until you have full understanding and faith arises for you to act on your faith and receive.

13. Watch out for discouragement from the enemy. Even if the time was short and dry, keep on keeping on. God

says if we seek Him we shall find Him. Don't give up. Keep pressing in, until your time with your heavenly Father, builds a better relationship that is more intimate and special than before. Grow in and develop your relationship with God by acknowledging that the Holy Spirit dwells in you and wants to live and love through you (John 14:16; 17, 26). Continue your fellowship with your Father also by praying in the Holy Ghost. He will build you up (Jude 20) and give revelation knowledge and the mind of Christ on matters of your life. He will show you God's plan for your life and teach you how to walk step by step in His plan to give you victory and success (1 Corinthians 2:10-16).

14. Defer to God the Holy Spirit for help every time you are in need. Spend time praying in the Holy Ghost and ask God for the interpretation. Listen for when He speaks. Get familiar with His voice. This is not easy, and I am still in the learning process myself, so persevere. God gave us the Holy Spirit so we can be dependent on Him, and go to Him. You will never have to be ignorant about an issue in your life ever again.

15. Depend on the Holy Spirit to help you balance your reverence for God, and your deepening friendship with Him. Never let familiarity breed contempt. (Number 12) Miriam and Aaron had contempt for Moses but David had honor for God.

Psalm 27:4, "*One thing have I desired of the Lord, that will I seek after, that I may dwell in the house of the Lord, all the days of my life, to behold the beauty of the Lord and to enquire in his temple.*"

This Psalm speaks of David's relationship with God. He had a great desire for the Lord, and he wanted to seek Him, dwell with Him, go into the house of the Lord and gaze on His beauty, worship Him, enquire of Him, talk and listen to Him. David's graciousness and desire for relationship, as well as his consistency in worship, prayer, praise, and supplications and repentance were some of the reasons God declared him as a man after His own heart. Even when he sinned with Bathsheba, he did not run away from God, but was close enough to be corrected by the prophet. He repented and went on with God. In good times and bad, stay with God, trust Him, and depend on His Grace and His goodness in blessings or His mercy in repentance, and correction (Psalm 23:6; Hebrews 12:6-11).

If God related to these Old Testament saints in love and friendship in this way, He will do the same for us. His Word says that He's no respecter of persons (Romans 2:11). He will be your friend. Jesus has shed His love abroad in your heart and He is in you and for you. The Holy Spirit in you is yearning after God crying "Abba, Abba Father." He is knocking on the door of your heart, non-believers and believers, inviting you to sup (feast) with Him (Revelations 3:20). Proceed to draw near and receive what you need to develop an intimate relationship with your heavenly Father.

The blood of Jesus has purchased Christ's divine life to be your life.

In addition to your closet prayer mentioned above as you go about your daily life, 1 Thessalonians 5:17, says "pray without ceasing" Wherever you are, whatever situation you find yourself in saturate it with prayer. Talk to God continually about everything. Involve Him in everything as you in turn listen and respond to Him. Enjoy His companionship throughout the day and at night give Him thanks for His loving care and protection as you sleep (Psalm 4:8; 138).

Will you draw closer? The blood of Jesus has purchased Christ's divine life to be your life. You and God are one life, one spirit (Deuteronomy 30:20; Colossians 3:3, 4).

Your Commitment to God,
Be faithful to the life of God in you

Jeremiah 3:14, *"Turn, O backsliding children saith the Lord; for I am married unto you: and I will take you one of a city and two of a family, and I will bring you to Zion."*

Hosea 2:19-20, *"And I will betroth thee unto me forever; yea, I will betroth thee unto me in righteousness, and in judgment, and in loving kindness, and in mercies. I will even betroth thee unto me In faithfulness: and thou shalt know the Lord."*

John 10:11, *"I am the good shepherd: the good shepherd giveth his life for the sheep. But he that is an hireling and not the shepherd, whose own the sheep are not, seeth the wolf coming and leaveth the sheep and fleeth: and the wolf catcheth them, and scattereth the sheep."*

Jesus committed to love us as the Shepherd loves His sheep. We see the Father's commitment in the story of the prodigal son (Luke 15:11). We are to be fully committed to our walk with God. This commitment will keep us in relationship and fellowship with our Father, so we can go through the good and the bad together with Him in faith and without despair. We can walk hand in hand with God through trials or difficult times. Through the process of overcoming each of these trials we build faith, commitment and trust (Genesis 22:7- 14).

If you know He took you through the first time, you know He will do it again (Psalm 37:3-5). God is looking for your commitment to allow the Holy Spirit to help you to yield to His Word and obey His voice as He leads and guides. We are committed when we remain constant in our fellowship with and worship unto the Lord, yielding to the anointing of the Holy Spirit and depending on His power to help. As fellowship and communication increase, intimacy will also increase. God is pleased when we are looking to Him, talking, listening, and joyfully yielding to Him, expecting Him by faith to fulfill His purposes and promises in and for us.

Be consistent. Your consistency in fellowship, the word worship and praise to God daily will demonstrate your faithfulness and will increase God's power in your life. God will speak to you and revelation and knowledge will increase. Give Him time to speak back to you. In His power and strength, you will become as He desires of you. God wants your commitment, which He will reward (2 Chronicles 16:9; Esther Chapter 8).

What it takes to follow Jesus: (Matthew 16:24; Luke 9:23; Luke 9:62; Luke 14:33; 2 Peter Chapter 2).

To follow Jesus, it takes commitment to step out of your comfort zone and learn to depend on Jesus. Spiritual commitment will, spur, time in the word, prayer, consistent fellowship with your Father and being faithful throughout the day to engage Him in everything you think, say or do. As you commit to fellowship, eventually you will get more intimate. Somewhere in your time together, take some time to ask? *"Lord, is there something you have to say to me today?"* Then practice listening. You may seem to hear nothing for a long while, but stay with God and over time you will begin to hear as the noise of your soul diminishes and it becomes quieter so your spirit can ascend and lead you.

> *Give Him time to speak and fully listen to Him with expectancy. Relax in His presence, rest in His peace. Don't be in a hurry.*

Give Him time to speak and fully listen to Him with expectancy. Relax in His presence, rest in His peace. Don't be in a hurry. Just as committed couples love to spend time together and time goes by without realizing, the same is true with God and yourself. It may seem difficult at first especially in the quiet and long silences, but be patient; in due time you will be more secure in Him and learn to desire Jesus' presence more and more. Desire Him He will come and meet with you and talk to you.

Some results of a personal and intimate relationship with God are:

- You will come to know the true love in God and now you can genuinely love others (1 John 4:11).

- You will have peace and contentment in your heart and in your life. The fruit of the Spirit and the work of righteousness will improve your love relationship with God and others (Isaiah 32:17, 18; Romans 13:8-10; Galatians 5:22).

- Security and assurance (Hebrews 13:5).

- Sensitivity to His nature, His voice, His will in His word, His desires, His ways and His needs (John 10:27; Philippians 2:13).

- Greater spiritual understanding, "till we all come …unto a perfect man, unto the measure of the stature of the fullness of Christ" (Ephesians 1:17; 18; 4:11-13, Colossians 2:9, 10).

- Intimacy as you will be led by the Holy Spirit, who relates to each person, individually and personally. You will become a friend of God (Exodus 33:11; Romans 8:14; Ephesians 3:19-21).

- God answered prayers (Psalm 34:4, 1 John 5:14, 15).

- Manifestations of the presence of God Himself (Colossians 1:26, 27).

- Guidance:

"Cause me to hear thy lovingkindness in the morning; for in thee do I trust: cause me to know the way wherein I should walk; for I lift up my soul unto thee" (Psalm 143:8).

- Joy: *"Thou wilt shew me the path of life; in thy presence is fullness of joy; at thy right hand there are pleasures for evermore."* You will show me the way of life, granting me the joy of your presence (Psalm 16:11).

- Eternal life making us sons of God, like Jesus, able to demonstrate the knowledge and power of God to a hurting world (John 17:3, 14:12).

You are God's friend. Friends love one another and make time for each other. Friends meet together and share thoughts, even disclose secrets as they have mutual confidence in each other. Sharing confidences and being vulnerable cause friendships to grow, and a friend is the main person who can often show you that you are wrong and you will listen and accept it. Receive God's Word to you today and do not spend even one more day without a relationship or a better relationship with Him. Don't be religious, seek to be His friend.

It was J S Parks who said "A religious person says, "I'm following the rules and I'm doing good." The true Christian says, "I'm in a relationship with God and He makes me good."

CHAPTER 11

ETERNAL LIFE

S tep into relationship of eternal life with God.

John 3:16 *"For God so loved the world, that he gave his only begotten Son, that whosoever believeth in him should not perish, but have everlasting life."*

Eternal life is having the life of God in you and through you from the day of your salvation, until eternity as you remain in Christ. Eternal life is having a new identity full of the life of God, full of the newness of life, and the resurrection power of His Spirit. It is being destined through all things to have the goodness of God in your life.

1 John 5:11-13, *"And this is the record, that God hath given to us eternal life, and this life is in His Son. He that hath the Son hath life; and he that hath not the Son of God hath not life. These things have I written unto you that believe on the name of the Son of God: that ye may know that ye have eternal life, and that ye may believe on the name of the Son of God."*

John 1:4, *"In him was life; and the life was the light of men."*

The life of God will not only bring light to your path but it will also shape your life and your destiny for good.

John 5:26, *"For as the Father hath life in himself; so hath he given to the Son to have life in himself;"* According to the Word, eternal life is having the life of Christ in you when you believe on the name of the Jesus the Son of God. God further extends His life to us through His eternal Words in the Bible which enter our hearts by His Spirit. A believer's life is eternal, because the eternal God lives within. God said His Words will never pass away and neither will His presence when we believe on Him because He is the living Word (John 1:1).

John 17:3 puts it this way, *"And this is life eternal, that they might know thee the only true God, and Jesus Christ, whom thou hast sent."*

Here we see the word *"know"* also used in 1 John 5:13, *" These things have I written unto you that believe on the name of the Son of God; that ye may know that ye have eternal life, and that ye may believe on the name of the Son of God."*

The Greek word "Ginosko," translated, *"know"* is the knowledge of God beyond mere intellectual capacity. It is knowledge gained from your intimate union relationship and experience with God (Genesis 4:1; Luke 1:34). God's Word to you is life, as you get to know Him and develop relationship with Him through His Word. The Holy Spirit, by faith will arise from your spirit to bring the fullness of God's eternal life into you and into your daily life (Romans 10:17; 12:3b).

We can partake in God's eternal life.

- Genesis 1:27; 2:7 *"So God created man in his own image, in the image of God created he him; male and female created he them. And the Lord God formed man of the dust of the ground, and breathed into his nostrils the breath of life; and the man became a living soul."*

- Colossians 1:12, *"Giving thanks unto the Father, which hath made us meet to be partakers of the inheritance of the saints in light;"*

- Philippians 1:7b, *"… Ye all are partakers of my grace."*

- 2 Corinthians 4:16, *"For which cause we faint not; but though our outward man perish, yet the inward man is renewed day by day."*

- Revelations 21:27b, *"... but they which are written in the Lamb's book of life."*

A person has eternal life when he becomes born again.

"But God commendeth his love towards us, in that, while we were yet sinners, Christ died for us" (Romans 5:8)

"Therefore if any man be in Christ, he is a new creature: old things are passed away: behold all things are become new" (2 Corinthians 5:17; John 14:16, 17; Galatians 4:6, 6:15).

Salvation is not just being cleansed through the forgiveness of sins to get us to Heaven, but it is the life of Christ living in our human spirit which makes us new creation beings from the heart, here on Earth. God expect us to inherit, inhabit and experience His eternal life and all His blessings now.

"I had fainted, unless I had believed to see the goodness of the Lord in the land of the living" (Psalm 27:13).

This life of Christ, His Zoe life, makes us both natural beings, living by the senses in this world and supernatural beings living by faith and also accessing the spiritual world. As spiritual beings, eternal life leads us into a superior quality of life that is full of wisdom, healing, deliverance, protection and provision; it is here that our soul is quickened, strengthened, illuminated, and become full of God's abundant overcoming life led by the Holy Spirit.

God's plan is to bless us through His life in us.

John 3:16 – *"For God so loved the world, that he gave his only begotten Son, that whosoever believeth in him should not perish, but have everlasting life."*

- John 10:10b, *"... I am come that they might have life, and that they might have it more abundantly."*

- 3 John 2, *"Beloved, I wish above all things that thou mayest prosper and be in health, even as thy soul prospereth."*

- John 20:31, *"But these were written, that ye might believe that Jesus is the Christ, the Son of God; and that believing ye might have life through his name."*

If you have never heard of Jesus and that He died to save you from sin, death and Hell, or if you have heard of Jesus but have turned your back and choose to neglect or reject Him, He still died for you because He loves you. Right now you may feel, miserable, lost, and alone, out of balance in life, in pain, or in need of relief and peace.

If that's you, Jesus is waiting for you to call out to Him for help. Just as the devil and his evil spirits made your life a living hell, Jesus is real and He is ready to give you peace. He will turn your situation around for your good. Read John 3:16 again, and turn back to the end of Chapter Three on the topic of the gospel, and sincerely pray the prayer of Salvation. If you were a believer once, pray for restoration. Your sincere belief in God through Jesus His Son has now saved you or restored you. His eternal life now lives in your recreated spirit. Go forward and live as His new creation. Let His Word in the Bible continue to change your thinking, feelings and your choices to line up with the new person you have now become.

If you are Already a Believer, God Desires that you Grow and Mature in Christ-Likeness.

1 Peter 1:9, *"Receiving the end of your faith, even the salvation of your souls."*

1 Peter 2-1, 2, *" Wherefore laying aside all malice, and all guile, and hypocrisies, and envies, and all evil speakings, As newborn babes, desire the sincere milk of the word, that ye may grow thereby."*

Eternal life is God's truth of all He has secured through Jesus on the cross for you. When you believe, you have salvation which is embodied in His healing, deliverance, joy, peace, provision, protection, and all His promises to you deposited on the inside within your human spirit. Faith, which is your belief in God's Word, forms the bridge to cross over into the spiritual realm and pull spiritual blessings into the natural realm here on Earth where you live and is in need of them.

God has allowed Satan to remain on Earth with us to challenge us, just as he did Adam and Eve thereby giving us the opportunity to choose Satan or Him Jesus, as our Lord (Romans 6:16; Revelation 20: 1- 10). Satan will be bound for 1,000 years after which he will be loosed to test those born in the dispensation of the millennial reign when there was no evil on Earth. Love is a choice and the millennials must be given a choice to choose Jesus or Satan just as we have this choice now. Our choice for God through Jesus proves our love for Him. Unfortunately even after being with Jesus with no evil from Satan for 1,000 years, when Satan was loosed to test these born during the millennial reign many were deceived as seen in Revelation 20:10. By faith we must turn from Satan and run to God at all times especially in times of testing and in the dark and difficult times. God gets His greatest heart's desire when as our Father He can embrace us with His love and be the One to love and help us mature in faith so we can receive all His blessings. God's heart is to love and bless us.

> *Your sincere belief in God through Jesus His Son has now saved you or restored you.*

The devil will always continue to try to accuse you trying to rob your faith, and block your blessings. The Bible tells us the devil is defeated; you must believe that truth, and daily enforce his defeat so that you can enjoy all the good in eternal life God has for you. God wants nothing more than for you to choose Him, through His Son Jesus Christ. His desire is to fill you up with His eternal life.

Manifestations of Eternal Life

Eternal life: Zoe, when received and developed, brings newness of life and maturity in the things of God and blessings.

- Eternal life: makes us new beings; or new creatures in Christ (Romans 6:6; 2 Corinthians 5:17; Galatians 6:15; Ephesians 4:23, 24).

- Eternal life: makes us one with God through Jesus Christ (John 6:56; 15:15; 1 Corinthians 6:17; Colossians 1:27).

- Eternal life: makes us righteous, loved and acceptable to God (Jeremiah 31:3; 2 Corinthians 5:21; Philippians 3:9, 10; 1 John 4:10).

- Eternal life: delivers us from Satan's dominion, and the kingdom of darkness (Luke 10:18, 19; John 8:12; Romans 6:14; Colossians 1:13, 14; 1 John 5:18).

- Eternal life: makes us more than conquerors and victorious in Christ Jesus (Romans 8:37; Colossians 1:16, 17; Revelation 3:9).

- Eternal life: gives us God's Grace, power and ability, His goodness and His mercy (Psalm 23:6; Romans 8:11; John14:10, 16, 17; 2 Corinthians 13:3, 4).

- Eternal life: in us gives us power to receive the promises of God (Psalm 103:1-5; John 7:38; Romans 5:10; Galatians 6:8).

- Eternal life: causes us to be always victorious overcomers being prepared for heaven (1 Corinthians 15:57, 58; 2 Corinthians 2:14; Ephesians 3:14,15; Philippians 2:13; 1 John 5:4; Revelation 12:11).

Receive Jesus Christ and receive eternal life. Receive the fullness of your life through Jesus. In relationship with Christ, you no longer have to be alone trying to figure out life on your own. Instead your dependence on Him will cause you to succeed in all aspects of your life and allow you to fulfill your earthly destiny. Talk to Him as Father about everything, listen for His leading follow and let His life work on your behalf to bless you.

"When Christ who is our life, shall appear, then shall ye also appear with him in glory." (Colossians 3:4.)

The eternal life of Christ can be your life if you humble yourself, forsake the way of self-will, your own ways, the world and then turn to God by faith in Jesus Christ.

Let Christ be your life. The hope of His glory in you, your salvation into God's presence in Heaven, love, joy, peace, long-suffering, gentleness, goodness, faith, meekness and self-control. There is also Healing, deliverance, power, love and a sound mind and much more treasures for you to discover as you in relationship worship God.

When Christ is your life, He alone will be the first focus of your spiritual eyes. You will seek Him and find Him with the eyes of your heart, in His Word and by His Spirit, as He is a God of pure love.

Do not let your self-will, others, the world, religion, the church or denomination be the god of your salvation. Let Jesus Christ be your redemption, your Savior and Lord, the source of eternal life to you.

He will be enough for you because He will fill you; with all the treasures you need through His life eternal and in time He will turn your heaviness into joy, your mourning into dancing, your weeping into laughter, and your torment into peace.

Let Christ be your life and fill you with life eternal.

CHAPTER 12

GIFTS: GOD GAVE GIFTS UNTO MEN

"But unto every one of us is given grace according to the measure of the gift of Christ. Wherefore he saith, WHEN HE ASCENDED UP ON HIGH, HE LED CAPTIVITY CAPTIVE, AND GAVE GIFTS ONTO MEN" (Ephesians 4:7, 8).

God gave the world His best gift; which was the gift of His Son Jesus Christ to die and bring redemption, in salvation to mankind in order to raise them from spiritual death to spiritual life.

Jeremiah 33:15, *"In those days, and at that time, will I cause the Branch of righteousness to grow up unto David; and he shall execute judgment and righteousness in the land."*

John 3:16, *"For God so loved the world, that he gave his only begotten Son, that whosoever believeth in him should not perish, but have everlasting life."*

Christ lived for approximately 33 years on Earth, and for approximately three of those years, He was walking, teaching, healing, and delivering all who came to Him in faith. He went to the Cross and died to secure mankind's salvation, by executing judgment on Satan and delivering mankind from his grasp. Jesus shed His blood cleansed the heart, forgave sins and gave mankind His righteousness, which therefore opened the way for salvation in restored love and for the Father to give many other gifts to His believing children (Psalm 68:18, 19).

- He gave the gift of salvation and forgiveness in repentance: (Ezekiel 11:19, 20; Acts 4: 12).
- Faith (Mark 11:22, 24; Ephesians 2: 8).
- Righteousness (Romans 5:21; Ephesians 4:24).
- Grace and Rest (Ephesians 4:7, 8; Hebrews Chapter 4).
- Gift of the Holy Spirit reproving the world of sin unto eternal life (John 1:12; John 16:8).
- All Spiritual blessings (Romans 8:32; Ephesians 1:3; Philippians 2:9; I Timothy 6:17; II Peter 1:3 10; Revelation 1:5).

John3:3, *"… Verily, verily, I say unto thee, Except a man be born of water and of the Spirit, he cannot enter into the kingdom of God."*

The Kingdom of God is both in the here and now on Earth possessing the life of Christ and all His goodness, as well as in our future eternity when we get to Heaven. For you to enter both you must be born-again. The Kingdom of heaven may be accessed without water baptism for example the thief on the cross (Luke 23:39-43).

Water baptism is the symbol of death to old self and the world and being alive unto God. In addition to being born again baptism is a command requirement for entrance into the spiritual life of the kingdom here on Earth (Matthew 3:13-16)

Once born again, we receive the Spirit of God into our human spirit. God sent the Holy Spirit to dwell in our bodies, His temple, to make us children of God (Ezekiel 11:19; Romans 8:16; 2 Corinthians 5:17; I Corinthians 3:16).

A. The Holy Spirit abides within us at the new birth or born-again experience and changes our heart to make us ready to meet God (John 3:16, 14:17).

B. The Holy Spirit builds within us the Christ -like Character of Jesus (Galatians 5:22, 23)

C. The Holy Spirit also abides as the anointing within, to destroy yokes and burdens within us (Isaiah 10:27; Romans 8:11; 2 Corinthians 4:7; I John 2:27).

D. The Holy Spirit is our comforter, helper, and guide in the inner man of the heart (John Chapter 14).

E. He is the operator and distributer of the gifts of God in and through believers for the benefit of believers and the growth of the church (1Corinthians chapters 12-14).

F. The Holy Spirit also comes upon a person at the experience of the "Baptism of the Holy Spirit" to give power to live the Christian life and for service.

Receiving the Gift of the Holy Spirit

(Luke 24:49; Acts 1:4; 5; 2:38, 39; Mark 16:17, 18)

Study and meditate on the above and the following scriptures and believe them to be true, pray the prayer, believe and receive the Baptism of the Holy Spirit with evidence of speaking in tongues.

1. Be born again (John 3:16, 4:14).

2. Baptism of the Holy Spirit is subsequent to salvation; examples in the Bible, (John 14:16-18 ; Acts 2:1-4; Acts 10:44-46; 19:2-6).

3. Some ways the Holy Spirit helps us (John 14:26; 15: 26; 16:13; 17:3; Acts 1:8; Romans 8:26).

4. You receive Him by faith (Mark 11:24; James 2:17).

5. God's responsibility is in the giving (Mark 16:17; Luke 11:13; Acts 19:6).

6. Man's responsibility is to believe, receive by faith, respond and speak (Galatians 3:11b, 14; Acts 2:4).

INSTRUCTIONS:

God will give you the gift of the Holy Spirit because you asked (Luke 11:13).

- You may sense a prompting or an urge flowing from your belly to speak. Yield and begin to move your lips and your tongue. Speak those syllables that you are sensing.

  They are coming from your spirit to your mouth. Your brain will not understand because they are not words. Because of this, do not judge the language God gives you as gibberish or foolishness. Receive Him and His language as your Father's gift to you.

  Refrain from speaking in English or any other known language. Speak the utterance the Spirit is giving you. Speak by faith. You are the one who will have to put sound to the utterance. Open your mouth and speak from your spirit (Acts 2: 4).

- There is not just one way to receive. I have seen the ministering of Baptism for the Holy Spirit where the Word is preached to build faith. Then the minister ask persons after saying the prayer for baptism of the Holy Spirit to close their eyes, concentrate on Jesus and with a fervent heart begin to praise and worship God by saying Hallelujah! Hallelujah! Hallelujah! ... Very soon the Holy Spirit comes to a yielded heart and tongue. The person will begin to speak as the Holy Spirit gives utterance.

- I have also seen ministers lay hands on people and they begin to speak in tongues instantly. Jesus is the baptizer and He is God the Holy Spirit, let Him lead according to His power and the faith of the person receiving. If you are ministering be led by the Holy Spirit.

Prayer for the Baptism of the Holy Spirit:

Lord Jesus, you promised if I asked you for the baptism of the Holy Spirit, you would give Him to me. I am asking you now to baptize me in the power of the Holy Spirit with the evidence of speaking in tongues. Pour out your Spirit upon me, and fill me with your power and your presence, in an overwhelming way. Father, I believe you have given Him to me, and by faith I receive Him now in Jesus's name. Amen.

Minister lay on hands and say: Receive the Holy Ghost!

Person in their heart: I receive in Jesus' name.

Minister: Keep encouraging the person to yield, to open their mouth, move their tongue and speak.

Minister: Pray quietly in your own tongue to encourage them, as they hear you pray in your language. Tell them their language given to them will be different and unique to them.

- If one did not receive instantly, tell them to remain in faith, and continue to thank God for the manifestation of the baptism of the Holy Spirit, because you believed that you received Him when you asked. God may correct you about something, receive it and make the adjustment. For example, you might need to forgive someone. He will reward you with your desire for the gift of baptism in the Holy Spirit. Even while at home as you fellowship with God, continue to thank Him for the utterance which can begin to flow. Remain in faith expecting to receive.

If necessary, speak with someone more experienced than you in this area for more help. Once you have received, pray in tongues daily, and watch your relationship with God soar to greater heights.

The Holy Spirit and supernatural gifts

The Holy Spirit comes with power and gives supernatural gifts, in offices of administration, to whomever God chooses.

Ephesians 4:11 *"And he gave some, apostles; and some, prophets; and some, evangelists; and some, pastors and teachers; For the perfecting of the saints, for the work of the edifying of the body of Christ…"*

In I Corinthians chapter 12, He also gives gifts to the believer as He pleases, for the building up of the believers personally and for the church. These are:

- Gift of word of wisdom
- Gift of word of knowledge
- Gift of faith
- Gift of healing
- Gift of the working of miracles
- Gift of prophecy
- Gift of discerning of Spirits
- Gift of tongues
- Gift of interpretation of tongues

It is said that God the Father is the owner, Jesus is the CEO, and the Holy Spirit is the manager on Earth. He was given to help us live victoriously as we use these gifts to improve our everyday lives, and to make us the church ready for the second coming of Jesus. We are not left on our own (John 14:18; Epheisans 4:11,12).

"That he might present it to himself a glorious church, not having spot, or wrinkle, or any such thing; but that it should be holy and without blemish " (Ephesians 5:27).

In our daily lives when we enter a time of fellowship, whether at home, church, or in prayer believe God is actively working through the Holy Spirit to work in you and through you to build you up:

- He is leading you into truth, revealing the things of God (John 16:13).
- Pricking hearts (Acts 2:37).
- Opening eyes and hearts (Luke 24-32; Acts 16:14).
- Quickening your mortal bodies (Romans 8:11).
- Helping your infirmities and weaknesses (Romans 8:26).

- Teaching and bringing all things to your remembrance (John14:26).

- Testifying of Jesus (John 15:26).

- Giving guidance, and showing you things to come (John 16:13-14; 1 John 2:20).

- Reproving the world of sin, the believer of righteousness, and reproving Satan, who is judged as defeated (John 16:8-11).

- Helping us to pray as He makes intercession for us (Romans 8:26).

- Giving us power to witness, and speak in other tongues (Acts1:8; 2:4).

- Leading us into fellowship and closer relationship with the Father (John 16:13; 17:3).

- Working in us, to help us obey the Father (Philippians 2:13; Hebrews 13:21).

- Leading us continually (Romans 8:14).

- Helping us to walk in and be kept by God's grace (Psalm 23; Galatians 2:20; 1 Peter1:5).

- Helping us to please God (Philippians 2:13; Hebrews 13:21; Hebrews 11:6).

Fellowship with the Holy Spirit

The Holy Spirit does more than just cause us to be born- again, more than speaking in tongues, and more than power abiding within. He is the third person of the God-head and is worthy of being in fellowship and having a close intimate communion or relationship with (2 Corinthians 13:14).

John 14:16, *"And I will pray the Father, and he shall give you another Comforter that he may abide with you forever;"*

The Holy Spirit is a person referred to as "He" in John 14:16 above. He is the one who dwells with you and shall be in you

(John 14:17). He is the greater one that is in you (I John 4:4) He, the anointing, the Spirit of God, is greater than any power of the enemy. As the third person of the Godhead, He is to be acknowledged, welcomed as a partner, and honored when we exalt Jesus. Give Him welcome, love, recognition and fellowship. He will take you into the presence of Jesus. God is in Heaven and Jesus, after His ascension, arose to be seated at the right hand of the Father. The God we have continuously and relationally on Earth is the Holy Spirit who is living in you and me and in each and every one who is a believer. Our God is a great God!

So honor His presence and He will testify of and bring you to Jesus and the Father. Pray in tongues often to experience His presence.

David Yonggi Cho, Pastor of the largest church in the world in South Korea said, "I began to nurture an even greater relationship with the Holy Spirit. I realized that the Holy Spirit had been given to me to work with me, not just to sit in a corner... Today I treat the Holy Spirit as the most important person in my life...I praise Him, and I tell Him that I love Him. "Dear Holy Spirit, let's together pray to the Father. Let's together pray to Jesus Christ. Let's together read the Scriptures. Always my fellowship begins with the Holy Spirit. Then with the Holy Spirit I worship God and His Son Jesus Christ. So now I feel the presence of the Holy Spirit intimately and that is when the Spirit speaks... I understand..."

I always say, "Dear Holy Spirit I welcome you, I recognize you, and I love you. I depend on you. Dear Holy Spirit, let's go!

He continues, "Before ministering I always force myself to recognize the Holy Spirit, to welcome the Holy Spirit and to worship the Holy Spirit, because He is a person... I always say, "Dear Holy Spirit I welcome you, I recognize you, and I love you. I depend on you. Dear Holy Spirit, let's go! Let's bring the glory of God to the people' .... After finishing the sermon, I will sit down and say, "Dear Holy Spirit we did a wonderful job together, didn't we? Praise God! "10.

I took the time to make this lengthy quote, because I believe we all can learn to be more intimate with the Holy Spirit, whether ministering or just fellowshipping with Him. Let us take the time to fellowship with the Holy Spirit, talk with Him, listen to Him, and yield to Him. Ask for His help, to recognize and yield to His voice when He speaks to us. Receive from Him insights, wisdom, revelation, the hope of your calling, the riches of the glory of His inheritance, and knowledge of the greatness of His power. Let Him fill us up with God's eternal life and power (Galatians 4:19; Ephesians 1:17-19).

Let Him the Holy Spirit:

- Help you with all things. Ask for His help? (John 14:26; 15:7; 16:13; 1 John 5:14, 15).

- Help you to be transformed (Romans 12:1-2; I Corinthians 1:30; 2:16; 3:23; 6:11).

- Equip you with gifts to do the work you are destined for (Ephesians 4: 11-15).

- Help you to minister with supernatural help and power (Acts 1:8; 3:6).

- Help you to grow in Christ -likeness (Galatians 5:22; Hebrews 13:20-21).

- Lead you into all of God's goodness (Romans 2:4; 8:14).

- Help you to yield to God's grace using His strength not yours to please the Father (Romans 10:3,4)

Philippians 2:13, *"For it is God which worketh in you, both to will and to do his good pleasure."*

Whatever you read in the Bible that you don't understand, find difficult doing, or any personal difficulty that you encounter in life with a bad habit, look to the Holy Spirit, give it to Him and ask His help to give you the answer. Pray in tongues and listen for His direction. Do not quench the Holy Spirit (Matthew 23; 1 Thessalonians 5:19-22). We can quench the Spirit as the religious leaders did, despising prophesyings, failing to prove all things, and holding on to what is good. We quench the spirit also by ignoring Him, trusting our own abilities (self-will or law mentality) rather than God's grace and ability in us, walking in the flesh, being prideful, doing our own thing in your own way and time, and resisting Him in disobedience as He tries to lead.

Walk in the Spirit. Walk according to the written Words of the Bible, and the spoken Word of the Holy Spirit. Walk in God's grace, through faith, walk in God's love, and walk in the power of the Holy Spirit always looking at the things which are eternal (2 Corinthians 4:18). Learn to rely on the Holy Spirit as your helper. Pay attention to Him. He has a voice, He speaks so listen keenly when He prompts you to action, and respond.

The Holy Spirt will orchestrate and bring together things, people, places, and resources to accomplish the will of God for your life. He did before in creation.

Genesis 1:2, 3 *"And the earth was without form, and void; and darkness was upon the face of the deep. And the Spirit of God moved upon the face of the waters. And God said, Let there be light: and there was light."*

The Spirit of God hovered over the face of the deep and hearkened to God's voice to form creation. Let Him hover over you as you walk by faith in God's grace believing, embracing, and desiring all that the blood of Jesus purchased for you. Allow Him to create life eternal, full of abundant life in you and for you, and for others through you. The Holy Spirit orchestrated all things for the birth of Jesus and His protection into manhood (Luke Chapters 1, 2).

The Spirit of God hovered over the face of the deep and hearkened to God's voice to form creation.

The Holy Spirit orchestrated and put in place everything for baby Moses' protection and sustenance (Exodus Chapter 2). The Holy Spirit also directed and protected Joseph to live and fulfill his destiny to save Israel (Genesis 37 onwards).

These are examples for us. If the Holy Spirit orchestrated their lives to bring success, He will do the same for you and me if we trust and rely on Him to do it. We are in the age of the Holy Spirit, to depend on Him. Will you acknowledge, receive, fellowship, and yoke yourself with God through Him in relationship? He will take the Word of God that you read, meditate, and speak using it to stir your faith (Romans 10:17). He will take you into the presence of God your Father, and into His blessings and His peace.

The voice of the human spirit is your conscience. When your soul is aligned with God and His Word, your conscience will be at peace and your soul at rest and you will begin to flow with the Holy Spirit more and more.

> *"Now the God of peace, that brought again from the dead our Lord Jesus, that great shepherd of the sheep, through the blood of the everlasting covenant, Make you perfect in every good work to do his will, working in you that which is well pleasing in his sight, through Jesus Christ; to whom be glory forever and ever Amen* (Hebrews 13:20, 21).

> *"And let the peace of God rule in your hearts, to the which also ye are called in one body; and be ye thankful"* (Colossians 3:15).

HOW TO PRAY OUT MYSTERIES
(THE UNKNOWN THINGS IN YOUR LIFE
TO WHICH YOU NEED UNDERSTANDING)

Pray in tongues, expecting God to give you direction or the answer. I Corinthians 14:1-15 Read scriptures first, make confessions, and become assured in your heart before you pray. Feel free to make up your own words relating to each scripture.

- 1 Corinthians 2:16; 14:1-15, Father, I know I have the mind of Christ.

- John 14:17, I know the Holy Spirit of truth dwelleth with me and is in me

- John 16:13; I Corinthians 14:4 & Jude 20, therefore, I pray in tongues to edify and build myself up, to get understanding and an answer towards my situation.

- I John 2:20, The Holy Spirit is in me and I have an unction from the Holy One, and I know all things in my spirit, so I thank you for wisdom and understanding (Ephesians 1:16-18).

- John 14:26 & 15:13, The Holy Spirit, my Comforter shall teach me all things. Ask Him your question. Thank you lord for hearing me. Please help me to listen expectantly, and to hear you as I wait while fellowshipping with you.

- I Corinthians 14:13, Father I pray for interpretation, make my mind fruitful for the things I need to know, thank you for the answer in Jesus name Amen.

PRAYER

"Thank you Father, I know my spirit has the answer, because the Holy Spirit dwells there and He knows and teaches me all things. Father I thank you for revelation knowledge and for the truth of your heart and mind in this matter. I thank you in advance for your answer and for your help and I praise you for your goodness in Jesus' name Amen."

Now pray in tongues, worship and praise God. Keep expecting to hear or know the answer or be led in the way go.

Listen to your heart, expecting to hear. If you believe you didn't hear, speak 1 John 2:20; 5:14, 15 and remind God of His promise as you keep on expecting to hear.

If you have waited, and still feel you haven't heard, this is what I do. I tell God, Father I know by your Word you, answered, but I didn't hear. Please tell me again and this time, please make it easy for me to understand. For the rest of the day and night, and the

next few days I keep listening, He will answer and you will hear
(1 John 5:1, 15).

- Your answer may come as a thought in your heart from the Holy Spirit.
- A scripture in the Bible.
- Through nature or creation Romans 1:20
- A dream or a vision, or a strong desire.
- An audible voice, usually rare, as when this happen it often is a grave or very important situation God does not want you miss to miss hearing correctly.
- Another person speaking the answer to you.
- Providence or circumstances a path or door of opportunity, In line with your prayer opens for you.
- If you're young in the Lord, do not be afraid to ask the Lord for confirmation or reassurance (Isaiah 7:11; Psalm 31:3; John 13:23, 24).
- Any other help the Holy Spirit gives you.

You have the precious gift of the Holy Spirit your helper, along with the promise that He will never leave you nor forsake you, but will keep you connected to God your Father through Jesus. We all can depend on The Holy Spirit to help us in all the ways we need.

"But the manifestation of the Spirit is given to every man to profit withal." (1 Corinthians 12:7)

Will you let Him help you in all the ways that only He can?

CHAPTER 13

SATAN
A DEFEATED FOE

1 John 3:8 b "... *For this purpose the Son of God was manifested, that he might destroy the works of the devil"* (Hebrews 2:14, 15).

Satan is God's arch enemy, and by extension, also ours. His whole effort is to see people go to Hell and believers busted, disgusted, and defeated. He thwarts Christlikeness and spiritual maturity to the point of ultimately causing some to lose their salvation by rejecting Jesus, who is their only source of eternal life. (Hebrews 6:4-6) Satan works hard to keep people in bondage in their spiritual life and all realms of the natural life: physically, emotionally, mentally, and financially.

Satan is defeated, totally defeated, stripped of all power over mankind, humiliated, and was made a spectacle for the whole world to see. As believers, we must have faith to believe Satan is a vanquished foe.

Colossians 2:15 *"And having spoiled principalities and powers, he (Jesus) made a shew of them openly, triumphing over them in it."*

When Jesus died on the cross and rose again from the grave, He demonstrated mighty power over death, Hell, and the grave. I want you to know about the great and mighty power that God has given us as His followers. It is the same wonderful power He used in Ephesians 1:20 when He raised Jesus from the dead and caused Him to sit at His Fathers' right hand in Heaven. In verse 21, Christ rules over all forces, authorities, powers, and rulers. He rules over all beings in this world and will rule in the future world as well. Verse 22 tells us that God has put all things under the feet of Jesus for the good of the church (Ephesians 1: 19-22).

Satan Was Defeated and Victory Was Won When:

- God kicked Satan out of Heaven, and Jesus saw him falling like lightening. When we stand in Christ we too will see him bow and fall (Isaiah 14:12-16; Luke 10:18; Philippians 2:9-11; Revelation 12:9).

- God sent Jesus who came in the flesh and, in His death, burial, and resurrection as a sinless man, destroyed Satan's power over mankind by taking sin into Himself and giving us freedom with authority in His word, repentance and forgiveness in His love (Romans 5:9; 10;10; 2 Corinthians 5:21; Ephesians 1:7; Hebrews 2:14,15).

- People who become born-again as believers, and allow Jesus to control their hearts with His word ends Satan's power and rule over them (Jeremiah 31:33, 34; John 1; 14,16; 1 Corinthians 15:54; Hebrews 2:14,15).

- Jesus nailed the Law to the cross, the weapon that gives sin strength and Satan power over us controlling our self-will. In His grace with the power of the Holy Spirit Jesus destroyed sins power as well as all its effects of guilt, shame, rejection, accusation, condemnation, judgment, punishment and death (Luke 11:13; Romans 8:1,2;1 Corinthians 15:56; Colossians 2: 14-17).

- Sin lost its power and dominion over us as Jesus justified us and gave His gift of righteousness (made us innocent and loved) by depositing His Spirit within. This made us New Creation beings having His nature of love deposited in our hearts which cancels all fear (Romans 5;5; 6:4-6; 8:14; 2 Corinthians 5:17; Hebrews 2:14).

- Jesus' death on the cross brought judgment to Satan (John 12:31; John 16: 8, 11; Revelation 12:11; 20:10).

- When God gave us power to overcome the enemy in the name and blood of Jesus (Luke 10: 18,19; Ephesians 6:13; Philippians 2: 9-11; Revelations 12:11).

- The Holy Spirit, the greater One, the Anointing within, was given to dominate within and guide God's people into truth that sets them free from Satan (Isaiah 10:27; John 8:32, 36; Acts 1:8; 1 John 1:27).

- Jesus defeated Satan, by Faith in the Word and the Spirit in the wilderness. We can read this in Matthew Chapter 4, and we are to enforce his defeat in the same way. Jesus demonstrated His union with the Father, His faith and character of righteousness, which caused Him to speak the Word in power and defeated Satan.

- Satan was defeated when God raised Jesus from the dead, far above every name that is named and every demonic power. Ephesians 2:6 says we are raised up "IN CHRIST" and are seated with Him in heavenly places. Every force of darkness is under Jesus' feet and because we are "In Him" Christ Jesus, demons are under our feet also. (Ephesians 1:16-23)

We triumphed over Satan in the victory Jesus won for us, when He rose from the dead. He defeated the whole hosts of Hell, took the keys of death and Hell and gave us power and authority over all demonic powers

Matthew 16:19, *"And I will give unto thee the keys of the kingdom of heaven: and whatsoever thou shalt bind on earth shall be bound in heaven; and whatsoever thou shalt loose on earth shall be loosed in heaven".*

Philippians 2:9-11, *"Wherefore God also hath highly exalted him, and given him a name which is above every name: That at the name of Jesus every knee should bow, of things in heaven, and things in earth, and things under the earth..."*

Luke 10: 19. *"Behold, I give unto you power to tread on serpents and scorpions, and over all the power of the enemy: and nothing shall by any means hurt you."*

Revelation 1:18, "I am he that liveth, and was dead; and behold, I am alive for evermore, Amen; and have the keys of hell and of death."

Other related Scriptures: Isaiah 14:19-24; Ezekiel 28; 16-19; Matthew 12:29; 16:19; 28:18-20; Mark 16: 15-18; Luke 10:18-19; 11:20-22; 22:53; John 12; 31, 32; Romans 10:9,10; Ephesians 2;12-14; Colossians 1:13,14; 2:14,15; 1 John 4:4; Revelation 12:11.

God's Word is truth. Truth defeats Satan and his lies every time it is believed and spoken and acted on in faith.

"Then said Jesus to those Jews which believed on him, If ye continue in my word, then are ye my disciples indeed; And ye shall know the truth and the truth shall make you free (John 8:31, 32).

Before the truth can set you free you must know, speak, meditate and act on the truth you believe and you will see your supernatural God work on your behalf to set you free.

(John 17: 17 ; 2 Corinthians 4:13, 14; Revelation 12:11).

Jesus rose victorious, giving us complete victory over Satan when we stand in His Word by faith and rest in His grace believing and expecting to receive (Mark 11:22-24; Ephesians 2:8).

1 Corinthians 10:13: *There hath no temptation taken you but such as is common to man: but God is faithful, who will not suffer you to be tempted above that ye are able; but will with the temptation also make a way to escape, that ye may be able to bear it.*

Satan is a created being, he is not the creator of new ideas and everything he does is a perversion of God's ideas. Satan has no new tricks to use on people he hasn't used on Jesus.

Because Satan has no power, and nothing new, he uses lies, trickery, deceit, temptation, accusation, bluffing, condemnation and deception to get you out of faith in God and to enter onto his territory of the flesh, self-will, self-effort, unbelief and fear. Satan has no power unless you give it to him when you believe his lies and get out of faith and enter into worry, unbelief or fear. We get into fear through believing and speaking and reacting to Satan's faithless thoughts, ideas, suggestions, feelings and actions. Only when you fall for his tactics mentioned above and get into fear can Satan gain power over you.

There are only two forces in this world: God with Love and truth resulting in good, light, and life and Satan with fear and lies, resulting in evil, darkness and death. Any step you make away from God (His Word and His Holy Spirit) is a step away from His love and a step towards the enemy' fear darkness and death there is no middle ground except Jesus (John 3:36; Romans 6; 16; 14:23; 1 John 5:17a).

Every time you fear, you have believed a lie of Satan opposing God's truth to you.

John 8:12, "… *I am the light of the world: he that followeth me shall not walk in darkness, but shall have the light of life.*"

John 8:32, And ye shall know the truth, and the truth, shall make you free."

Some of Satan's personality traits

- He is a confirmed sinner: Revelation 14:10,11
- He is an adversary: 1 Peter 5:8, 9
- He is a tempter: I Thessalonians 3:5
- He is a liar and a murderer: John 8:44
- He is an accuser: Revelation 12:10
- He father of lies: John 8:44

Satan is not the God of Earth.

Satan got his power over mankind from fallen Adam when Adam forfeited his authority, giving up dominion over the earth. Satan continued to perpetuate his evil through sin and its consequences of guilt, shame, the law with self-will and control, condemnation, sickness and death, but he is not the God of this world, which is the Earth.

2 Corinthians 4:3, 4, *"But if the Gospel be hid, it is hid to them that are lost: In whom the god of this world hath blinded the minds of them which believe not…"*

In this verse Satan is referred to as the god of this world, the world of them that are "lost" the sinner "them which believe not." (The collective group of people who rejects Jesus) He is not the God of the world we call the Earth.

1 Chronicles 29:11, *"Thine, O lord, is the greatness, and the power, and the glory, and the victory, and the majesty: for all that is in the heaven and in the earth is thine; thine is the kingdom, O Lord, and thou art exalted as head above all."*

Psalm 115:16, *"The heaven, even the heavens, are the Lord's: but the earth has he given to the children of men."*

Psalm 24:1 *"The earth is the Lord's, and the fullness thereof; the world, and they that dwell therein."*

Psalm 89:11, *"The heavens are thine, the earth also is thine: as for the world and the fullness thereof, thou hast founded them."*

All believers, living on Earth when in faith, activate God's power over Satan and all evil.

Many times people refer to God as the ruler of Heaven and all things good and to Satan as ruler of Hell and evil. But he, Satan is not the ruler of Hell, neither is he God's counterpart. Satan was created an Archangel in the league of other Archangels such as Gabriel and Michael. Let's cut him down to size in our eyes, so we do not give him the same stature as we do the God of heaven, because God also rules over Hell (Psalm 139:8-10; Matthew 16:18,19; Acts 2:30-35; Revelation 1:18).

As a created being and a fallen angel, Satan is very limited in power because he is not omnipotent, omniscient, and omnipresent nor is he infinite, because he has a beginning and he has an end. God has placed limitations on him (Job 1:12). He can also be successfully resisted by believers (James 4:7) and his end is in sight (Revelation 20: 2, 10). When Satan attacks you remind him of his powerlessness and of his impending demise.

> *Satan is a created being, a fallen angel, and is very limited in power because he is not omnipotent, omniscient, and omnipresent.*

Some of Satan's Weapons, Power Sources and Attacks against People:

Satan's main weapons of power are used to deceive you into believing his lies starting with the thoughts of your mind and pictures in your imagination. He continues his attack in your feelings, your emotions, and the choices of your will. He tries to get you to yield to him instead of God's truth in the Bible. Defeat Satan by refusing to listen to his voice when he speaks to you, and tries to contradict God's nature, and His will in His Word. Reject him. Instead, choose to believe God's Word as the only source of truth (John 10:10; 2 Corinthians 10:4, 5; Ephesians 4:21-24; Philippians 4:8).

John 10; 10a *"the thief cometh not, but for to steal, and to kill, and to destroy."*

Satan Attacking People from Within:

(1) **Doubt:** makes you question your God and His Word.

(2) **Fear:** activates Satan's power, which if left unchecked, blinds you to God's love for you and cancels faith leading to discouragement. You then begin to look at yourself, your problems, and dwell in the darkness worry, anxiety,

intimidation, accusation, condemnation, despair, depression, and ultimately oppression is produced.

(3) **Bait:** Satan goes fishing to capture the human soul. For his bait, he brings thoughts pictures, suggestions of negative scenarios to the mind and imagination tempting and coercing you to get into fear. Once you swallow the bait, he progressively leads you into bondage and ultimately deception. For example he will put a feeling or symptom or sickness on you if you ignore it you will get sick, if you cast it down (2 Corinthians 10:4,5) you will be well.

(4) **Bluffing**: Satan further uses compromise, deceit, trickery, pretending he has the upper hand. He will attack with force pretending he is too strong for you that you cannot do anything about him.

(5) **Lies and Accusations:** attacks your love, identity, significance, and security before God and man causing negative or low feelings inside, which leads to sickness, guilt, shame, low self- esteem, worthlessness, insecurity , condemnation, depression and oppression.

(6) **Wounds:** Satan enters and operates through hurts, offence, bitterness, un-forgiveness, anger, resentment, jealousy, rejection, shame and injuries.

(7) **Religion:** Satan seeks to keep peoples belief in self-will of the law instead of God's will of His grace (Romans 4:3-5; 14:23)

(8) **The occult:** witchcraft or any practice or behavior which exalts Satan

Satan's Power Affecting Us from Without.

1. **Distractions:** bring thoughts into the mind with fear and torment and leads us to focus on things of little or no importance, keeping you from the main things like, faith, love and maturity in Christ. For example materialism.

2. **Delay:** attacking the human Will, causing procrastination, confusion, indecision and disobedience and living in self-will.

3. **Temptation:** lust of the eyes, world, and flesh. He shows pictures and gives thoughts, suggestions, ideas and feelings to look at and be captivated by so you can be ensnared into sin. For example, overspending and pornography.

4. **Deception:** actually believing the lies of the devil, and living by those wrong beliefs.

5. **Instigations:** stir up trouble and strife in your thoughts towards other people or vice versa.

6. **Spirit of slumber:** sleepiness; works well for him against Christians in church and at devotional times, reading the Bible and in prayer.

7. **Sicknesses, disease and death:** pain or sickness to kill and remove you from the face of the Earth.

8. **Demon- focused rather than Jesus- focused:** excessive focus and preoccupation with binding and loosing Satan and his demons demonstrates a lack of faith, and will increase demonic activity in your life. Whatever you focus on grows and multiplies. So focus on God and the sacrifice of His Son.

9. **Disguise.** He will attack in one area for example accusation and condemnation but disguise it with pain in the body. He tries to keep your focus speaking to the pain in your body, but is doing the greater damage in your soul. It takes the Holy Spirit to help you to differentiate as he tends to attack in pairs or multiple troubles at each time disguised as an angel of light. (2 Corinthians 11:14; Galatians 1:8)

How Do We Give Satan Power Over Us?

"Be sober, be vigilant; because your adversary the devil, as a roaring lion, walketh about, seeking whom he may devour" (1 Peter 5:8).

- Failure to read, meditate and speak the Word in faith causes weak faith which easily walk in the flesh and yield to fear.

- Failure to believe all your sins are forgiven and that you're justified thus causing you to remain in sin-consciousness, having feelings of unworthiness, and condemnation and fear. This further leads to double mindedness and the inability to appropriate all that Jesus purchased in your redemption. You really do not believe you have been fully redeemed (James 1:5-8).

- Failure to receive the gift of righteousness, the ability to stand in God's presence, and know who you are " In Christ" that you are fully loved and be free from guilt and all condemnation. Lack of righteousness leads to feelings of insufficiency, unworthiness and insecurity before God and man.

- By falling from God's grace back to self-will walking out your Christian life under the law. This shortchanges you from receiving the full effect of God's power of grace that is working on your behalf to help and deliver you. You have reverted to living by your own strength and means instead of God's. (Galatians chapter 3)

- Failure to guard your mind, resulting in a negative mindset and a wild unsanctified imagination, one that is not aligned with God's Word. Satan then freely injects negative thoughts, suggestions and ideas, pictures and bad dreams all designed to bring fear which is his entrance to bring your destruction.

- We listen to his lies and speak them, then taking it one step further we believe his lies and yield to the flesh and his deception. Stop listening to him and worse, repeating to others what he said. Reject it immediately and completely.

- You believe his bluffing and bullying tactics that he is too strong for you, or that you cannot get rid of him or that you are not healed or not freed. Instead of confronting him and telling him that he is a liar you give into lies and fear therefore prolonging his attack against you. Stand your ground in the midst of his roaring, and let him know you have knowledge of your God, of His love for you, of your inheritance in Christ, and whom the Son has set free is free indeed. Let him know that you know he Satan is defeated. Stand and resist he's, stubborn but will flee.

- Failure to forgive and instead continue to live in anger, resentment or bitterness.

- Failure to repent of missing the mark of righteousness and remain in sin.

We Enforce Satan's Defeat By:

God said of Satan in Isaiah 14: 15, 16, *"Yet thou shalt be brought down to hell, to the sides of the pit. They that see thee shall narrowly look upon thee, and consider thee, saying, Is this the man that made the earth to tremble that did shake kingdoms."*

- Knowing how big your God is and speaking His Word as truth (Psalm 89).

- Knowing who you are "in Christ," and whose you are, protects you from being the "whom person" in (1 Peter 5:8).

- Know that you have been made a new Creation in Christ, qualifies you to receive by faith (Galatians 3:11-14; 1 timothy 6:12).

- Know your inheritance and blessings which were promised to you by the blood of Jesus and that you must partake or receive your desired blessing in the presence of the enemy despite your feelings or the circumstances. (Psalm 23:5)

- **Recognize** the weapons and the strategies the devil is using against you and believe that he and his demons are defeated. Beware of opening the door yourself with anger, sexual sin, lying, un-forgiveness or any works of the flesh (Romans 1:24-32; 2 Timothy 3:1-7; 2 Peter 3:3-4). Pray and also pray in the Holy Spirit who will reveal exactly what tactic is coming against you.

- **Reject or resist.** Reject the voice, attacks, lies and threats of the enemy. Humble yourself and Submit to God as His child by believing His Word as truth, speaking it and obey by doing what it says. Now resist the devil, *Say,*

- *"Satan I reject you and command you to leave from my head/ soul /body in the name of Jesus. Get out!"*

  Father in the name of Jesus let your anointing raise a standard against every force of oppression coming against me and put me over, into your peace. Amen
  (Isaiah 10:27; 54:17; Matthew 18:11,19; Luke 10:19; 2 Corinthians 10:4, 5, 1 John 4;4; Revelations 12;11).

- **Replace:** Replace by speaking God's Word, His truth that you believe concerning the attack against you (John 8:31,32,36; Philippians 4: 4,8, Philippians 4:19; 1 John 4;4;).

- **Remain.** Sit and receive resting in the Lord rejoicing. You remain free as you receive God's word and promises as true and fill your heart with His truth. When Satan tries to mimic the symptoms as if he is still there after the Word says you are healed, or that you are free. Rest in Christ and continue speaking the truth of the Word, the blood and the Name of Jesus believing you received, say: *"Satan I resist you in the Name of the Lord Jesus Christ my redeemer, the blood is against you, I rest by faith in God's grace and I believe what the Word say…. I am free, I am healed, I am delivered and I will REMAIN FREE IN JESUS' NAME. NOW I CHOOSE TO REJOICE AND WORSHIP THE GOD MY PROVIDER FOR HIS GOODNESS."*

Knowing what God's Word has to say about all of the above and speaking them in faith will enforce Satan's defeat and reduce his stature and power in your own eyes as God strengthens you to believe and teach you by His spirit to trust His power to help you to stand and overcome.

Remember you have to partake at the table in the presence of the enemy. So expect to believe you are healed in the midst of pain or delivered in the throes of torment until freedom comes.

God has Given us Spiritual Weapons to Enforce Satan's Defeat.

- Humility having Faith in the Word of God, (Mark 11:22-24).

- The Word of God (Matthew 4:1-11)

- The Name of Jesus, (Philippians 2:9-11).

- The Blood of Jesus, (Revelations 12:11).

- The Power of Casting Care, (1 Peter 5:7).

- The Gift of Righteousness in God's love not Judgment, (Matthew 7:1-2; John 3:17; Romans 3:22, 14:17, and 5:17).

- Truth You Believe and Speak and act on in Authority (2 Corinthians 4:13; John 8:32, Philippians 2:9-11.)

- Keys to His Kingdom, (Matthew 16:19).

- Spiritual Armor, (Ephesians 6:10-18).

- Power of the Holy Spirit to discern how the enemy is attacking and to give God's salvation. (John 16:13)

- Rest of faith to remain in the freedom God gave you in His Word, (Mark 11:22-25; John 8:32, 36; Hebrews 4).

Grace, the person of Christ Himself

John 1:16, 17, "*And of His fullness have all we received, and grace for grace. For the law was given by Moses, but grace and truth came by Jesus Christ*

Satan cannot overcome a person who is walking in the Spirit and in faith yielded to the truth of God's Word, walking in forgiveness, repentance and total dependence on God.

(John 1:17; Galatians 5:16; Ephesians 3:2-4, 4:7; 1 John 1:9; Titus 2: 11-13; 2 Timothy 2:1; 1 Peter 1:10-13).

God's grace and truth in Jesus ended the law of commandments with self-will and self- effort, thus releasing the power of the Holy Spirit within to help us be overcomers in Christ.

Jesus gave us in Himself power, love and a sound mind (2 Timothy 1:7). He gave us a sanctified imagination (2 Corinthians 10:3-5; Philippians 4:8).

Christ Himself is our spiritual armor. We overcome when we put on Christ, Total dependence on God (Ephesians 4:20-24; 6:11-18).

Exercising the use of your spiritual weapons will bring truth to the heart. The Word says,

"And you shall know the truth, and the truth shall make you free: If the Son therefore shall make you free, ye shall be free indeed" (John 8:32, 36).

Every believer will go through spiritual battles, times of trials, troubles, darkness, and testing. God will not always relieve you immediately by taking you out. Sometimes He allows you to go through so you can see your weakness and lean on Him.

God however will always be with you to see you through until you are delivered. We have spiritual power and authority over Satan; Speak the Word to him as a firm command, wield the sword of the Spirit, use your authority, listen for God's instructions by the Word and by the Spirit. Follow God's instructions and exercise your dominion over Satan to enforce his defeat. God leads us through the battle because every believer in order to live victoriously must stand against and overcome Satan and fear, which is ultimately his greatest power influencing your life.

You can resist fear and Satan, not by constantly binding and rebuking over and over again, but by binding Satan by your authority and command him to go! Then immediately turn towards God in trust speak and act on His Word in faith. Loose your faith by now turning your attention to magnifying God with praise and thanksgiving. Thank Him for the blood of Jesus and all it did for you.

Remember His goodness and thank Him for the Word of God given to bring deliverance in all the situations you face. **Stand** and believe **sit** and receive. Worship and praise God as you minister unto Him and remind Satan how Jesus, by His blood, completely destroyed him, gave you the victory and made you free.

Acknowledge the Great Power
That Is In the Name of Jesus
And The Blood of Jesus.

See yourself in CHRIST, in union with Him. **Stand** in Christ as the New Creation being you have been made (1 Corinthians 1:30). Confront the enemy and speak of your exaltation "In Christ" over him. **Believe,** God by His Word about everything He says about His greatness, His love and care for you and your qualification to receive of Him all His blessings and lastly, speak to Satan of his defeat. Now that you believe and is in faith empowered, **Sit,** be seated in heavenly places, rest in God's anointing in your spirit and claim your blessing as yours and claim Satan's defeat then **Receive** your desire from God's grace in His blessings as you rejoice in His grace and goodness.

Satan is under Jesus' feet and consequently is under your feet too, so now you can tread on serpents and scorpions (Luke 10:19) using Jesus' feet as your own. Receive Jesus' Word as true, because you know He loves and cares for you. Bring every situation you face to rest in His GRACE, POWER, and STRENGTH for your deliverance.

James 4:7, *"Submit yourselves therefore to God. Resist the devil, and he will flee from you."*

You submit to God by believing His character and His love in His Word given for your situation because of the finished work of the Cross. Jesus did it for me. It is already done, it's true, and I believe there is power in the name and the blood of Jesus for me to receive. Abide in Him, and focus on all He did for you and have faith to receive in His name. I am God's son/daughter, a child of God, I have relationship with Him, I yield and obey His Word to me, and therefore I believe and receive in Jesus' name.

For example, in the area of healing: I believe that what Jesus accomplished on the cross was for me. I believe the Word given in Isaiah 53:4, 5, "... *By his stripes I were healed,*" Jesus said it, He bore my pains, I speak the word and I believe it, I stand in faith and patience to believe and receive my healing in Jesus' name. The name of Jesus and the blood of Jesus are greater than sickness. I do not have to bear any of this because Jesus already bore for me. I believe I am healed and I rest in faith and rejoice as I remain healed in Jesus Name (Nehemiah 8:10; Isaiah 53:4, 5; Jeremiah 32:27; Matthew 8:17; Galatians 3:13, 14; 1 Peter 2:24).

> *The name of Jesus and the blood of Jesus are greater than sickness.*

When the devil attacks you, your first response should be:

1. Jesus loves me and has already done something about this. I have relationship and trust His love for me. Pray for wisdom concerning the attack.

2. What does the Word and the Holy Spirit have to say about this? Find God's Word that speaks to your situation. Hold that situation up with the truth of God's love in the Word. Hold firm until faith in God's grace releases power in the anointing to overcome. In faith believe the Word, that the devil is completely defeated.

3. Stand in faith, believe, speak and act on the word and receive God's Word as true, including that Satan is defeated. You have overcome him and the evil one cannot not touch you (Romans 14:23; 1 John 5:18).

4. Let your faith in that Word you believe make you unmovable, unshakable, and confident as you rest in your relationship with a faithful Father, knowing that your help from the Lord will manifest in your natural life in due time.

5. Stand in the authority of the name of Jesus and in the power of Jesus' blood as an overcomer enforcing Satan's defeat until the harassment and torment of the devil ceases. He may try to be stubborn and keep his attack going with thoughts in your head such as, "Is this ever going to end, when is this going to stop." He's bluffing you, take your stand, *Devil you are a liar, this ended at the cross when…"* (Speak the Word concerning your victory)

6. Let your faith abiding in Christ causes the power of the Holy Ghost within, to flow like rivers of living waters from your belly or spirit. Then you shall ask what you will and it shall be done unto you…. that, your joy may be full (John15:7, 11). Now I believe Mark 16:17 can become a reality in your life.

Mark 16:17, 18, *"And these signs shall follow them that believe; In my name shall they cast out devils; they shall speak with new tongues: They shall take up serpents; and if they drink any deadly thing, it shall not hurt them; they shall lay hands on the sick, and they shall recover."*

(7) Guard your mind, rejecting Satan's thoughts, suggestions, and negative imaginations. Choose to speak the thoughts of God's Word instead (2 Corinthians 10:4-5; Philippians 4:8).

We should never be asking God to do what He has already done in Jesus and we should never ask Jesus to do what He has given us authority to do. Jesus has already defeated Satan and has already given us the authority to keep Satan defeated.

Paul had asked God three times to relieve him of Satan's attack something Paul living in the presence of Jesus had authority to do. When Jesus replied to him "My grace is sufficient" He meant Paul had God's grace, His power and ability within him to resist by standing in faith to defeat Satan (Judges 2:3; Mark 16:17; Luke 10:19; 2 Corinthians 12: 6-9; James 4:7).

Give God your situation, in faith believing His Word and character, while taking a stand against the devil. In your relationship listen, hear and do as God instruct trusting Him unwaveringly to cause you to overcome. Rest, let go and let God and receive.

Had Jesus instantaneously removed the trials and persecution Paul faced, he would have believed he was some "big shot" in the kingdom and be overcome by pride again. God allowed his flesh to bear the pain of those trials so by faith, he would exalt the Spirit by putting faith in God's grace, learning to depend on Jesus through the Holy Spirit to overcome his self-righteousness. By this Paul learned to live by grace through faith and became the blessing he is now to us today (2 Corinthians Chapters 11, 12).

Believers, never let the enemy trick you by using, "My grace is sufficient" as a reason for you be passive and to tolerate or endure the devil's evil attacks against you waiting for God to move from heaven and deliver you. He already moved when Jesus died on the cross for your salvation and deliverance giving you power over Satan. Stand your ground with faith in God's grace and in your new creation identity. Stand in your authority and resist Satan and overcome him. Trust in God's grace to overcome your persecutors, His stripes for your healing and the power of His blood for your deliverance and protection. As Paul grew in God's grace, his faith overcame his sin of religion and self righteousness as well as his adversaries. He became one of the most prolific writers and preacher on God's grace in the New Testament, teaching us how to walk grace through faith.

It is God's responsibility to work and He already did through Jesus. He continues to work on your behalf as Priest, Mediator, Intercessor, and Advocate only as you stand in faith through His grace. It is your responsibility to stand in faith believing, speaking and acting on God's word to enforce Satan's defeat. Stand in faith in God's grace and believe in the knowledge of who your great God is and the overcomer your God made you "In Christ" and command Satan to leave because he is defeated. Then sit, rest your faith, in God's grace and receive the promises of God. Receive out of God's grace all the finished work of the cross accomplished for you. Receive and claim your victory in Christ Jesus in every area of your life. Meanwhile rejoice and remain in joy speaking the Word and warding off Satan until your blessing manifests (Romans 15:13)

> Revelation 12:11, *"And they overcame him by the blood of the lamb, and by the word of their testimony; and they loved not their lives unto the death."*

Rejoice always, worshipping, and praising God because you have the power of the Holy Ghost the power of God in you, to enforce Satan's defeat. We have the same power in the Holy Spirit that Jesus the Son of man had when he lived on Earth.

> Romans 8:11, *"But if the Spirit of him that raised up Jesus from the dead dwell in you, he that raised up Christ from the dead shall also quicken your mortal bodies by his Spirit that dwelleth in you."*

> Psalm 149:6, *"Let the high praises of God be in their mouth, and a two- edged sword in their hand."*

Like Jesus, we too can say and move in the anointing and gifts to do as Luke 4: 18, 19, says,

> *"The Spirit of the Lord is upon me, because he hath anointed me to preach the gospel to the poor; he hath sent me to heal the broken hearted, to preach deliverance to the captives, and*

recovering of sight to the blind, to set at liberty them that are bruised, to preach the acceptable year of the Lord."

We have been freed from Satan and every force of demonic oppression from Hell. Let us by the power of the Holy Spirit, which is God's anointing within, enforce the devil's defeat. Stand against every force of fear and demonic oppression within the soul, just as you would against the sickness of cancer in the body.

"*Stand fast therefore in the liberty wherewith Christ hath made us free, and be not entangled again with the yoke of bondage* (Galatians 5:1).

Satan is already a defeated foe. As believers and overcomers we must believe this, despite whatever the devil is throwing at you, despite what it looks or feels like. We are equipped and empowered to enforce his defeat so that we can become the overcomers in Christ that we have already been made. God made us to do great exploits and greater works in the power of the Holy Ghost.

WHERE THE SPIRIT OF THE LORD IS THERE IS LIBERTY. WE ARE FREE AND WE HAVE THE VICTORY!

Confessions:

"*And they overcame him by the blood of the lamb, and by the word of their testimony; and they loved not their lives unto death*" (Revelation 12:11)

- I am redeemed from the curse of the law, Christ being made a curse for me... that the blessing of Abraham can be mine by the blood of the Lamb; greater is He that is in me than he that is in the world (Galatians 3:13).

- In Him was life and the life was the light of men. He dwells in me, He is my God and I am His child.

- As the Son is in the Father and hath life so I am in the Son and hath life everlasting (John 1:4; 5:26; 2 Corinthians 6:16).

- Jesus has given me power and authority over all. In Him I live, move and have my being. No weapon formed against me can prosper, so devil leave in Jesus name (Isaiah 54:17; Luke 10:19; Acts 17:28;).

- My God is greater than Satan, greater than my present feelings, greater than this situation that I am facing, because God hath highly exalted Jesus and given Him a name higher than every name. At His name ___ must bow as my tongue confesses that Jesus is Lord over me to the glory of God the Father.

- By the blood of Jesus, *"Surely He hath borne my griefs and carried my sorrows…He was wounded for my transgressions He was bruised for my iniquities: the chastisement of my peace was upon Him: and with, His stripes I am healed"* (Isaiah 53:4, 5).

- I overcome by the blood of the Lamb and by my testimony that Jesus the Spirit of the anointing in me is greater than all, and Christ in me is exalted above all. I reign in this life by Him, Christ Jesus (Romans 5:17; Acts 5:31; 1 John 4:4; Revelation 12:11).

- Jesus is the light of this world I am a follower of Jesus and I shall never walk in darkness but shall be full of light (John 8:12).

-I walk in, the light and I am in fellowship with Jesus by His Spirit and the blood of Jesus Christ cleanses me now and continually from all sin (1 John 1:7).

-Through the blood of Jesus I am washed, I am sanctified, I am justified made holy and set apart from sin and guilt unto God and His righteousness (1 Corinthians 1:30; 6:11; Hebrews 10:10).

-Jesus purchased me by His precious blood and through the blood of Jesus I am redeemed out of the hand of the enemy. The blood makes me free and I am free indeed therefore I rejoice, I rejoice the blood makes me free (Psalm 107:2; John 8:32)

-Greater is He that is in me than he that is in the world. God word says it and it is truth. I believe the truth that the greater one in me is greater and therefore every knee of____ must bow and leave in Jesus name (1 John 4:4; John 8:32, 36).

- Jesus loves me just as He loved and protected the children of Israel by placing blood on the doorposts for their protection and

THE BLOOD

deliverance (Exodus chapter 12) I now sit and rest in the power of the blood of Jesus and receive my healing from His stripes / deliverance from His blood. His anointing absorbs and removes every oppression and sickness from my body, and soul. I rest and remain healed in Jesus' Name.

"Who hath delivered us from the power of darkness and hath translated us into the kingdom of his dear Son" (Colossians 1:13

There is power in the name of Jesus. There is power in the blood of Jesus. By faith, I stand in Jesus Christ and His great love for me full of light, in Him I live, move, and have my being. (John (1:4; Acts17:28a,) I Resist your oppression devil and stand in the Name of Jesus and command you to bow your knees and leave. I believe I am delivered and remain delivered in Jesus' Name.

- I stand on Matthew 18:18 and I bind you Satan from my life and I loose the resurrection power and life of Christ as I Thank you Father, for /deliverance/ provision/protection. I cover myself, my mind, my thoughts and every person and every possession that concerns me, with the blood of Jesus and receive your peace in the Name of Jesus.

- The blood of Jesus cleanses my conscience from sin and from dead works to serve the living God (Hebrews 9:14; 10:2)

- I plead the blood of Jesus against you Satan, and I command you to cease in your attack because no weapon you for against me can prosper (Revelation 12:11).

- I walk in the light of God's word and I plead the blood of Jesus and claim divine protection on myself, my family, my house/ car, and my finances. I draw a blood- line around us as I thank you father, in the Name of Jesus that your love in Jesus' blood is my safety and my protection. Amen

CHAPTER 14

FAITH IS LIVING OUT OF THE RELATIONSHIP

"I am crucified with Christ: nevertheless I live; yet not I, but Christ liveth in me: and the life which I now live in the flesh I live by the faith of the Son of God, who loved me, and gave himself for me." (Galatians 2:20).

This topic was given to me to search out, so that as a Christian I could better live by faith in God's grace. This verse of Galatians 2:20 that is used to expound on this topic is the reality of how a Christian should live a life of grace in today's present-day church age. The Old Testament parallel for Galatians 2:20 could be Psalm 23, because when a person sincerely confesses Jesus as Lord using Romans 10:9, 10 the Lordship of Jesus puts Him over us as our shepherd and us as His children, or His sheep (John 10:14).

For the Christian life to be fruitful and victorious, we must be dead to the old life and the old person we used to be. We must be crucified with Christ.

Crucified with Christ

Romans 6:11, tells us exactly what crucified with Christ means: *"Likewise reckon ye also yourselves to be dead to sin, but alive unto God through Jesus Christ our Lord."*

The moment Christ came into your heart, at the born-again experience, you became forgiven of all sins. The old sinful heart and its nature were removed. The Spirit of Jesus, the Holy Spirit, moved inside, and you are now justified and made righteous. You belong to Jesus. If you believe this by faith, you are saved, or restored into relationship with God. Satan and sin is longer your master. You are freed unto God.

Being dead to sin means that sin no longer has any power or dominion over you as you can now say no to sin. You can do this because Jesus provided forgiveness as well as the Holy Spirit within to keep you from temptation and to keep you righteous. Let me explain further. The strength of sin is the law, and Jesus fulfilled and ended the law and sin which lost its strength in the grace of forgiveness. When you receive forgiveness, the devil's right to attack you based on that sin is cancelled and you are free in the Holy Spirit's power within to lead, guide and keep you in Christ (John 16:8-10; Romans 10:4; 1 Corinthians 15:56; Ephesians 1:7; 1 Peter 1:5).

Secondly, the blood of Jesus justified you, or made you innocent before God, just as if you never sinned, righteous and loved before God. Your innocence and being restored unto God frees you from the stain of sin (Romans 6:14; 2 Corinthians 5:21; 1 John 1:7). Sin repented of cannot be counted against you, because Jesus paid the price for it (Psalm 32:1, 2; Romans 4:8; 5:13).

God, who is pure and holy, can now have closer relationship and fellowship with you, because Jesus' blood dealt with and removed sin in His body, when born-again His Spirit came to live in your heart and made you holy. Believe you have been made pure, holy, and innocent in your spirit by the blood of Jesus and can now come boldly to the throne of grace for mercy and to live a holy lifestyle if you live from your spirit where you are holy as God is holy.

Peter 1:15, 16 is truth to you. *"But as he which hath called you is holy, so be ye holy in all manner of conversation: Because it is written, Be Ye Holy; for I am Holy."*

When forgiveness is received, you are cleansed or purged of all that is ungodly in your heart. When there is sin in your soul, by His grace, the Holy Spirit living within will convict of righteousness; if you yield to Him, He will keep you from sinning or lead you back to God and righteousness to keep you free.

The old is gone and, in replacement, we are made new creatures in Christ; we are made loved and acceptable to God, capable of living a victorious resurrected life in Christ. In Christ Jesus, all is done for you at the cross and it is enough, He continues to do for you according to your faith. Romans Chapter 6 and Ephesians 4:17-24 are telling you to believe God's grace, and see yourself living by faith in the newness of life given to you.

Now that you are born-again and believe you're a new creation in Christ Jesus, the relationship of walking in the spirit has started because you are walking by the Word as to who you are "In Christ." As a believer, you are now freed from Satan, sin and the law. You are embodied with the Spirit of God and full of eternal life, made innocent and righteous as a child of God; you are qualified to enter God's presence anytime and begin to have a living and a right relationship with Him as your heavenly Father. God has granted you access into relationship with Him by the blood of Jesus. The question is, will you reciprocate His love and come boldly to God just because Jesus died for you?

A relationship should to be two ways. God as our Father wants us as His children to give ourselves completely over to Him and give Him unrestrained access to our whole being, spirit, soul and body so that He can, by His power of grace, as we depend on Him to change us into being the best people we can become as He transforms our soul and body (2 Corinthians 6:14-18; 1 Thessalonians chapter 5).

The relationship God desires is for Him to be our Father through Jesus His Son, and we are to live and act like we are His children in dependence on Him. The Holy Spirit within us is to be our connecter to Him. We are to acknowledge, recognize and honor the Holy Spirit, as we exalt Jesus and call upon Him, His

Spirit will come to and bring God's presence to give all the help we need. He is to be listened to, yielded to, and obeyed. As we do this, He in turn will testify and point us to Jesus (John 15:26).

As we exalt Jesus and call upon Him, His Spirit will come to and bring God's presence to give all the help we need.

His presence within has recreated our human spirit to be God's dwelling place, which is now 100 percent God and will abide with us, and keep us in God forever.

We involve the Holy Spirit by reading and meditating and speaking the Word of God as we practice abiding with God through fellowshipping with the Holy Spirit in prayer. We activate Him as we speak and act on God's word and being filled with and praying in the the Holy Ghost, fasting, praying or any other discipline mentioned in the Bible. Fellowship will increase your awareness of God's presence in and with you, and He will begin to commune and communicate with you more and more. The Holy Spirit will begin to use the Word of God you read and meditate and speak, to bring them to your remembrance and begin to direct your soul and body to relate and yield to God your Father in better way.

1 John 5:2 *"By this we know that we love the children of God, when we love God, and keep his commandments."*

As children of God we want to keep His commandments, but you do not have to stress by trying to obey God for Him to accept you. He already accepted you in Christ. By faith, acknowledge you are in a Father and child relationship trusting the Holy Spirit to help you to obey God.

Philippians 2:13 "For *it is God which worketh in you both to will and to do his good pleasure"*

Other related scriptures (Psalm 143:10; Haggai 1:14; Philippians 1:6; Hebrews 13:20, 21; 1 Peter 1:2, 5).

Saul, whose name was changed to Paul the Apostle (Acts 13:9), became dead to himself as he allowed Christ to be formed in him (Philippians 3: 5-14). How? We know it is by the power of the Holy Spirit, as he explained in the scripture, Galatians 2:20 above.

After his, Damascus experience (Acts chapter 9), Paul began a growing relationship with God, full of the Spirit and led by the Holy Ghost. As a child of God, he became heir of God and a joint heir raised up in heavenly places. In oneness with God, he now saw himself "In Christ" so much so that we heard him say, "Receive us we have wronged no man, we have corrupted no man, we have defrauded no man" (2 Corinthians 7:2). How can he say this after he was murdering Christians in (Acts 9:1, 2)?

He became crucified, dead to that old person and became new in Christ. He also drew so close to God and began trusting God's grace, and so he was able to hear the Holy Spirit forbidding him to go and preach in Asia in Acts 16: 6 (Romans 6:4; 8:14-17; 1 Corinthians 6:11-17; Ephesians 1:3; Colossians 3:3, 4).

Confess the Word and believe that you are dead and raised up, seated with Christ in heavenly places on the very throne of God in Christ Jesus. This will cause you to become established in Christ and "Be" in God. This is why, we cannot stop at the cross. Jesus was resurrected and raised up, seated at the right hand of the Father, and we are in Him raised up also. Establish yourself in the exalted Christ by meditating on "in Christ" scriptures, thereby abiding in Christ. Abiding in Christ is the way to keep the old man under, keeping the old man dead (John Chapter 15; 1 Corinthians 9:27). Some "in Christ" scriptures have already been given in chapter 7, *Union and Confessions*. Meditate on them and be raised up in Christ Jesus, walking as the new creation being we have been made alive in Christ.

> *Jesus was resurrected and raised up, seated at the right hand of the Father, and we are in Him raised up also.*

The Christian life is to be lived in union with God as a Father and child relationship. God through Jesus is your good Father and he wants you as His child to live by faith out of this relationship in total dependence on Your Father to take good care of you.

Jesus lived by faith out of His relationship with His father as Father and Son together.

"Then answered Jesus and said unto them, verily, verily, I say unto you, the Son can do nothing of himself, but what he seeth the Father do: for what things so ever he doeth, these also doeth the Son likewise" (John 5: 19).

Jesus is in complete unity with God His Father. They are one in Spirit. His union was so complete; Jesus said He could do nothing of Himself but only what He saw His Father do. Because Jesus knew His Father, and knew His Father's character of love, He had a close intimate relationship with Him. He could imitate every thought, every word, every understanding, and every feeling of compassion in order to reproduce them into miraculous actions here on earth.

John 14: 11, *"Believe me that I am in the Father, and the Father in me: or else believe me for the very works' sake."*

Jesus, in relationship with the Father, lived by His faith, yielded to the Holy Spirit, and was obedient and sinless. He went about teaching, preaching, and was mighty in working miracles in hea-lings, deliverances, raising the dead, feeding the hungry, and loving and comforting all those in need.

Jesus told us that we can have the same relationship with God as He did, because we also are one in Him, Christ Jesus.

"That they all may be one; as thou, Father, art in me, and I in thee, that they also may be one in us: that the world may believe that thou hast sent me (John 17:21).

We have union with God through the blood of Jesus, and Jesus is saying here that we can be one in God and with each other (John 13:35). When we live from the position of our union with

God through the Holy Spirit, we become free to see situations and others through Jesus' eyes of love, compassion, mercy and grace. As members in the body, we should become more able to live by faith and be able to be tolerant of each other's differences and weaknesses as we learn to release them to the Lord who Himself will deal with them appropriately. He may use others in authority above them to discipline or otherwise, but He will do what is best for them, in His way and His time. We do not have to take on the care and the worry about another person's need to walk in righteousness. These may be your parents, adult children, pastors, or family members or enemies. We can hand them over to God and trust Him to make things right for them.

Living by God's grace and learning to release others to God through confession, and prayer and blessing them, some scriptures God gave me were: Jeremiah 17:7,8; Luke 6:36-42; Romans 14:4-9; Ephesians 2:13-16; Philippians 1:6; Colossians 3:12-15; 2 Timothy 1:12; James 4:12; 1 Peter 2:23-24; 5:6-8.

Prayer: *Father in the Name of Jesus I destroy, cancel, and render null and void all judgments I may have made against _____. Father, please forgive me for pronouncing judgment on_____. You are the only rightful judge and have called us unto grace. I decree and declare these judgments as null and void, broken off. I command all evil spirits that have attached themselves to me or _____ through these judgments to go to the feet of Jesus. In the name of Jesus, demons of judgment Go! And I declare and decree ourselves free from all resulting accusations, condemnation and oppression in Jesus' name.*

We should remain dead to self and the desire to be god in ours and in other's lives. Instead, be dependent on your relationship with God, by His grace, to release others who are in need of God's help or who have wronged or disappointed you. You should also release those whose cares and burdens you may be carrying, especially your children. Instead cast the situation to God and trust Him to make things right in them and for them. In relationship we pray and listen and do only what God says to you by the word or as led by the Holy Spirit.

Living by faith and trusting God's grace in difficult times and even in differences with others, one can still maintain peace and unity. Grace brings peace in our own hearts, our home, and in the body of Christ as we crucify self. Law, which activates self-will, is often judgmental, demanding and controlling, and brings disharmony and division.

"Nevertheless I live yet not I but Christ liveth in me." "It is no longer I who live, but Christ lives in me." NLT

This verse speaks of "REST." When we reckon ourselves dead in Christ, walking by faith and abiding in God, we begin to rest, allowing Jesus to live not only in us but through us by the power of the Holy Spirit. As your dependence on Him increases, your relationship and trust increases and you become less worried about your life or the situations you face. You rest in faith, because you are more assured that God's got you in the hollow of His hand and will never let you go.

Many present day Christians may be, as I was, trying to chump up faith by knowing doctrine, reading and memorizing the Word, speaking and confessing the Word without a sound foundation in what the blood had done for me. I was trying to get the word to move from the head to my heart without the blood. We may study spiritual laws, biblical principles, know the standards of behavior to walk in love, study the correct attitude on how to respond, all of which in themselves are good, but they will not be very effective unless they are rooted and grounded in the love of God for you as a good Father, through Jesus Christ and His shed blood at the very core of your spirit.

"That Christ may dwell in your hearts by faith; that ye, being rooted and grounded in love" (Ephesians 3:17).

When you rest in God's love in relationship based on the blood, His righteousness flows and releases the Holy Spirit to move in God's grace and power on your behalf to build truth you will believe. When your faith lives out of relationship with the father and your heart truly believes you will be at rest and at peace. We do not have to work, strive or chump up faith to believe. Instead as children we turn to and depend on God our Father just as a natural child would to their natural father.

When you rest in God's love in relationship based on the blood, His righteousness flows and releases the Holy Spirit to move in God's grace and power on your behalf.

As we trust God, He will bring it to pass. This is what it means when God says,

"*Be still and know that I am God*" (Psalm 46:10).

Faith: "*And the life which I now live in the flesh I live by the faith of the Son of God...*"

As we live by faith in relationship with God through Jesus, we will also be full of love and compassion as Jesus was. We will hear God speak, see what He is doing with the eyes of our heart and also do, by the Holy Spirit, what Jesus does, because "*... the Just shall live by faith*" (Romans 1:17). And we too can and should live by faith, out of a close intimate relationship with Jesus through the Holy Spirit, responding to the Holy Spirit as Jesus did to His Father.

John 14:12 "*Verily, verily, I say unto you, He that believeth on me, the works that I do shall he do also; and greater works than these shall he do; because I go unto my Father.*"

"And the life which I now live in the flesh I live by the faith of the Son of God." Faith is dependence and confidence in the character and the Word of God. Faith is belief in Jesus, the one who makes us sure that the thing we hope for, but cannot see, will become evident and manifest in His time. Hebrews 11:1-6, explains it to us and further states that, it is the only means by which man can please God.

"*But without faith it is impossible to please him: for he that cometh to God must believe that he is, and that he is a rewarder of them that seek him*" (Hebrews 11:6).

It is said that faith is the currency with which we can withdraw blessings from the spiritual realm into the natural realm and into our everyday physical lives. By faith, we can exchange our sickness for God's healing, our poverty for His wealth, our bondages for His deliverance and any other blessings we may desire.

Many believers over the years have been trying to live a life of faith, void of a close relationship with God as their Father. They have seen faith as standards or principles to follow, methods and steps to follow, reading, studying and memorizing, and speaking the Word. While all these have their rightful place, relationship must precede them because it was Jesus' relationship with the Father which produced the promises we are expected to believe. We must "BE" in Christ before we "DO" The lord said this to me, "Do you know why you're called HUMAN BEING? Of course my answer was "no." He went on to say, "Because you're made to BE- IN- **G (OD)**." Be in God, and put Him first in relationship before you "Do" works.

- 1 Corinthians 1:30: be made wise, accepted, holy, and free.
- Colossians 1:9: be filled.
- Romans 12:1, 2: be transformed.
- Ephesians 1: 3: be raised up in heavenly places.
- 2 Corinthians 5: 17: be a new creation being
- 1 Corinthians 3:23: be Christ's
- Romans 8:6: be spiritually minded
- Romans 8:14: be led by the Holy Spirit
- Psalm 46:10 be still

"Doing" out of your own thinking, self- effort, and own-strength without God's input is a law mentality of self-will. Doing through God in relationship and the power and leading of the Holy Spirit is God's grace or God's will.

Matthew 26; 39, *"…O my Father, if it be possible, let this cup pass from me: nevertheless not as I will, but as thou wilt"*

Old Testament examples representing Law and grace include King Saul representing the law and David representing God's grace (1 Samuel chapters 15 and 26; another example is 2 Chronicles chapters 16 and 20).

It's very important to anchor your identity in whom the blood has made you and rest in God's Word to you. We have relationship with God the Father because of the shed blood of Jesus, and it is in this relationship, that every need you have can be met by faith in the Jesus, the living Word.

Hebrews 11: 1 says "Now *faith is the substance of things hoped for, the evidence of things not seen.*"

Notice the Word 'hope.' Hope must be placed in someone or something greater than the person hoping. Since we are made to be in God, He must be the source of your desire and your hope, because Christ is in us, and we are full and complete in Him. When your heart become aligned with God's heart, then whatsoever you ask, you can receive of Him (1 John 3:22). We can expect to see our desires manifest. It is Psalm 42:11 which says, "Hope thou in God…"

Faith is an eternal hope in an eternal source, which is God through Jesus. His Word etched in the blood, believed and acted upon, builds faith in God through Jesus His Son. Faith is the lifestyle of the Kingdom of God. As we relate to God and maintain relationship, perpetually living the gospel from the place of oneness, choosing to believe and act on His Word, faith comes alive and makes us ready to receive.

> *His Word etched in the blood, believed and acted upon, builds faith in God through Jesus His Son.*

How do you obtain faith?

Faith is a gift deposited in your human spirit when you are born again.

Ephesians 2:8 "For *by grace are ye saved through faith and that not of yourselves it is a gift of God.*"

This gift was given to us, deposited within by the Holy Spirit "according as God hath dealt to every man the measure of faith" (Romans 12:3; Galatians 5:22).

Faith is of the Spirit, as you fellowship with and listen to the Holy Spirit and the word of the Bible, this personal communication builds faith so you can please God (Hebrews 11:6). Also as you meditate on the Word or listen to ministers preach the Gospel, you will hear God's voice speak to you, and as you believe what you hear, faith rises from your spirit. When exercised, or acted on your faith grows to manifest and receive your desire.

Romans 10:17, "*So then faith cometh by hearing and hearing by the Word of God.*"

For faith to come alive there needs to be hearing, speaking, and a desire for relationship with Jesus by believing, and acting on what you believe according to the Gospel. We must have faith in the blood. Faith is living out of the relationship of Love first, for God and His grace Jesus, before we start doing.

John 13:34 "*A new commandment I give unto you, That ye love one another; as I have loved you, that ye also love one another.*"

Galatians 5:6b, "*… But faith which worketh by love.*"

Love is of the heart involving at least two people relating to each other. Faith works by love in the heart. The heart is for relationship, so as you love God in relationship with your hope in Him, faith will arise up in your heart to believe and receive from God. So, talk to Him in prayer, and let your love in relationship and fellowship with the Holy Spirit and the Word increase your faith In God. When He speaks, listen and hear Him then do as He says. The abundant life God promised will be yours.

> **Love is of the heart, faith works by love in the heart.**

Now we understand why Jesus said to the Centurion whose servant was sick in Luke 7:2 -9,

"*… I say unto you, I have not found so great faith, no, not in Israel.*"

Why? Because the Centurion had no relationship with Jesus, yet he had faith to believe. As a believer you already are in relationship, draw near to God, He says He will draw near to you. He will speak to His beloved, and out of this relationship, you will hear. One Word from God will cause faith to arise for you to believe and do as God says, in order to receive His blessings. Faith is living out of the relationship; as you receive God's love and blessings, now you are capable to give the same love and blessings to others, fulfilling God's command to love.

Relationship

Relationship in the Oxford English dictionary is defined as the state of being connected. It is how groups regard and behave towards each other. Relationship therefore is not static as with standards and principles to follow, but it is relational, it is more of an experience as one person relate to another.

Relationship is a product of:

(a) Choice: People in relationship choose each other (Ephesians 1:4).

(b) Union or connected hearts (Genesis 2:24; 1 Corinthians 6:17).

(c) Relating or communicating together (Luke 15:32).

(d) Fellowshipping or continually drawing closer (Matthew 26:18-29).

(e) Getting on with life together and reproducing oneself (Genesis 1:28; Mark 16:15, 16; 1 Peter 1:16, 22).

What is your level of relationship with the Father? Is it a distant relationship, seeing God as "My God"? Is He only Savior and Shepherd but not Lord? Or have you identified with Him as your loving Father, or even better still, as your friend? You and I as God's friend is His highest heart's desire, and this can happen when we give the Father God first place in our life and make greater relationship and fellowship with His Son our priority.

When you choose to relate, and depend on God, He will come to you and will prosper you in every area of your life: in your family, work, finances and everything you put your hands to. When you seek the Word, and find your Father's heart full of love and kindness, you will find true riches; as in God through Jesus, you'll find all you need.

Seek to grow in relationship daily until you know you are God's friend. We grow in this relationship with our precious Lord and Savior in the process of SANCTIFICATION; that is, with the Help of the Holy Spirit continually purifying us by putting on Christ unto holiness as well as separating ourselves from evil (John 15:2;1 Thessalonians 5:23; 2 Timothy Chapter 2; 1 Peter 1: 2,22; 1 John 3: 3).

> Ephesians 1:4, "According *as he hath chosen us in him before the foundations of the World, that we should be holy and without blame before him in love."*
>
> John 17:17, "*Sanctify them through thy truth, thy word is truth."*

Sanctification is learnt from God's Word, experienced with the Holy Spirit and should be pursued earnestly by every believer (Romans 12:22; 2 Timothy 2:15; Hebrews 4:12). Sanctification occurs as we read and become doers of the Word. Then, we allow the Holy Spirit, by God's grace, to help in transforming our minds (Legalism is the opposite, seeking sanctification by self-will or the flesh, self- effort or works). Sanctification God's way continues as one puts faith in the Word of God and acting on what you believe as well as by the Holy Spirit's power to cut off and change those areas of bad habits, weaknesses, addictions and failures. The more you fellowship and receive the leading of the Holy Spirt, the more you're being changed into the character-likeness of Jesus. As you grow in the Word and in fellowship, a closer relationship will develop as the Holy Spirit will help you to declutter the soul so that you hear and obey God more accurately and quickly from the heart.

Jesus loves us so much. He will not leave us in our need if we run to Him in faith. If a believer is ignorant of the truth or fails to walk in truth of the light of God's Word that they already know, then sanctification can also come through the "fire" of suffering, trials or oppression. God did not cause the suffering but will allow the trials in your life to expose weaknesses as He did my failure to trust Him fully. He is giving an opportunity to earnestly seek Him and to find Him to help you out of your weakness. A believer who has gone through the fire and overcomes will emerge refined as pure gold, stronger, a deeper relationship and of greater faith as he or she learn to trust God more (Judges 2:22,23; Romans 2:7,5:3-5; James 1:2-4; 1 Peter 1:3-9).

> *The more you fellowship and receive the leading of the Holy Spirt, the more you're being changed into the character-likeness of Jesus.*

It is the love and the grace of God that reached out to us through Jesus His Son, to rescue us from separation, religion, self-will and distanced relationship with God and to draw us, by the blood, into a loving relationship with Jesus who gives us access. Genuine Faith starts with a love relationship with God through Jesus. Relationship starts with accepting forgiveness and the gift of righteousness, which is faith in God's love. When anchored in fellowship in the Word and the Spirit, faith comes which releases God's grace to walk as new creation beings, who are blessed with all spiritual blessings, and will prosper in health as the soul prospers (3 John 2).

NEW CREATION LIVING

- Acknowledge and believe by faith that Jesus lives within your heart and you are born-again by faith in His grace (Ephesians 2:8).

- Acknowledge that you are made righteous by faith, acceptable and restored into a loving relationship with God, sealed as righteous in your human spirit by God's grace and not by any good works (2 Corinthians 5:21; Ephesians 1:13).

- Acknowledge and believe by faith that you are dead to the old self and are in union, oneness, with God through Jesus, abiding in Him. Self-will is discarded and God's will is chosen. This takes time so trust God to help you daily (John chapter 15; Romans chapter 6).

- Know your God by His true nature of love and forgiveness and as your good Father as shown to you in face and life of Jesus (John 17:3).

- Be filled with the Holy Spirit and be led by Him (Luke 24:48,49; Acts 1:8; Romans 8; 14-17).

- Know the new person God has made you to be; know who you are "in Christ" (1 Corinthians 1:30; 2 Corinthians 5:17) while remembering that only your spirit is saved. You must transform your soul (mind and imagination, will, and emotions) by the Word, the Holy Spirit and fellowship with the Father (Romans 12:1, 2).

- Grow in relationship by sanctification, renewal, and transformation. Put on the new, while dropping off old thinking, attitudes and behaviors (Romans chapter 12).

- Acknowledge by faith that Satan is defeated. "In Christ" you are now his master (Ephesians 1:19-23; Colossians 2:10; 1 John 4:4).

- Seek to walk your entire life as grace through faith or as a new creation who is being raised up and seated with Christ on His throne and is growing daily in closer relationship, authority and power (Ephesians 2: 8; Colossians 2:6 ; Galatians 2:20; Psalm 23; Hebrews 10:22-25).

- Let Christ be formed in you until He is your life (Galatians 4:19; Colossians 3:2-4; John 7:38).

Hindrances to relationship.

- Lack of Knowledge of the truth of God's Word and not becoming doers of the Word.

- Religion or legalism: Distortions to the truth of the character of the believer, God, and His Word and the power of the devil.

- Old-man remaining alive with self-will in charge instead of new man seeking God's will.

- Not knowing the character of love of the one true God.

- Not spending enough time fellowshipping with God.

- Not knowing who you are in Christ: A new creation who accepts the gift of righteousness and God's love and walk by faith.

- Not living from the throne, seated with Christ, in authority and overcoming.

- Not knowing the role of the Holy Spirit to guide you into greater relationship and use of His gifts.

- Lack of knowledge of the truth that Satan is defeated, and failure to resist him, allowing him to ride roughshod over you.

- Any others the Lord may bring personally to you…

Jesus had no hindrances in His relationship with His Father. At every instance, He acted out of faith and therefore brought blessings to those He ministered to. In Matthew 14: 15-21, we saw Jesus feeding the multitude with two fishes and five loaves. Being confident in His relationship, He looked up to heaven, blessed the food and gave it to His disciples. As they distributed the food, it multiplied to feed the whole multitude. Jesus also calmed the roaring waves and raised His friend Lazarus from the dead.

Jesus' miraculous life demonstrates relationship: the place of union, authority and dominion, trust and confidence that God wants all believers to personally recognize and achieve, so that, like Jesus, we can have the confidence,

"... That, if we ask anything according to his will, he heareth us: And if we know that he hears us, whatsoever we ask, we know that we have the petitions that we desired of him" (1 John 5:14-15).

Every one of the persons mentioned in what is referred to as the "Hall of Faith" in Hebrews Chapter 11 had enough belief and or relationship to act in faith, which pleased God. We too in this present day church age can develop relationship with God through Jesus Christ and, by faith, we can fulfill our God-given purpose and destiny.

Maintaining your relationship.

Matthew 11:28, 30 *"Come unto me, all ye that labor and are heavy laden, and I will give you rest. Take my yoke upon you, and learn of me; for I am meek and lowly in heart: and ye shall find rest unto your souls. For my yoke is easy, and my burden light."*

- Have personal devotions by reading, meditating and speaking the Word. Jesus was the living Word (John 1:1-4).

- Fellowship with God in prayer, worship and time spent in His presence. His yoke is His love, it is easy to love Him and His burden for you to believe Him is light.

- Confess often your righteousness is by faith in the blood to create union relationship and peace with God (Romans 5:1).

- Thank God often for His grace in His righteousness giving you boldness and full asurance to enter His presence knowing He loves and welcomes you (Hebrews 10:19-23).

- Be continually filled with the power of the Holy Spirit; depend on Him and pray often in tongues to be edified, or charged up.

- Abide: "*If ye abide in me, and my words abide in you, ye shall ask what ye will, and it shall be done onto you*" (John 15:7). Speak the words of God and His fullness and power into your spirit. For example, Colossians 2:9, 10.

- Do not forget to assemble yourselves together for worship and praise. In relationship with each other in love and unity, God can in corporate worship manifest in greater dimensions (Hebrews 10:25).

- Remember to acknowledge the presence of God minutely, hourly, daily in everything in your life (1 Thessalonians 5:17).

- Remember God's blessings of yesterday; remember His faithfulness, and praise Him for it. You do this to build your faith for the next challenge you will face (Psalm 77:11, 12).

- Keep your eyes upon Jesus. Let your every thought, word, attitude and action be directed by the Word of God and His Spirit.

- Any other the Holy Spirit may give to you personally.

RESULTS:

The results of allowing your faith to live out of your relationship with God through the Holy Spirit.

- You will walk in whom God has made you as new creation beings (Romans 6:4). Right relationship starts with God. He is to be first in your heart.

- Righteousness, rightness with God in a love relationship, brings peace (Isaiah 32:17, 18).

- The wicked one toucheth you not. He will attack and bring trouble, but he cannot destroy you (1 John 5:18b). God's love has freed you from the enemy's fear (1 John 4:18).

Without fear, the devil cannot touch you. Because the love of God is shed abroad in your heart, love is greater than the fear of the enemy.

- Christ is your life. Colossians 1:22, 3:4a: You become holy, faultless, and innocent so that you can be dependent, assured, anchored, unmovable, trusting, full of peace and rest in your God. He is your strength, your wisdom, your every-thing, and you're satisfied with Jesus because He is the author and finisher of your faith. See Him on the mountain in the good times and in the valley of hardships, see Him in the light and see Him in the darkness. He is your all in all.

- You truly believe you're one with the greater one inside, and He is truly greater than all the bad circumstances that the devil on the outside can throw at you. You stand in faith, knowing that you are indestructible in your spirit, whether in sickness, lack, pain, bondage or in the face of death. God's grace brings true freedom here on Earth or on the other side in heaven (Revelation 12:11b).

- CHRIST IS YOUR LIFE. He is immortal and eternal and faithful, we can rest in Him and be at peace, because as He is, so are we in this world (1 John 4:17). When Christ is your life, you will be, hear, rest, have faith and "do as God says and live to fulfill your destiny in Christ.

- You live in and flow with the Holy Spirit. You do this in your own life, and as God wills in ministry. Your faith is no longer one of struggle, but of assurance in God's grace believing and receiving.

- Attacks will come but you will overcome by your faith in relationship as the Holy Spirit helps us to overcome (Joshua 6; Job 7:21; Psalm 104:29).

- You possess the resurrection power and life of God to live and do what He has called you to do. This is so that, like Hosea called to marry a prostitute, when instructions to you seem contrary to your belief of the Word, you can trust your relationship with God and yield to Him (Hosea chapter 1). Like Gideon, when self seems insufficient, we can stay in the process of our relationship with God and ask and trust Him to bring us through victoriously.

Father, I receive your grace through the blood of Jesus and His finished work on the cross. I have relationship with God my Father. I stare in the mirror of His Word and in the face of His Spirit, the Holy Spirit, and I see myself for who Christ says I am. I am accepted, worthy, approved, justified, righteous, loved, and I stand boldly in His grace a new creation being, under His New Covenant of grace, in union with God, redeemed, delivered and free, looking unto Jesus the author and finisher of my faith.

In relationship with you my Father, I take hold of the Comforter and Helper, which is the Holy Spirit whom you gave to me, to walk and navigate this life. I will walk the same way I received Jesus, grace through faith, trusting in all He has already done for me at the cross.

As a child of God, I am filled with the fullness of God; the same resurrection power that arose Christ from the dead also rose me up and seated me in Christ in heavenly places, as an anointed, believer standing in faith. I will prosper and be in good health, walk in love with others, and do the work that Christ has called me to do in whatever form that may take. I have Jesus, and I have all I need. He is my all in all. I'm satisfied with Him, He is enough, and I trust in Him.

With Him I am victorious, because in Him all things are possible.

In relationship as I gaze in my Fathers wonderful face:

All flaws, shortcomings, and insufficiencies are absorbed in the perfection of His love.

All weaknesses are absorbed in His strength.

All failures in His possibilities.

All darkness of the past in the light of His presence

All evil in His goodness.

All death in His resurrection power and life.

Christ in me is the hope of Glory, for I am dead and my life is hidden in Christ. As I live by faith out of my relationship with God, CHRIST IS MY LIFE.

ONLY BELIEVE

"…Be not afraid, only believe" (Mark 5:36b).

To believe means to, "remain steadfast," to be persuaded of God's revealed truth. To adhere to, or to rely on God's promises. The story is told in Mark 5:22-43, where a ruler of the synagogue named Jairus fell at Jesus' feet and pleaded with Him greatly to come and lay hands on his sick daughter that she may be healed and live. Jesus was on His way to perform this request when news came from the ruler of the Synagogue's house saying, *"Thy daughter is dead, why troublest the master any further?"* As soon as Jesus heard the negative word that was spoken, He said unto the ruler of the synagogue, *"Be not afraid, only believe"* (Mark 5:35, 36). Jesus quickly summoned Jairus to continue believing God, because He needed Jairus' faith to be working in order to cooperate with the anointing needed to release his daughter from the bondage of death.

As Jesus continued on His journey, He allowed only three of His disciples to go with Him. They were the ones most likely to remain in faith with Him to cause the miracle of this child to be raised from the dead.

Jesus did not want the unbelief of the others as well as of the mourners He met at the house to hinder His faith. Jesus commanded the young girl to arise and to the amazement and astonishment of all onlookers, she rose from the dead. This ruler of the synagogue heeded Jesus' instruction, to ONLY BELIEVE, and his daughter was delivered from death. We have the same instruction, to put our faith in Jesus and to only believe.

Mark 11:23, 24, "For *verily I say unto you, That whosoever shall say unto this mountain, Be thou removed, and be thou cast into the sea; and shall not doubt in his heart, but shall believe that those things which he saith shall come to pass; he shall have whatsoever he saith: Therefore I say unto you, What things so-ever ye desire, when ye pray, believe that ye receive them, and ye shall have them."*

Any believer can have what they say when they believe in their heart the Word of faith spoken from their mouth and acted on. To believe is to acknowledge and accept God's Word as true, then choose to act on the Word by faith by putting action to what you believe, do something you couldn't do before or something you find difficult to do for example rejoicing. Your healing or deliverance is embodied in everything the blood of Jesus has accomplished for you. Believe and rely on Jesus to use the power of His Spirit to bring about the desired change so you can receive His blessing. God, your Father, through Jesus and His shed blood, is to be the source of your believing.

> *To believe is to acknowledge and accept God's Word as true, then choose to act on the Word by faith.*

"These things have I written unto you that believe on the name of the Son of God; that ye may know that you have eternal life, and that ye may believe on the name of the Son of God" (1 John 5:13).

Believe On The Name Of The Son Of God

- Believe the love of the Father for you through His Son Jesus Christ. Believe you are in union relationship in the heart.
- Put your faith in the finished work of the cross. All the promises that Jesus accomplished for you were on the cross. He is the fulfilment of all promises made by God to you. As you put faith in God your Father, and keep your eyes

on Jesus, you can believe and receive. (Romans 10:9; 10; 2 Peter 1:4).

- God's Word is His "will" for you, put faith in His Word based on Jesus' blood shed on the cross, and claim your desired blessing, cast aside religion and self-will (Matthew 26:39).

- God has put a new heart in you, full of His Spirit, which enables you to believe, reach into the supernatural realm and claim your inheritance by faith (Jeremiah 31:33, Romans 12:3).

- When you call upon the name of Jesus, you are calling on God's power through the living Word, which is dwelling within you. Jesus will be Lord and Father of your life as the written Word dominates your being (Matthew 7:21).

- The Holy Spirit will be released for miracles to the level of your relationship with the Word you believe and speak. It is the truth you believe, speak and act on in faith that will set you free (John 8:32).

Start believing. The purest and best way to believe is when you hear the Word of God; you draw on the blood, the finished work of the cross, and what was accomplished for you to anchor your faith. Immediately, believe in your heart that because of the shed blood of Jesus, the promise given is true. Let your spirit be at rest and be in full confidence and assurance towards God that He will bring it to pass in your life. No matter what the circumstances look like, or how you feel, hold God's Word as the truth. For example, in some cases like tithing or healing, even a non-believer can believe the promise and receive from God because God says He causes the rain to fall on the just and the unjust. They should, however, upon being blessed, let His goodness lead them to repentance. How much more should a believer believe God and receive His promises (Matthew 5:45; Romans 2:4)?

THE BLOCK THE BLOOD

Romans 15:13, *"Now the God of hope fill you with all joy and peace in believing, that ye may abound in hope, through the power of the Holy Ghost."*

Mark 11:24, *"Therefore I say unto you, what things so-ever ye desire, when you pray, believe that ye receive them, and you shall have them."*

For you to have pure faith in your heart and believe, you must know your God. You must know His character of grace, full of love, compassion, goodness, and mercy towards you.

According to Mark 11: 22-24 you must be fully assured in your heart that God's Word about your situation is true, and believe you receive the promise in your heart before you pray.

In the midst of your trouble, to be fully assured of your blessing, you must know that the devil, who is trying to rob you, is defeated. He has no power to keep you in bondage because the blood of Jesus has set you free from all things evil. Resist him! The prison door is open. Jesus opened it, so believe and walk away healed and free.

As you stand in faith believing God, you must exercise self-control over the negative thoughts of your mind, your emotions, feelings, and your will. Know who you are "in Christ" and stand as the redeemed. Your challenge is to look past all the negatives you may hear, see, or feel towards your situation, and remain steadfast, believing in God. Resist falling back to focus on what the devil is doing. Instead speak how loving and good your God is, speak of yourself as the overcomer He has made you "in Christ." Stand in your relationship with God as Father, and against the devil, remind him that he is defeated. Continue resisting the devil and his evil report by resting on the finished work of the cross and the promises your Father God gave you in the Word concerning your situation. Believe God's Word is true.

Start your rejoicing giving worship, praise, and thanksgiving to God, as by faith, you have already received your desired blessing. Paul and Silas did just that when they were imprisoned. They sang and praised God in prison as if they were already free. God responded to their faith and sent an angel to set them physically free (Acts 16:16-31).

The Holy Spirit May Lead You to Put Action to Your Faith:

Start your rejoicing giving worship, praise, and thanksgiving to God, as by faith, you have already received your desired blessing.

- Trials and oppression of the enemy, to rejoice (Philippians 4:4).

- Lack of finances, to give (Luke 6:38).

- In difficult relationships, walk in grace of God's love, and forgiveness (Jeremiah 17:7, 8; Romans 5:17; 14:4).

- Sickness: Get up and walk (John 5:8).

- For any need you have, listen to God for His particular leading to you. Yield and obey Him (Romans 8:14).

Develop Your Faith:

The best way to start developing consistent faith believing is to be born- again. Enter into a personal relationship with God through Jesus Christ His Son and His work on the cross. Acknowledge the relationship with Him as your Father and you as His child. Seek to pursue fellowship daily to increase and strengthen your relationship and faith in the written and spoken Word of the Holy Spirit.

Romans 10:17, "So *then faith cometh by hearing, and hearing by the word of God.*"

In your relationship with God your Father, let your faith in believing arise out of your communion and fellowship with God. As you hear the Word, know the Holy Spirit is at work opening your heart to believe and receive. Further solidify your relationship by not only reading the Word, but meditating on the Word, speaking the Word to your heart until the Holy Spirit quickens you to really believe them to be true.

Confess the Word until the Word is quickened, becomes alive and the reality of the cross imprints God's blessings in your heart that you believe and receive. Begin to rejoice even though you have not seen your manifestation as yet.

"If ye abide in me, and my words abide in you, ye shall ask what ye will, and it shall be done unto you." (John 15:7).

Refrain from being double minded by making negative confessions and saying the opposite of what you believe. It will negate your faith (James 3:11).

Speak the Word of promise connected to the Blood, pray, rejoice, until illumination and revelation comes. That is the point when you know that you know you've gotten your desire.

"Therefore it is of faith that it might be by grace; to the end the promise might be sure to all the seed…" (Romans 4:16).

Receive your desired promise by an act of faith, "I know that I already have it because I'm in relationship with Jesus who came down, procured it by His blood and gave it to me." Believing is always supernatural and of the Spirit. You must first receive it on the inside, in your spirit, before it will manifest on the outside, in your life.

Now that you believe, pray and command that mountain or sickness to move out in Jesus' name. Receive your desire in the spirit as a done deal because of your relationship with Jesus. He purchased it for you, start praising God, and rejoice until your blessing manifests. I am convinced that many believers pray too soon before they fully believe in their heart, and as a result, they do not receive. Pray when you believe (Mark 11:24) Amen. When you become discouraged, remember and pinpoint the day and time when your heart became fully persuaded you receive the revelation of your desire in your spirit. "I GOT IT." Remind yourself and be encouraged that despite the present negative situation, the blessing that I received in the spiritual realm on this date_____ is on the way to me in the natural. I will rejoice for it shall come to pass.

Hannah, a childless woman in 1 Samuel chapter one, is a very good example of believing God. Hannah prayed for a child, her desired blessing. The Prophet gave her a Word,

"...*Go in peace; and the God of Israel grant thee thy petition that thou hast asked of him*" (1 Samuel 1:17).

Start praising God, and rejoice until your blessing manifests.

Hannah believed and replied, "*Let thine handmaid find grace in thy sight...* So the woman went her way, and did eat, and her countenance was no more sad.*" Sometime later, she became intimate with her husband, and the Lord remembered her and she conceived.

Some hindrances to your believing:

- Not having a close relationship with God as your Father through fellowshipping with the Holy Spirit. Hannah did.

- Not enough time reading and meditating in the Word and in prayer concerning your need. Hannah spent much time in prayer.

- Expressing doubt, murmuring, complaining, and fear by wondering how and when?

- Wrong teaching. For example, that healing has passed away.

- Spiritual warfare fighting the devil, constantly binding and loosing this is in fear, making the situation worse. Instead, fight the good fight of faith, casting down imaginations, believe God and rest in what Jesus did on the cross. God gave you power and authority, so use it! (2 Corinthians 10:4, 5).

- Failure to Speak the Word (Matthew 12:34-37; 2 Corinthians 4:13).

- Passivity, expecting someone else to do it for you, such as your Pastor or prayer partner or even Jesus Himself to come down and do it for you. Act on your faith (Romans 10:6-8).

- Focusing on the circumstances, feelings, or the devil instead of keeping your eyes on Jesus and His Word, God's truth (2 Corinthians 5:7).

- Failure to exercise patience (James 1:4).

- Failure to confront the devil in faith that he is defeated; resist him, and take back what God says is yours through the blood of Jesus. Speak it into being that he is defeated and Christ is exalted in your situation. As Jesus is free so are you, free. Now REMAIN healed, delivered, provided for (1 John 4:17b).

- Failure to stand in and believe the love of God and walk in love with others. Perfect love cast out all fear (Romans 5:5, 1 John 4:18).

- Failure to trust God.

- Failure to receive. In Acts chapter 10, Peter had difficulty receiving from God.

Some signs you really believe

- You believe that you receive right then when you pray. You must believe the moment you pray no matter how you feel. Take time to assure your heart before you pray (Mark 11:24; John 15:7, 8).

- You are fully convinced because of His love that God your Father can and will do what He says. "Abraham" staggered not at the promise of God through unbelief but was strong in faith, giving glory to God (Romans 4:17-21).

- You are resting in His grace, faith in the blood and the finished work of the cross. Keeping your eyes on Jesus, as you fellowship with Him in Word, worship and prayer. Believe you receive when you pray and not being in a restless or in a panic mode by watching the promise or the time frame. When in relationship, keep your eyes on Jesus, rest and trust your Father completely. The reasons, the time, or the details do not matter. Transfer all trust from yourself to

God's ability through the Holy Spirit and the finished work of the cross.

- Remain consistent in faith believing.

"That ye be not slothful, but followers of them who through faith and patience, inherit the promises"(Hebrews 6:12).

Faith is the lifestyle of a believer. Never yield to the temptation to complain, be in a hurry, get upset, be in strife, or wanting to give up or to blame God. Enforce Satan's defeat. What the devil has to say or do has no significance to you.

- You know you believe when you hold fast to your confession, speaking the Word that you believe, day in and day out, listening to the Holy Spirit for any instructions, and becoming a doer, acting on the word rejoicing until your manifestation comes.

- You are resting with joy and peace, believing in the power of the anointing in the Blood of Jesus and continuing to rejoice. Christ will come to you as He remembered Hannah and fulfill your heart's desire because every situation, every circumstance you will ever face is subject to Him (Mark 4:4-10).

NOW RECEIVE

Receive: Definition in the Oxford Dictionary, "To be given, presented with…" This gives the picture of someone accepting, taking possession of what is given.

As a young believer, in the natural, I was a very self-motivated, independent, and high-achieving person. I was willing to work hard for all I needed, and I did not like to beg or feel obligated. This was the perfect scenario of self-will for the enemy to push me into a legalistic, self- sufficient, law mentality of works and trying hard. The result was difficulty in resting and receiving from God.

Although aspects of this personality are God-given, they must be given over to God for Him to control, correct and direct. Only then can they be used as representative of Christ.

God, by His grace, plunged that old me into complete darkness and gave me the topics in this book as well as others. As I studied out the topics, He gave me light, and more light came as I progressed along. Deliverance from self-will and into His grace with ever growing dependence on Gods will was the result.

Exodus 23: 29,30, *"I will not drive them out from before thee in one year.....By little and little I will drive them out from before thee, until thou be increased, and inherit the land."*

For all God has done by His grace, through Jesus, we must humble ourselves, not only to believe, but to receive.

To help me understand this, the topic that God gave me was Psalm 23:5,

"Thou preparest a table before me in the presence of mine enemies...."

I was binding and loosing the enemy as well as fasting for him to leave me alone. God however, was more interested in developing my faith, especially against the enemy and his evil forces.

Jesus is God's table that was prepared for us, prophesied in the worldly tabernacle in Exodus chapter 25. He was represented in the tabernacles of the Holy of Holies in Numbers chapter 4 and manifested as the perfect tabernacle in Hebrews chapter 9 and John Chapter 6 as the bread of life. Jesus is the Bread of life,

"For the bread of God is he which cometh down from heaven, and giveth life unto the world" (John 6:33).

God has spread the table with good things, wonderfully good things. Many have been mentioned up to now: power in the blood of Jesus, power in the name of Jesus, forgiveness, righteousness, grace, union, authority over darkness, all spiritual blessings, healing, deliverance and eternal life.

Adam had been given a table spread in the presence of the enemy Satan, and he yielded to the enemy and sinned, eventually forfeiting his blessings on the table. He lost God's plan to rule, reign, dominate and propagate God's goodness and blessings here on Earth.

Jesus, the last Adam, came and succeeded and has given us the same opportunity (1 Corinthians 15: 45, 46). If you are like I was, your first response in the face of an attack may be spiritual warfare by quoting scriptures, binding and loosing, fasting, seeking to get the devil to leave you alone so you could be in peace. Needless to say Satan didn't leave me alone because as long as there is any aspect of your belief system, your character, your personality or behavior, that Satan has a hold on, he has a legal right to stay. God's Word, believed as truth and acted on in your life, is righteousness and removes Satan's right to stay.

Jesus spread that table for us with His blood,

"Whoso eateth my flesh, and drinketh my blood, hath eternal life; and I will raise him up at the last day" (John 6:54).

1 Peter 3:18, *"For Christ also hath once suffered for sins, the just for the unjust, that he might bring us to God…"*

1 Corinthians 10:17, *"For we being many are one bread, and one body: for we are all partakers of one bread."*

Jesus now sits at the head of the table in the company of the Holy Spirit and tells us to partake in the presence of the enemy. Our Father is with us and the devil is defeated and cannot stop us from receiving, despite what the situation is currently showing you.

Here's the take away:

- You must know your Father God. Know Him personally as your Emanuel, God with you, and your great I am. He is full of love and grace and is your almighty; He is full of power and is your all sufficient one. He is your heavenly Father, supplier of your needs, your Shepherd, the greater one in you, and your provider. He will never leave you nor forsake you. When you get closer in relationship with your Father, you are in a better position to know and trust Him, so you can receive from Him.

- Know who God made you "in Christ", a qualified partaker, because of your union one spirit with the Father. Stand in your position of righteousness, all that the Word says you are, and have in Christ.

- Whatever blessing that you are seeking to receive must be anchored in and received from the blood. Jesus did it all, it's already done at the cross. Believe that His blood, through the stripes of Jesus, provided your healing and everything you will ever need. It is more than just confessing scriptures; you must believe what the blood did for you.

  Speak the Word of His promise to yourself. Simultaneously be raised with Him in His resurrection power, seated in Christ on the throne, and reigning over Satan and whatever he's bringing against you. Having believed, rest in what Jesus has done for you, holding up by faith the end of your desire in your heart, receive and walk out from sickness as the healed (1 Peter 2:24). Thank God for the sacrifice of His Son, thank Him for the blood, thank Him for His power, and His anointing in His blood to bring healing.

- Now, sit down at the table, the very throne of God, and eat. Rejoicing He is your Provider. Jesus Himself sat when He was finished. Sit, it is time to rest from works and binding the devil; rest from confessing scriptures in order to believe. Instead, confess scriptures as praise and thanksgiving, because you believe. Rest from trying not to offend anyone, so your love walk will keep your faith going. Faith is about knowing and loving your Father in relationship that He is good and that He took your sickness, so you don't have to carry it. His great love for you frees you from fear to partake of His flesh and His blood for your own healing or deliverance as well as to walk in love with others. Your life flows from the life in His blood, in relationship, not your self-will and self- effort and what you do.

Father, I rest in the power of Jesus' blood and I believe by His stripes I am healed, delivered, provided for and claim it. It's mine and I have it. Healing is mine because Christ purchased it with His blood and gave it to me. I am the healed of the Lord; I receive my deliverance through the blood of Jesus from all oppression, in Jesus' name, Amen. (Hebrews chapter 4:1-12).

• Refuse to be moved.

Psalm 16:8, *"I have set the Lord always before me: because he is at my right hand, I shall not be moved."*

My Father had to really help me to sit down, rest and receive. He said this to me *"Sit down on the inside."* He meant for me to rest in what Jesus has already done in my spirit/ heart. He's the greater one on the inside. and where the Spirit of the Lord is there is liberty. Pull up your chair and sit with Jesus, He is good; be one in union with Him, eat His flesh and drink His blood. Everything His body was broken on the cross for is yours to take by faith. He did it for you. It is the gospel, so believe and let healing flow from your spirit into your body. Receive and be made whole in the name of Jesus (John 6:53-58; 1 Corinthians 11:24, 25).

• *Father, I honor the blood of Jesus and I sit and rest in the chastisement He took for me, and in exchange, I receive my healing, deliverance, or provision and peace. Whom the Son has healed is healed indeed. I am free from this sickness in Jesus' name.*

• Never let the devil lead you into fasting just for fasting sake to get God to move on your behalf or to get rid of him the devil. He can use fasting to keep you locked into works, instead of believing God. If you read, meditate God's Word, believe that you have received, what reason is there to fast at this point? (Samuel 1:17,18) The real reason to fast is to remove unbelief or clutter from your soul so you can hear from your spirit what God has to say to you about your situation. Do you remember, when the Jews asked Jesus why His disciples didn't fast, He replied why should they fast when He was with them (Matthew 9:14, 15). When you believe the word, because of the cross, Jesus is formed in your heart; having believed and waiting to receive. He is now with you, so there is no need instead, rise up and receive your desire by faith not by works (2 Chronicles chapter 20).

- Now call those things which are not as though they are (Romans 4:17): Fractured bones (John 19:36; Ezekiel 37:3-5; Psalm 34:20) Bleeding to cease (Ezekiel 16:6, 8, 9), provision to come Philippians 4:19; Hebrews 1:14).

- To receive deliverance from the voice of the devil, the accuser, speaking in your head or those he uses to bear bad reports or speak against you. Speak, My Jesus *"He was oppressed, and he was afflicted, yet he opened not his mouth: he is brought as a lamb to the slaughter, and as a sheep before her shearers is dumb, so he openeth not his mouth"* (Isaiah 53:7)

Father, In Jesus' silence, He bore the pain and death in the voice and words of the accuser, and he opened not his mouth, so father I rest in Jesus' silence and command every negative voice speaking against to me to cease and every words spoken to or against me to fall powerless to the feet of Jesus. Now quote Romans 8:1,2; 2 Timothy 1:7. I receive freedom from the accuser in Jesus' Name.

- Jesus loves me, Jesus loves me, His love is shed abroad in my heart and I receive His love. Through His love for me in His shed blood, I receive healing, deliverance etc. I know He loves me and His perfect love cast out all fear and I am free from fear. I am healed, I am delivered, I am free in Jesus' name.

- With any hindrances along the way, ask your Father for clarification and help in understanding your specific situation. He will gladly give it to you.

- You will have to dig deep to rest in the midst of turmoil and all you may be feeling and rejoice in order to receive (Hebrews 4:11). The devil is going to fight you to keep going, binding, rebuking, confessing without faith, because the feelings of torment of the evil one is to get you doubt that you really received. He will come at you with his barrage of pain, symptoms, feelings of torment, confusion, hopelessness, just as a loaded train pulling into a station, except this is your soul. Stand your ground in who you know your God is and who you are "In Christ," and rest rejoicing in the blood and its promises; remind the devil of the Word that you believe concerning your situation. Rest and resist the temptation to get into fear and board Satan's loaded train of dread and fear and prolonging your situation. Sit and partake at the table in the presence of the enemy, hold the mindset you are healed, delivered, and free because of the blood and because the word says so (Psalm 107:2). Now you're walking in grace through faith, face Satan square in the face and REMAIN. Speak the Word you believe concerning your situation. Tell him you are free because of the blood despite how you feel and remain free. He will flee, rolling on by and away with his fear, sickness, torment, lack, depression and cannot unload on you. Let the anointing in the blood take away now what Jesus carried away for you 2,000 years ago. Whatever ails you, Jesus already made you whole. Only believe.

Habakkuk 3:17-19 "Although *the fig tree shall not blossom, neither shall fruit be in the vines; the labor of the olive shall fail, the fields shall yield no meat; the flock shall be cut off from the fold, and there shall be no herd in the stalls, Yet will I rejoice in the Lord, I will joy in the God of my salvation…*"

Partake of your blessing in the presence of your enemy and overcome by the blood.

BELIEVE, REST AND RECEIVE IN JESUS' NAME.

Confessions:

- The love of God is shed abroad in my heart. He loves me, and I receive His love. God's love in my heart drives out all fear. His love for me caused Him to take the punishment of stripes on His back for me. He took sickness from me, and I refuse to be sick now. I rest in the stripes of His blood and claim my healing. It is mine. I receive it in Jesus' name. I am healed and I remain healed (Do the same for deliverance, lack or any other need).

- I John 4:4, *"Greater is He that is in me than He that is in the world."* God, who is love, lives in my heart, with His anointing power in me, He is greater than fear. The anointing within me is greater than the oppression of the enemy without. I rest in the love of God and His anointing and thank you Father. The anointing raises a standard against all oppression and drives it out in Jesus' name. I claim healing, freedom, and wholeness. I receive freedom and peace now in Jesus' Name. Amen.

- I draw a blood line around my mind, my thoughts, my emotions and my will, my family, my possessions and my destiny. I claim and receive divine protection in Jesus' name. AMEN.

CHAPTER 16

THE WAY:
THE PATH TO LIFE

John 14:6 *"Jesus saith unto him, I am the way, the truth, and the life: no man cometh unto the Father, but by me."*

Psalm 16:11, *"Thou wilt shew me the path of life: in thy presence is fullness of joy: at thy right hand there are pleasures for evermore."*

Salvation, procured through the blood of Jesus on the cross is not a 'once and for all' cure to your problems for the rest of your life. It is a mistake to believe that once you receive Jesus you will never have any more trouble and all should be bliss. Salvation is your cleansing by the forgiveness of sins, which is the door that leads to your justification, the Lordship of Jesus and all of His great blessings: love, healing, deliverance, protection, provision, peace, joy, and faith. Jesus said,

"I am the door: by me if any men enter in, he shall be saved, and shall go in and out, and find pasture" (John 10:9).

Salvation does not absolve you from temptations, trouble, or from the attacks of the enemy. The blood of Jesus grants you access into relationship with God and you have the assurance of your Father God who is in and with you at all times. We have been given everything that pertains to life and godliness, because God is interested in relationship with you. Within Adam, Eve existed (Genesis 1: 27) and within every baby everything is given to him/

her to make that baby an adult, including hair for the arm pits, tissue for breasts and muscles, even a second set of teeth. Within every young fruit bearing tree, the fruit already exists.

Likewise in Christ, we have everything needed for our entire life which has been given to us at salvation in Jesus Christ. It will take your entire lifetime to learn all you can about your God and all He accomplished for you and even that time will not be enough because He has more. He is an infinite God. You can daily learn of Him, apply and grow in all what He has done for you to obtain your inheritance. He has made inheritance blessings available through Christ, so that you can mature in your spiritual life as you do naturally in the physical. Often times you will learn through the Word, the Spirit, and learn as you go through natural circumstances, or in trials and difficulties. Whatever form learning takes to grow, if you stay with God you will grow and experience a greater depth of His Grace, His love, goodness, and His mercy (John 17:17; James 1:2-4, 1 Peter 1:6,7).

The Gospel from the birth of Christ through the Cross to His ascension is the truth about Jesus. Faith in the Gospel is the solution to every problem a person will ever have in this life here on Earth. Have faith in His blood and believe Jesus died and shed His blood to save you from sin and all its emerging problems. You, however, have the responsibility to believe and receive all that Jesus gave to you and continue the process of sanctification or spiritual maturity... *Go in and out and find pasture* (John 10:9).

Believe Jesus died and shed His blood to save you from sin and all its emerging problems.

If you believe on Jesus, accept and acknowledge by faith that you are saved, a new creation, being "in Christ," and made righteous and reconciled into relationship with your Father who loves you very much. You should receive His love for you, which has been shed abroad in your heart. As His child when you are wrapped up in Jesus' love and following

His commandments, you will have no need to fear (Romans 5:5; 1 John 4:18)

> John: 13:34; *"A new commandment I give unto you, That ye love one another: as I have loved you, that ye also love one another."*

You have a God who has given you a covenant of love. He is a covenant keeping God. Trust that His covenant of love will always point you to His grace. As you fellowship over time, your level and quality of relationship with Him will become more intimate. Let your love for God keep you continuously turned towards Him in faith, even though receiving your inheritance from God will not always be quick and neither will it be always easy. Why, you may ask? Sometimes God withhold or delay giving you your desire because it may not be aligned with His plan for your life. You may not be mature enough to handle the blessing or He's growing your faith more as you seek Him. Withholding can also be God's way of proving Himself as Father to you. When you lack, He can show up as your provider, or when sick, as your healer. It can also be His way of protecting you from the enemy, Satan, in your weakness. When God sees weakness in us, by withholding, Satan is not given power to cause you to fail in your destiny (Acts 16:6, 7) Have faith in God and trust your relationship with Him. Satan will fight you every step of the way to prevent you from succeeding, but God is greater and is with you in every step (Exodus 23:29-30; John 10:10; Hebrews 13:5; 1 John 4:4).

> *Trust that His covenant of love will always point you to His grace.*

Once saved, do not believe that Satan and all his temptations and evil against you will end or that he will never trouble you again. We are free from Satan's power over us because we have this greater power of God, the anointing living within us.

> *"… greater is he that is in you than he that is the world"* (1 John 4:4).

Temptations will come,

James 1: 2, *"...when ye fall into divers temptations..."*

This is a matter of "when" not "if." The God of our salvation, by the power of the Holy Spirit, gives us His life, His power, and His authority to command Satan and to enforce his defeat in every area of our lives. We are not given a pass or an exemption from Satan's attacks; we are given power over him! Stay in union relationship and stand in faith as the redeemed and let your Father fight for you.

By faith in God's grace, work out your salvation with fear and trembling, submit to God, trust the Holy Spirit, resist the devil, and he will flee (Philippians 2:9-11; James 4:7). Satan will try every trick in his book to defeat you in every area of your life. He will try temptations, fear, doubt, lies, accusations, sickness, accidents, discouragement, religion, guilt, condemnation, demonic harassment, persecution, torment, oppression and more. A believers' job is to know, by the Word of God, that he is a defeated foe and to live as if he is.

Diligently guard your mind. Don't give Satan space in it. You overcome Satan when, through the blood, you **Recognize:** him and his attacks, **Reject:** him with the commands in the Word you believe, stand victorious and **Replace:** Satan's suggestion, lies and ideas with God's Word and His truth and **Remain:** rest rejoice and receive (Romans 5:17b; 1 Corinthians 15:57; 2 Corinthians 10:4, 5; Philippians 4:8; 1 Peter 5:8; Revelation12:11). Find the relevant scriptures that match these categories in your need and speak them as true from your heart.

A person can only receive salvation after they have heard the gospel (Romans 10: 15, 17). Having believed, the believer places their faith in God's grace (what was done on the Cross), and is saved and restored into relationship with God. He becomes the Father and you the child of God.

Ephesians 2:8, *"For by grace are ye saved through faith: and that not of yourselves: it is a gift of God."*

This means you did nothing for yourself to be saved. Jesus did it all. You only believed and did what the Bible says in Romans 10: 9, 10. You are saved grace through your believing by faith. Likewise for the rest of your Christian life, you are to follow the same pattern. For example, do not think that if you go to church only on a particular day that will get you to Heaven. No, you need to believe only on Jesus. Or do not think that you can solve all your own life problems yourself neglecting your Father. If your boss is discriminating against you, for a promotion that you can retaliate by cussing him out. No, grace says you look to God, cast your cares about the situation (1 Peter 5:7), and pray for God to solve or lead you into the solution. Your response is to then do only as God says. While you wait on your answer, pray for your boss, show love and bless the person, or obey the word and walk away from cussing him because a soft answer turns away wrath.

Colossians 2:6 says *"As ye have therefore received Christ Jesus the lord, so walk ye in him."*

The above scripture means that you should be continuously walking your Christian life grace through faith, in dependence on God through the help of the Holy Spirit, just the way you were saved grace through faith. The Holy Spirit is to be your closest friend. Cultivate His friendship. It was George Williams who said, "The whole Christian life, from beginning to end, day by day and moment by moment is simply learning what it means to live grace through faith in Christ alone." It is all about letting your faith arise out of your relationship with God your Father through His Word and the Holy Spirit as you depend on Him. It's all about your complete dependence on your Father through Jesus and His presence in the Holy Spirit, honoring Him daily with genuine and intimate times of fellowship, so that He can lead you to do as God your Father says. This is living the true gospel, trusting God always.

Failure of the believer to walk grace through faith, as Galatians 2:20 tells us, will frustrate God's grace, His power and ability working for you, and will cause you to fall back to living under the law of self-will or self- effort. Living with this law mentality of relying on one's own resources, efforts, abilities, own performance, is a recipe for frustration, and failure. Under these circumstances, operating under the law when there is success, one is often elated, resulting in self-congratulation, self-exaltation, and pride. The Bible says whatever is not of faith is sin, and a law mentality lacks faith. The lack of faith and sin exposes one to the tactics of the devil with pride in success or despair in failure. When the crash comes, the devil will bring fear, accusations of worthlessness, hopelessness, insecurity, discouragement, anxiety, condemnation, and depression.

"Pride goeth before destruction and an haughty spirit before a fall" (Proverbs 16:18).

This will happen because you were relying on your own strength and it failed, as it always will. As humans, you will not do everything perfectly correct at all times. With failure, the devil will accuse you of not being perfect, not measuring up, being unworthy, pathetic, eventually bringing, in addition to those mentioned above, low self- esteem, guilt, shame, and condemnation. Now you will have to go back to the scriptures on the blood of Jesus to remind yourself who is your great, big God and who He made you in Christ. Instead of remaining prideful you should humble yourself and receive God's grace to re-establish your identity in righteousness. When your faith is in Christ Jesus, by grace, it is His responsibility to keep you stable and grounded in His righteousness so that no condemnation can come to you and no weapon formed against you can prosper (Isaiah 54:17; Romans 8:1, 2; 1 Peter 1:5).

Romans 8:1, 2, *"There is therefore now no condemnation to them which are in Christ Jesus, who walk not after the flesh, but after the Spirit. For the law of the Spirit of life in Christ Jesus hath made me free from the law of sin and death."*

There can be no condemnation for a believer because God made us loved, innocent, righteous and acceptable by the blood of Jesus and not of ourselves. Satan cannot successfully accuse us because we are not righteous by our actions, behavior or performance. Jesus' innocent blood made us innocent and acceptable in our spirit before

God. Furthermore, Jesus was accused and condemned granting us forgiveness in repentance that we should not be condemned. He has made a way of escape from all condemnation (John 5:24, Romans 4:5; 1 Corinthians 10:13; 11:32; Colossians 1:22).

There are two paths before the born-again believer:

- The life of God in His grace with faith - righteousness in dependence on Christ Jesus through the Holy Spirit.

- Law mentality and carnality in self-righteousness - living by self-will and one's own effort.

(1) **Path 1, Born Again:**

- Acknowledge by faith that you have a rebirth in Christ, grace through faith and that the old man is dead. Christ now lives within and begin to see yourself as a New Creature in Christ. Begin your Christian journey, walking in the spirit of who God made you to be in Christ Jesus.

- Christ is now enthroned in your heart as Lord. Receive His love, the gift of righteousness by faith, believing you are reconciled unto God into a union love relationship, one spirit and at peace with God. He is now your Father. Stand as the new person you've been made "In Christ always looking to your Father in love."

- Get to know the God of your salvation as your loving Father (Isaiah 12:1-4).

- Be in complete dependence on the Word of God and the power of the Holy Spirit, seated in heavenly places. As a son/daughter of God, you are to be filled and led by the Holy Spirit.

- Take authority over all darkness and enforce Satan's defeat (Luke 10:18, 19).

- Enter and embrace the process of sanctification, transformation or spiritual growth by faith and a willingness to let God change you, and others and not of yourself.

- The result of your union with God your Father will be righteousness, peace, and joy in the Holy Ghost, power, love, and sound mind, quietness, and assurance forever (Isaiah 32:17; Romans 14:17; 1 Corinthians 6:17; 2 Timothy 1:7).

(2) **Path 2, Born Again**

- This entails failing to reckon the old man as dead and continuing to yield to the old lifestyle dominated by "self-will." The old nature is still enthroned and being fed into the soul and body, resulting in a Carnal lifestyle, which is lived internally in religion and legalism or externally in carnality and immorality.

- Self-righteousness rule, with a law-mentality of dependence on self-effort, or one's own strength, and self-performance, because you lack union love relationship.

- You are a child of God. But this path is led by the self-directed tactics of the devil as he gives suggestions and ideas to the soul and body, which you yield to, instead of being led the Holy Spirit.

- One will not see the abundance, prosperity, overcoming victory or peace God says you should have, but instead fear.

RESULT of path #2: Is a Christian living in spiritual adultery, a mixture of law and grace (Genesis 21:9-21; Galatians chapters 1-3). This is a life of struggle, straining, striving, and trying harder to do good to please God yet never attaining peace. Here, there is not much level of victory as there often is anxiety, torment, anger, harshness, guilt, shame, conflict and condemnation, leading to fear and sometimes depression.

The consequence is seen in Romans 7 and the answer to spiritual adultery is in Romans 8; Galatians 4 and 5 which is grace through faith, walking by the power of the Holy Spirit.

There is a third choice, the path of the unbelieving sinner, or the believer who deliberately chooses to curse and reject Jesus and my hope is that no one takes this path. The one who rejects Jesus and all He has done on the cross will die in their sin. No one can get to God without Jesus. If you try, you will lose your way to Heaven and be lost for all eternity in Hell (Isaiah 52:14, chapter 53, Zechariah 12:10, 13:1, Psalm 22, John 3:16, 36, 14:6, Acts 4:12, 1 Timothy 2:5).

"I call heaven and earth to record this day against you, that I have set before you life and death, blessing and cursing: therefore choose life that both thou and thy seed may live." (Deuteronomy 30:19).

Choose God and His way through Christ because without Him, you are no match for the devil. But thanks be unto God through Christ, who has given us victory over the devil through the Holy Spirit (Luke 10:18,19; Romans chapter 8; Colossians 1:13; 2:14-15). Through Christ, Satan is a defeated foe. Let the resurrection power of Christ in you tell him this truth that you believe.

Jesus nailed the ordinance of the law to the cross, at which time, the law mentality of self-will, independence and self-effort in us died with Christ on the cross. Law demands that you "DO" or use your own skills and effort, in your own way to do right; it also means that you perform works to get saved in order to make yourself feel right with God. In the Christian walk, the law also means trying to solve your own needs or problems which often will result in strife and a lack of peace with self and others.

Christ, however, ended the first, the law of self-will, and established the second God's will. This He did in His covenant of grace, which is complete reliance, by faith, in God's power and ability to work on your behalf through the power of the Word and the Holy Spirit to deliver and to keep you (2 Timothy 1:12; 1 Peter1:3-5).

The true Gospel is the good news of Jesus and His finished work on the Cross all the way to the ascension. God gave the life of His Son for the forgiveness of your sins and gave the gift of righteousness to make you right and acceptable to God. He made you reconciled unto Him, complete and full of eternal life with the ability to live victoriously. In exchange, we are to give Jesus our entire life, and as Christ was baptized unto death and died on the cross, we were baptized in Him, as dead to self. We died with Him and were buried with Him.

Water baptism is a symbol of this. As Jesus rose again, you arose with Him into the newness of life. Accept by faith that you are raised up, seated in heavenly places where you reign as Priests and Kings over ALL through Jesus' righteousness and His abundant grace. (Romans 5:17; 6:1-5; Ephesians 1:3).

In relationship live, seeing God as your good Father and you as His child made good by the blood of Jesus.

Live a life sold out for Jesus in the Spirit to love Him and others, to reverence, bless, and honor and serve Him in all you say and do as you walk in faith through His grace. Believe, because of the blood of Jesus, that you have been forgiven and made righteous, by faith, and trust God to live in and through you by His Word and the leading of the Holy Spirit. He is the one helping you to walk in righteousness and holiness, conforming into the image of His Son Jesus. The Holy Spirit is continuing to make you pleasing to God and placing you on the path of a profitable Father, child relationship with God.

> *Live a life sold out for Jesus in the Spirit to love Him and others, to reverence, bless, and honor and serve Him in all you say and do as you walk in faith through His grace.*

The devil is always seeking to rob you of your righteousness by faith, therefore robbing you of relationship and intimacy with God. He seeks to push you back into self-will and self-righteousness, which is bondage to the law. But resist him and, instead, seek to maintain a thriving, loving relationship with Jesus living by faith. Believe God so that you can have all the benefits of being heir and joint heir with Him. Know that your inheritance, once born again, made you free from the power of Satan, the power of sin, the power of self-will in the law, and the power of death, including all sickness and disease. Deliverance is yours from Satan, forgiveness is yours from sin. Grace, through righteousness, is yours from the law and healing is yours from sickness and death.

God has many goals for our lives as His children: righteousness, the renewing of the mind, sanctification or spiritual growth, baptism of water and the Holy Spirit, continual transformation into Christ's character, and operating in His gifts and calling and glorification into eternity. All these are His paths, which lead us to Himself in His kingdom of righteousness, peace, and joy with Him, your Father, through the Holy Ghost. The Lord is your Shepherd, He makes you to lie down in green pastures, and He leads you beside the still waters. God is always leading towards His goodness and joy in His presence. God wants you to live by His life.

Colossians 3:3, 4, *"For ye are dead, and your life is hid with Christ in God."* **When Christ, who is our life**, *shall appear, then shall ye also appear with him in glory."*

By faith, Christ is your life, Christ is your righteousness, your healing, Christ is your peace, your joy, and your deliverance when you draw eternal life from the power of His blood shed on the cross for you. Galatians 2:20, *"I am crucified with Christ; nevertheless I live; yet not I, but Christ liveth in me: and the life which I now live in the flesh I live by the faith of the Son of God, who loved me, and gave himself for me."*

> **God is always leading towards His goodness and joy in His presence.**

John 1:4, *"In him was life; and the life was the light of men."*

Jesus is my light. I am a follower of Jesus, and shall not walk in darkness, but shall have the light of light (John 8:12).

Acts 17:28, *"For in him we live, and move and have our being; as certain also of your own poets have said, for we are also his offspring."*

Let your mind not confuse your path or the processes on that path in your life with the destiny or destination in your life. Just because the storm is raging and your situation looks dim does not mean you are not on the right path heading in the right direction towards your pot of gold of eternal life with Christ Jesus. Let the sacrifice of Christ Jesus bring you into an eternal relationship with God as your Father and healthy relationships with others as you love and trust Him. Trust in God by putting one foot in front of the other, daily walking through the good and bad by faith into your Father's love and His promise of an eternal destiny to meet your Savior and Lord one day.

Proverbs 4:18, *"But the path of the just is as the shining light, that shineth more and more unto the perfect day."*

The Christian walk in John 14:6 and in the book of Acts, was referred to as *"The Way"* (Acts 9:2 Acts 19:9; 23; Acts 22:4 24:14). In the Old Testament, Abraham killed a bullock and made a way through the blood for God to come to him. Moses sprinkled blood and the eyes of the people were opened for them to see God. In the New Testament, the blood of Jesus opened *The Way* for us to see God as our loving Father (Matthew 7:13, 14).

Let us as loving children choose to follow *The Way* of the blood of Jesus and the path of His grace through the power of the Holy Spirit into relationship, faith and victory.

Jesus walked and conquered for us and created the path to eternal life, victory, and peace. By faith in Jesus you can find the way, walk in it as pleasing to Him being the overcomers He made you to be. May God richly bless you on *"THE WAY"* through the blood of Jesus. May you find your path to Him and live victoriously in Him as His Word becomes a lamp unto your feet and a light unto your path. AMEN!

CHAPTER 17

TRUST IN THE LORD

"Trust ye in the Lord forever: for in the Lord JEHOVAH is everlasting strength." (Isaiah 26:4)

Trusting in God means an absolute and unwavering confidence in Him and His Word regardless of whatever negative circumstances you are facing. It means your faith in God's involvement and help remains resolute and unchanging.

Trusting in God is demonstrated when there is a strong commitment and dependence on the Word, character and integrity and timing of God. With unwavering faith, you take Him at His Word and believe it as true having, full assurance that everything will work out. It will be all right because your Father will never fail you.

All believers are children of God in a relationship with God their heavenly Father through Jesus His Son. The ultimate goal of this relationship is building trust. Most times, God will tell us the end result of the blessing He has for us. But as we wait for the blessing, the present reality of our life may be showing the opposite–a life full of trouble. When the present reality of your life does not match the promised blessing, you must realize that you are in *the process.* This means that you are in the trials that come between *promise* and *manifestation* and you must learn to trust God in order to have peace in your heart while you go through the processes of your life (Isaiah 26:3).

Trust is required at all times but especially when:

1. What is required of you is beyond your capability or control.
2. When you don't know what to do.
3. When the enemy launches attacks, especially those you don't understand.
4. In any new venture, situation or uncertainty which could paralyze you.
5. Any situation that seems impossible, or full of darkness.

When the situations you face are scary or the future is unknown, trust God with your whole life, both in good and bad times. Whatever is happening, God invites you to trust Him because He is big enough, wise and strong enough to help and deliver you from every trial. We can trust Him to work it out on our behalf because He promised His peace.

Philippians 4:6, 7 *"Be careful for nothing; but in everything by prayer and supplication with thanksgiving let your request be made known unto God. And the peace of God, which passeth all understanding, shall keep your hearts and minds through Christ Jesus."*

One of the highest callings and greatest privileges of a believer is to trust God. Trust is living day by day in union of our spirit to God's in a divine connection, which says like Jacob "I will not let thee go, except thou bless me"(Genesis 32:26).

You can trust God that He will bless your situations because He says He knows the plan He has for you, to prosper you and to give you an expected end, which is one of good (Jeremiah 29:11).

What do people trust in? And what does God say?

Psalm 20:7, *"Some trust in chariots, and some in horses: but we will remember the name of the lord our God."*

Psalm 118:8, 9 *"It is better to trust in the Lord than to put confidence in man. It is better to trust in the Lord than to put confidence in princes."*

The decision that lies before us in the trials we face daily is will we through self-will try to fix them ourselves, depend on others to fix them, or instead trust in God to fix them and when He responds, for you to do only what God says.

Many put their hope, belief, faith and trust in people or in temporary things like money, a job, fame, or even welfare but Psalm 18:2 says, " *The Lord is my rock, and my fortress and my deliverer; my God, my strength, in whom I will trust; my buckler, and the horn of my salvation, and my high tower."*

Another example, is a story in the bible of the rich young ruler in, Luke18:18 He approached Jesus saying "good master what shall I do to inherit eternal life?

Jesus answered him to obey the commandments, and the young ruler replied, "All these I kept from my youth up. Jesus then said to him, "Ye lackest one thing; sell all that thou hast, and distribute unto the poor, and thou shalt have treasure in heaven; and come follow me.' And when he heard this, he was very sorrowful: for he was very rich."

Money was his idol; it was more significant to him than the words of Jesus.

If truth be told, in the spiritual condition he was in not being born-again, if we were in his shoes, we would probably have responded the same way as the rich young ruler. Additionally, if the rich young ruler had willingness to obey, perhaps God could have stopped him the same way as He did with Abraham when He told him to sacrifice his only son. It is possible that God only needed for people to see their own heart and whether they are willing or unwilling to trust Him. Even if the rich young ruler had to give it all away, if he trusted God it would have been restored it to him just as He did with Job (Job: 42:12).

What are you committed to most? What do you spend most of your time, talent and money on? That will tell you what your trust is in. Then, listen to what God is asking of you to reveal your trust in Him, just like the young ruler.

Jeremiah 17:7, *"Blessed is the man that trusteth in the lord, and whose hope the Lord is.*

God can be trusted because:

1. He first loved us, even when we were sinners and unloved (Romans 5:8; 1 John 4;19).

2. Because of His character and integrity (Numbers 23:19; 1 John 4:16).

3. He is the Lord of righteousness. We can trust Him to take charge and do the right thing on our behalf (Jeremiah 23:6).

4. He is a mighty, awesome, great and everlasting Father who promised His goodness and mercy shall follow you all the days of your life (Psalm 23:6).

5. The word of God is truth which endureth forever (John 17:17; 1 Peter1:25).

6. His hands are not short because He is full of graciousness (Luke 9:16,17).

7. God is faithful. "Faithful is He that calleth you, who also will do it." Judge Him faithful as Sarah did (Psalm 34:22; 1 Thessalonians 5:24; Hebrews 11:11).

8. He is unchanging (Malachi 3:6), "For I am the Lord, I change not..." Jesus Christ is the same yesterday, today and forever in His character. His mind or methods may change (Judges 2:11-18; Hebrews 10:9)

9. He is the God of impossibilities (Jeremiah 32:27; Luke 1:37).

10. He can be trusted because He is your heavenly Father and He loves you to eternity.

We know we can trust God because His Word says so and His word is truth. But to really trust Him, you and I must *know* Him. After all, one can only trust someone who she/he knows. Do you and I really know him? Do we know He's our Father who loves us with unfailing love? Do we know His heart, His wishes, His needs, His desires, His plans for us, His plans for our children? Do you know Him as Lord? Is your relationship with Him as your Father getting closer each day?

Let me ask you a question, and I want you to think about it and give an answer: How do you see God? Complete this sentence. I see God as my _____ ?

You could have said many things here. You could see God as your God, your Shepherd or redeemer. You could see God as your Lord, your heavenly Father, or your friend. Here's how some people usually see God:

(1) Some people who can only say 'He is my God' are usually legalistic having have a long-distance relationship because they feel the love that God offers is too easy and they have a hard time doing nothing receiving His love. They are often led by their own self-will and feel that they have to earn His love and in answering prayer thinks that God will more quickly hear someone else's prayer. 'My God' people very often have the wrong concept of God, thinking that He is unreasonable, harsh and quick to punish.

At one time, I would feel fear every time I thought about drawing near to God. Filled with self-will and self-righteousness, I was not sure what He would say. I was not sure if I was ready to agree with what He said, or if He would rebuke me about something and I did not want Him angry at me.

(2) Some may see Him as 'my Shepherd.' God did not intend for us to forever be as mindless sheep, with no effort of faith or following on our part. That is why

His blood He gave us His Spirit within us so He can guide and lead us from within. We have the mind of Christ and are now His sheep with the mind of Christ (1 Corinthians 2:16). Now you follow by faith not mindlessly.

(3) Those even closer yet will see Him as Father, because they see His love and care in His Son Jesus, and believe He will bless them.

(4) Still, some have desired and pursued a closer relationship with their heavenly Father and call Him "Friend." A friend knows who they are "in Christ", and knows the heart, nature and character of their Father as they continually fellowship and have communion with Him.

It is not difficult to know the Lord because Hebrews 8:11 says, "And they shall no more teach every man his neighbor, and every man his brother, saying, know the Lord; for all shall know me, from the least to the greatest of them, saith the Lord; for I will forgive their iniquity, and I will remember their sin no more." (Jeremiah 31:34)

John 14:17, 18 say in part, "...*but ye shall know him; for he dwelleth with you and shall be in you. I will not leave you comfortless. I will come to you.*"

We will begin to overcome when we wake up and recognize that our sins are washed, cleansed and we are justified, sanctified by the blood, that all separation is removed and we are reconciled unto God in love, and is become bonded to God in a close Father/child relationship. The hindrances that sin and the repercussions it brought have been dealt with by God in Christ. Now your God-inside controlled human spirit can flow freely to the soul and body to receive Godly leading every time.

Think about it the birds know their time to migrate for winter, the trees know when to shed leaves for the fall season and when to put on leaves in spring. As human beings made to be in God we also know instinctively to hear and to follow God.

We have a God whose heart is full of power, compassion, care and a desire to bless. His call is for us to be in relationship, be dead to self-will and by faith, yield to and continually turn towards God.

To know God is to trust God.
Here are some ways we can come to know God:

1. We know God through His love, and we get born-again, receiving His love.

2. We know Him through putting faith in His grace and all Jesus did at the cross.

3. We know Him through creation and through His Word.

4. We know Him through fellowship and communion and prayer, where we get to build a deeper relationship and even intimacy.

5. We know Him through the experiences we have with Him where we sense His presence and hear Him speak to us as we listen.

6. We know Him through the workings of the Holy Spirit, who is leading, guiding and helping us to yield to Him. Jesus said in Luke 22:42, "Father, if thou be willing, remove this cup from me: nevertheless not my will, but thine, be done." Jesus, trusting God, released the power of the Holy Spirit, allowing Him to complete God's plan of redemption.

7. Know Him as Lord. Accept Jesus as Father, the one in control. Colossians 1:16-18; 3:17.

JESUS IS LORD

We cannot only receive Jesus as savior but must also receive him as Lord and head of our lives.

Throughout the Old Testament, the concept of Lord was pervasive. Subjects called kings lord, Sarah called Abraham her lord and all people refer to God as Lord. In the New Testament people and the disciples called Jesus Lord:

(Luke 2:11, Acts 10:36; Romans 14:9; 2 Corinthians 4:5, Philippians 2:10,11).

We are told in the word that to possess salvation we must confess with our mouth the Lord Jesus:

Romans 10:9, *"That if thou shalt confess with thy mouth the Lord Jesus, and shall believe in thine heart that God hath raised him from the dead, thou shalt be saved."*

Romans 6:23b, *"… but the gift of God is eternal life through Jesus Christ our Lord"*

For salvation to be genuine, Jesus must be acknowledged as Savior, who grants cleansing in forgiveness of all sins, but also as Lord, the possessor and head of your life. As a believer, you belong to Him.

1 Corinthians 6:19, 20," *What? Know ye not that your body is the temple of the Holy Ghost which is in you, which ye have of God, ye are not your own? For ye are bought with a price: therefore glorify God in your body, and in your spirit, which are God's."*

Jesus is Lord because:

- The elements yielded to His voice at creation and formed the galaxies, the universe and the earth, (Genesis 1,2; Colossians 1:16).

- Lord of mankind and sin, (Genesis 2,3, 3:15).

- The Lord of Righteousness, (Isaiah 45:24,25; Jeremiah 23:6).

- The Lord over a believer's life, to bless, builds character, strength, and power, plan for eternal life now and in the hereafter. Lord of everything that concerns us, family, finances, resources, successes, and our destiny (Psalm 84:11, 12; 2 Corinthians 5:21).

- Lord over death and the Lord of life. He raised Lazarus from the dead, and raised our dead souls unto eternal life (John 11:43, 2 Corinthians 5:17).

The superiority of Jesus as Lord is largely lost to us today, but when Jesus by His grace is Your Lord, it means He has authority and power over your life 1 Corinthians 6:20, *"For ye are bought with a price: therefore glorify God in your body, and in your spirit which are God's."* (Also Romans 14:7, 8; 2 Corinthians 6:16).

Give up ownership of yourself to God, exchange your Will for God's Will, exalt Him as Lord on the throne of your life, let Him lead as you follow.

Our response should be one of humility, submission, and commitment. We humble ourselves and, by faith, receive His salvation offered in the shed blood of Jesus on the cross. Be willing to accept that you are dead and your life is hidden in Christ in God in union relationship. Be willing to give up on all selfishness and let the life of Christ in you help you to surrender yourself to the leading of the Holy Spirit so you can please God (Philippians 2:13).

With Jesus in your heart, you become dead to yourself and your old life. You are alive unto Christ and are now placed "in Christ" and into God's kingdom. Now, you are heir; heir of God and joint heir with Christ Jesus (Romans 8:17; Galatians 3:29). You can possess in the spiritual realm everything Jesus purchased for you on the cross.

Jesus is Lord when you obey His commandment in John 13:34: *"A new commandment I give unto you, that ye love one another; as I have loved you, that ye also love one another."*

So settle in your heart who is in authority of your life. If Jesus is Lord, He is in charge and you honor Him, worship Him, and give Him first place in your life and in relationships. Let yourself be led by the Holy Spirit instead of living on your own terms. Yield to

God through the Holy Spirit daily as you seek a closer relationship with Jesus.

Yield to Jesus, submit all of your life, family, needs, desires, your body as a living sacrifice, holy, acceptable unto God, which is your reasonable service:

"I… Acknowledge you as Lord of my desires, my plans, my successes and failures, my place in the world, my friendships, my popularity. You are Lord of my present, my future relationships, health, money, possessions, and human approval. How good it is to yield to you, knowing that you withhold no good thing from your obedient children who trust you and call on you.[11]

What is the connection between Faith and Trust?

Mark 11:24, *"Therefore I say unto you, what things so ever ye desire, when ye pray, believe that ye receive them, and ye shall have them."*

According to Mark 11:24, the moment you pray, you should also believe.

Peter's faith nose-dived when he denied Christ. Jesus said "All ye shall be offended because of me this night." Peter replied, "Although all shall be offended, yet will not I." He said he would rather die than deny Christ, yet he did (Mark 14:27-30).

Jesus said unto him, *"verily I say unto thee, that this day, even in this night, before the cock crows twice, thou shalt deny me thrice."* We know the story: Peter denied Jesus three times. His faith stumbled when he became afraid of being identified and captured with Jesus and he denied Him before them all. Peter's faith caved in the moment of crisis (Matthew 26: 34, 35, 69-75).

A second time, we saw Peter's faith caved when he stepped out of the boat on water to walk to Jesus, when he forgot Jesus' command to COME and began focusing on the tumultuous waves. Why is it that Peter, in faith, so confidently stepped out onto the water then began to sink?

I believe by the Holy Spirit the answer is that when you have a need or desire; it is an expected manifestation in the future. To get to that manifestation, you must exercise your imagination to conceive your desire and believe that you have it NOW. If your imagination is not sanctified (fully lined up with God's Word) but is negative or wandering, the devil can get a hold of your imagination as he simultaneously raises adverse conditions and distractions to create doubt and fear, causing you to see yourself failing and you begin to lose faith.

When Peter took his eyes off Jesus and forgot Jesus' command to "Come," he looked on the waves and he imagined himself sinking. He did sink and his faith wavered. His faith did not fail because Jesus prayed for him (Luke 22:32). Like Abraham, Peter, after much trials and repentance, he learned patience to keep his eyes on Jesus and to trust God so much so that he was the front and center guy at Pentecost. Peter overcame his many trials and as his faith grew he learned to trust God more. He lifted up his voice boldly, preached the gospel so that hearts were pricked and three thousand souls were saved (Acts chapter 2:14-41). As with Peter, you can know how much you trust God by the circumstances that you allow to derail you and cause your faith to cave in. When your trust is solid, you will hold on to your promise and, despite the circumstances around you, will keep your eyes on Jesus alone until you receive your blessing.

Trust, therefore is developed over the long haul after overcoming many trials and failures designed by God to grow your faith. If you keep your eyes on Jesus, each trial will cause your faith to become stronger as you pay less attention to the circumstances having a more stationary focus on one person, the person of Jesus Christ as your best hope.

Peter's faith wavered, but Jesus' prayers kept him from giving up. Jesus prayed for us in John17 and is at the right hand of the Father still making intercession for us. When you trust in God you too will never fail. Psalm 37:5, *"Commit thy way unto the Lord; trust also in him; and he shall bring it to pass."*

Psalm 125:1, *"They that trust in the Lord shall be as mount Zion which cannot be removed but abideth forever.*

Psalm 34:22, *"The lord redeemeth the soul of His servants: and none of them that trust Him shall be desolate."*

When you trust God and His Word, to say yes to His will, The Holy Spirit comes alongside you and strengthens your will and your resolve to disregard all negative circumstances around you. The Holy Spirit helps you to obey and carry out God's plan for you, bringing forth the desired manifestation. Because of and through all the adversities you have experienced, you will learn faith and patience, trusting in Jesus alone to overcome. Your focus has shifted from the desire of a blessing to the one who blesses Jesus your Father and caretaker.

A gym instructor once said to me that in order to maintain your balance, you must find a stationary spot in the center on the floor before you and fix your eyes on that spot, as moving your eyes around creates imbalance. Let Jesus be that someone before you. Keep your eyes fixed on Him and you shall not be moved.

Psalm 16:8, *"I have set the Lord always before me: because he is at my right hand, and I shall not be moved."*

Psalm 112:7, 8 *"He shall not be afraid of evil tidings: his heart is fixed, trusting in the Lord. His heart is established, he shall not be afraid...."*

In faith with patience and with your eyes on Jesus and your imagination now sanctified you have become unmovable in your trust in the Lord and the devil has nothing in you to attack. Now these scriptures can now be yours.

Job 5:19, *"He shall deliver thee in six troubles; yea, in seven there shall no evil touch thee."*

Psalm 34:19, *"many are the afflictions of the righteous: but the Lord delivereth him out of them all."*

Psalm 91:10, *"There shall no evil befall thee, neither shall any plague come nigh thy dwelling."*

1 John 5:18, "*... And that wicked one toucheth him not.*"

God, through Jesus, is your only source of trust. Proverbs 3:5, 6 "*Trust in the Lord with all thine heart; lean not unto thine own understanding. In all thy ways acknowledge Him, and He shall direct thy paths.*"

God your Father will come to you with wisdom, strength, comfort, healing, deliverance and provision. Whatever your need is, He will fulfill your desire in His way and in His timing as you trust in Him.

Before one can really begin to trust, one must positively face and overcome the trials of your life. The Bible, speaking of Jesus, says "*though he were a Son, yet learned he obedience by the things which he suffered*" (Hebrews 5:8).

Peter too learned trust and obedience after he had gone through much trials when he offered to shield Jesus from the cross, when he nearly drowned stepping out to walk on water, when he denied Jesus three times, when he drew his sword and cut off the High Priest's servant's ear, and when, after Jesus died, he quit the ministry and went back fishing. But God, through Jesus, went to him and restored him by helping him to catch a net-full of fish. Jesus forgave him when He asked Peter three times if he loved Him, and Peter replied "yea, Lord; thou knowest that I love thee..." Jesus then gave him his new assignment to feed His sheep (John chapter 21).

Proverbs 24:16a, "*For a Just man falleth seven times, and riseth up again...*"

Peter fell and rose many times and came to a new understanding of the submission and yielding of his heart which is necessary to honor and trust Jesus as Lord of the New Covenant of grace, and be willing to follow.

To follow and honor Jesus, we must know the power of the Holy Spirit is in and with us as our helper (John 14; 16, 17)

Romans 8:26, "*likewise the Spirit also helpeth our infirmities: for we know not what we should pray for as we ought: but the*

Spirit itself maketh intercession for us…" we have a helper to help us to trust our Father. Follow His leading.

When we fail to trust God the results are:

1. Dread and fear and worry.

2. Questioning 'why me?' instead of embracing God in times of trials

3. Can lead one to think God is far and distant and when cannot hear Him one can feel abandoned and become upset or bitter toward God. Instead, turn your eyes to God's love in Jesus' eyes and find His love, His care and comfort in His Word.

4. Complaining, comparing ourselves to others, faultfinding, self-pity, anger, and judgment. All this will negate your faith causing you to walk by sight and not by faith as Thomas did in John 20:29.

5. Busyness. Keep busy working in self-will or in your own strength, rather than yielding.

6. Works of the flesh, Galatians 5: 17, 2 Timothy 2:22, 3:1-7, Ephesians 5:3-9.

7. Assumptions: Genesis 20:11-18 Abraham assumed king Abimelech was evil and would take away Sarah, his wife. He planned how to deceive him. God had to intervene to save Sarah. Never assume Gods response or non-response or what you think the outcome to your problem should be.

Give God your Father the situation and trust Him, by depending and relying on Him to come through for you His way.

Some ways that you can Grow in your Trust in the Lord:

*   Be born again, be baptized in water and the Holy Spirit

*   Honor the blood of Jesus and all He has done for you at the cross and believe His promises.

266

- **Believe** by faith that all your sins are forgiven and that you are cleansed, justified, dead to self, made righteous and restored into union relationship with your heavenly Father.

- Believe the love Jesus has for you in your relationship with Him as your Father.

"But God commendeth his love toward us, in that while we were yet sinners, Christ died for us" (Romans 5:8).

Realize the great privilege you and I have in yielding to God our Father, who in desiring your love, came to you His creation a sinful, disobedient, and flawed people, to fix the problem of separation between Him and us. By choosing to live inside our heart and to lead by His Holy Spirit, He takes us into an even greater intimate relationship with Himself.

- Know the true nature and character of your heavenly Father that He is good and desires only to bless. Believe even His correction and discipline is out of a heart of love to bring you out of sin and back into righteousness.

- Take hold of God's promises as truth and believe the Word as truth even when you don't understand. Seek not to figure out things or try to fix the situation yourself. Isaiah 26:3 says *"Thou wilt keep him in perfect peace, whose mind is stayed on thee: because he trusteth in thee."*

- Have faith in God, Mark 11:22-24, not yourself in self-righteousness (Ezekiel 33:13; Psalm 118:82; Corinthians 1:9). The same way, by faith, you trust God for your salvation, trust Him for everything else in your life, Grace through faith (Ephesians 2:8). Let your faith flow out of your relationship with God as Father to hear and understand what His love has to say about your situation (Proverbs 2:1-1-9; Galatians 2:20).

- Be led by the Holy Spirit. Remember, He leads one step at a time so be sure to grasp His incremental leading. He will provide leading to the next step and onwards to completion. God will not give you His entire plan at once.

He gives it in stages, so that we will choose to maintain our relationship with Him and keep trusting Him for the next step forward until He completes His plan in our lives (Genesis chapter 12, Mark 4:28, Romans 12:2).

- Remember that with every promise, there will be a period of testing to increase your faith in order to fully walk in the provision ahead. When trouble or testing comes, run to your Father for His heart and His mind and direction on the situation. This trial coming to you before your manifestation is the process God is using to cause you to seek Him, to draw near in a closer relationship. So, walk by faith and not by sight, always trusting God and His faithfulness to see you through (Deuteronomy 7:9; 1 Corinthians 10:13; 2 Corinthians 5:7).

- As you are faithful, stay in the process and be transparent with Him. Tell Him you don't understand, that you are afraid, but choose to depend on His wisdom. Ask for clarifications, receive His strength; receive His light and His peace. Hear God speak to you, yield to Him and obey His directions. Over time trust will be built in your heart toward God and rest will come to your soul.

- Whether in *the process* of waiting or in a trial, keep your eyes on Jesus, Numbers Chapter 12. When faith is wavering in the trial, keep going toward Jesus and give Him your failings: "…. Let the weak say I am strong" (Joel 3:10b). Let him strengthen you and show Himself strong in restoring you. He loves to take the nothings and makes something of them, to take the weak and show them strong. WHY? He wants and deserves to get the Glory, to be seen as the good Father He is to His children. So give Him your weakness and failures and let Him lift you up, He delights in doing good for His Children

- Meditate and speak the Word of God that you believe concerning your situation and praise and worship Him for what He's doing to bring your desired promise to pass. (Romans 4:19, 20).

- Along with faith in your relationship, allow God to develop patience in your heart so that you will have the endurance to be committed in order to stay the full course. James 1:2-4. To trust, you must foster good control of your thoughts, keeping them on the Word of God and His promise to you and away from distractions that cause fear, so you will not waver (Hebrews 6:12).

- You know you are trusting God when there are only two variables at work in your situation.

1. **God as your source.** (Matthew 6;31-34; 2 Corinthians 10:4,5; Philippians 4:6; 1 Peter 5:7) Jesus and God's word are one (John 1:1, 14). It is the faith relationship that you have with God's word through the person of Jesus and His shed blood that will release the power you need, to manifest your blessing.

2. **Your faith and patience in God.** All other components have been cast down: your feelings, bad reports, what you see in the natural, what other people have to say or what the devil is doing to make you question the how or the timing of your manifestation (2 Corinthians 10:4,5). You trust absolutely because the resurrection power of God in formed in you, and is greater than any power of the enemy (Galatians 4:19)

- If, because of ignorance, you failed to yield to God in the processing of your faith and you failed your test, God is merciful and will give you another chance to overcome. He will direct you back to where you missed Him and begin to help you move forward again. So, expect your test and stay in close relationship with the Holy Spirit so He can help you to remove the dross, fear, worry, cares, and your focus on self or temporal things. He will help you to mature spiritually with your focus on eternal things so you will overcome and learn to trust God (2 Corinthians 4:18).

- Proverbs 3 :5,6 says *"Trust in the lord with all thine heart; and lean not unto thine understanding. In all thy ways acknowledge Him, and he will direct thy paths."*

- You know you really trust when the why's, how's, when and where are not your primary concern. Instead, only your faith in God your Father becomes important. Stay steadfast in Jesus, your heavenly Father. You are fully committed with your trust in God's power and ability to get the job done on your behalf; knowing He will give you your breakthrough.

- Trust God's character, trust His salvation, trust His promises, trust His process, trust His goodness, trust His faithfulness, and trust His timing for your blessing.

- Rejoice in the Lord always while you trust God. Psalm 5: 11, *"But let all those that put their trust in thee rejoice: let them ever shout for joy, because thou defendest them: let them also that love thy name be joyful in thee."*

It makes the devil really mad when we trust God and rejoice in the midst of trouble. Praise God with songs in your heart (Ephesians 5:18-20).

When a train goes through a tunnel and it gets dark, it is said you don't throw away the ticket and jump off the train. Instead, you sit and trust the engineer that he will bring you out. Trust God in relationship today no matter what, no matter how dark the situation, God says He will bring you out.

Psalm 37:40, *"And the lord shall help them, and deliver them: He shall deliver them from the wicked, and save them, because they trusted in Him."*

What results can we expect when we trust God.

1. Increased relationship with God through the Holy Spirit. Confidence in your emotions and Joy in your heart (1 John 5:14,15).

2. Having a certainty that all things will work out for your good (Romans 8: 38-42).

3. The power of Satan to harm you is broken (Psalm 34:19, 22; Job 5:19; 1 John 5:18).

4. An enlarged tent expectant for blessings (Isaiah 54:1-3).

5. Peace, quietness and assurance (Isaiah 32:17, 18).

6. Joy in the God of your salvation (Habakkuk 3:17-19).

7. To be led by the Holy Spirit step by step into obedience. As you trust, steadfast faith makes it easier to obey (Philippians 2:13).

8. Trust spurs faith into action. Trusting God is not passive. Noah trusted God; he built the ark and was saved.

   -Abraham trusted God. He left Ur of the Chaldees on God's order and was willing to sacrifice His only Son. (Genesis 12, 22).

   -Four Hebrew boys trusted God, made a strong declaration "if *it be so, our God whom we serve is able to deliver us from the burning fiery furnace and He will deliver us out of thine hand O king.*"

   God delivered them out of the fiery furnace (Daniel Chapter 3) if you trust, you'll have a declaration!

   -David trusted God and did not kill King Saul in the cave (1 Samuel 24:1-12).

   -Hebrews 11 gives a very long list of people who trusted God. Their faith pleased God and worked victory for them over the long haul.

9. Overcome stress and fear as you cease trusting in the flesh. By trusting in God, you stop assuming, presupposing, judging on how the process is now and how the outcome will be also judging other people's reaction.

These are open doors for the enemy to bring fear and strife.

When you rest in faith with patience in God's grace, you can truthfully say you TRUST God through *the process* with all people in all things, in all ways, at all times and all is well.

Additional Scriptures: Job 12:5; 2 Samuel 22:3-4,31; Psalm 18:2,30 ;25:2; 31:19; 37:4,5; 73:28; 91:2; 118:8; Psalm 125:1, 141:8, 143:8,9, Isaiah 12:2,3, Isaiah 31:1, 57:13 26:4.

May God continue to bless you His child as you grow in a trusting relationship with Him as God your good Father.

ENDNOTES

Chapter 1
1. Richards James B, *Grace the power of change*, chapter 4 page 38.
Chapter 2
2. Chandler Matt, *Recovering redemption* Chapter 2 Page 25.
Chapter 5
3. Kenneth Copeland, *Covenant of Blood* Pamphlet. Page 4 Kenneth Copeland Ministries.
4. Lake, John G. *Spiritual Hunger*, the god-men, Chapter 7 page 71
Chapter 6
5. Lake, John G. *Spiritual Hunger*, the god-men, chapter 1 Page 5
Chapter 7
6. Lake, John G, *Spiritual Hunger*, the god-men, Chapter 1 page 17
7. Lake John G, *Spiritual Hunger*, the god-men, Chapter 1 page 18
Chapter 9
8. Hagin Kenneth, Jr. *The prison door is open* – mini book chapter 1
Chapter 12
10. Cho, David Yonggi, *Successful home cell group*
Chapter 17
11. Myers, Rutha Wamen, *31 Days of Prayer* page 71.

APPENDIX 1:

CONFESSIONS: UNION WITH GOD.

- Colossians 2:9-10, *"For in Him dwelleth all the fullness of the Godhead bodily. And ye are complete in Him, which is the head of all principality and power."* Living Bible: *"For in Christ there is ALL OF GOD IN MY HUMAN BODY so I have everything, because I am in Christ. I am filled with God through union with Christ. The Holy Spirit living in me is greater than any evil power that can come against me.*

  Confession: I am in Christ and I am one with God in Christ. I am complete in Him. I rest in oneness with God as I am filled with God and Jesus when the Holy Spirit came within. He will help me to reach my full potential in every area of my life and to be strong in the Lord and in the power of His might.

- Philippians 4:13, *"I can do all things through Christ which strengtheneth me."*

  Confession: There is nothing I cannot master with the help of Christ who gives me wisdom, strength and power by His Spirit.

- Ephesians 2:10, *"For we are his workmanship, created in Christ Jesus unto good works, which God hath before ordained that we should walk in them."* Confession: I am God's work of art created in Christ Jesus to live the good life of peace, assurance, acceptance, and confidence in God; the very life He intended for Adam from the beginning. I look just like Jesus to God, in my spirit and as I meditate on His Word I will begin to think and feel in my soul and body as I really am in my human spirit, completely restored into the image of Christ and made whole to do good works.

- Ephesians 2:6, *"And hath raised us up together, and made us to sit together in heavenly places in Christ Jesus."*

  Confession: I am in Christ, raised up from being dead in sin and lifted in Christ in the heavenlies. I now sit enthroned with Christ in the Spirit. I rule and reign with Him by His grace and His righteousness in me. Confession: I magnify Jesus, because I have been raised and is seated, in heavenly places with Christ Jesus. Greater is He that is in me than He that is in the world. My God is greater than Satan, greater than sin, greater than fear, and greater than condemnation. I am a new creation, and this is a new day that the Lord has made and I will rejoice in it and be glad.

- John 17:17, "Sanctify them through thy truth; thy word is truth."

  Confession: I know the truth and the truth now sets me free; because I am washed, sanctified, and is justified in the name of the Lord Jesus, the Spirit of my God is in me. "I belong to Jesus. • John 8:12, *"…I (Christ) am the light of the world; he that followeth me shall not walk in darkness, but shall have the light of life."* Confession: Jesus is the light of the world and He lives in me. His light floods my soul and my being more and more each day; driving out darkness and fear. I am full of His light.

- John 1:4, *"In Him (Christ) was life; and the life was the light of men."* His life is the light in my life. • I John 4:4, *"Ye are of God, little children, and have overcome them: because greater is he that is in you, than he that is in the world."*

  1 John 1:27):The anointing is the Spirit of God living in me and He is greater than any lie, and any force of evil the devil can bring against me. Greater is he that is in me than he that is in the world.

  Prayer: Father, I thank you that your anointing in me is greater than torment or oppression which the devil is trying to bring against me from the outside. Thank you, Father for rising up in me the anointing, a standard against all oppression, spirit of torment, and oppression. I command those things to go in Jesus name.

- Acts 17:28, *"For in Him we live, and move, and have our being..."*

  Confession: I am in Christ. I am in union; one spirit with Him. I depend on Him and trust Him for my highest good. In Him I live and move and have my being. I am dead to the old me. The old man died in Christ on the cross. Because of His great love He drew me to Himself. Jesus loves me, Jesus loves me, He loves me, and He loves me more! His love is shed abroad in my heart; I believe it and I receive it, In Jesus' name. I now rejoice in the God of my salvation and rejoice in His great love. I now choose to fill myself up with Jesus, so that His perfect love drives out all fear. I trust His love, His joy, and His peace rising up from my spirit, flooding my soul, and making me whole (Romans 5:8, 6:6, I John 4:18, Galatians 5:22). The old man in me is dead. I am a new creation, the righteousness of God in Christ. I am restored into a love relationship with God because of the blood of Jesus on the cross, not my performance or any negative life experiences. I am accepted by Him, approved, favored, and qualified for His love and all His blessings. I rest in His love, His care and His peace.

- Colossians 2:6, *"As you have therefore received Christ Jesus the Lord, so walk ye in him :"*(Grace through faith) (Ephesians 2:8). Living Bible: *"And now just as you trusted Christ to save you, now trust him too for each days need or problems. Live in vital union/relationship with him. Let your roots grow down into him and draw up nourishment from him establishing you in Christ.*

APPENDIX 2:

"Who am I in Christ?"

ON THE BASIS OF THE BLOOD:

1. I am a child of God; I am a Son of God. I am loved with an everlasting love. I am a partaker of His divine nature. (Romans 8:14,16; 1 John3:1-2; Ephesians 3:6)

2. I am saved by grace as I believe through faith, and have everlasting life (Ephesians 2:8,John 6:47, Philippians 3:9)

3. I am in Christ Jesus by His blood made new, and loved (Jeremiah 31:3; 1 Corinthians 1:30, 1 John 3:16)

4. I am God's child, born again of the incorruptible seed of the Word of God which liveth and abides forever (1 Peter 1:23)

5. I am brought near by the blood of Christ (Ephesians 2:13).

6. I am a new creation in Christ Jesus (2 Corinthians 5:17; Colossians 3:10; 1John 4:17).

7. I am a joint heir with Christ (Romans 8:17).

8. I am the righteousness of God through Christ Jesus (2 Corinthians 5:21).

9. I am adopted into the family of God, a fellow citizen (Galatians 4:5,6; Ephesians 2:19)

10. I am the apple of my heavenly Father's eyes (Psalm 17:8).

11. I am chosen (Ephesians 1:4; 1 Peter 2:9).

12. I am loved, accepted and holy and without blame before God (1 John 4:19; Ephesians 1:4,6; Colossians 1:22).

13. United into one body, I have access to the Father by one spirit; I am reconciled (Ephesians 2:15; 16-18; 3:6 ;2 Corinthians 5:18).

14. I am God's workmanship, created in Christ Jesus for good works (Ephesians 2:10).

15. I am forgiven of all my sins (Acts 13:38-39; Ephesians 1:7; Colossians 1:13-14).

16. I am redeemed from the curse of the law (Ephesians 1:7; Galatians 3:13).

17. I am justified, made innocent before God (Romans, 3:24; 5:1, 8:30; Exodus 23:7; Job 4:7; 33:9; 1 Corinthians 6:11).

18. I am sanctified, being changed into His image (1 Corinthians 1:30; 6:11; Philippians 1:6).

19. I am the temple of the Holy Spirit (1 Corinthians 6:19).

20. I am dead to sin and alive unto God (Romans 6:2, 11; Ephesians 2:5).

21. I am crucified with Christ (Romans 6:6; Galatians 2:20)

22. I daily overcome the devil by the anointing, which is the greater one in me (1 John 2:27; 4;4).

23. I cast down vain imaginations, bringing them into captivity (2 Corinthians 10:4-5.)

24. I am delivered from the power of darkness (Colossians 1:13-14;Psalm 107:2).

25. I have authority over the devil (Luke 10:18-19; Philippians 2:9-11).

26. I overcome by the blood of the Lamb. 1 John 5:4; Revelations 12:11)

27. I am no longer condemned, I have been set free (Romans 8:1-2; John 8:31-36).

28. I am made "the praise of his glory"(Ephesians 1:12; 1 Peter 2:9).

29. I am built for the Spirits' habitation (Ephesians 2:21, 22).

30. I am a partaker of God's promise, with a guaranteed inheritance (Ephesians 3:6; Colossians 1:12).

31. I am raised up with Christ and seated in heavenly places (Ephesians 1:3, 13,14; 2:6 ; Colossians 2:12).

32. I am a king and a priest unto God, reigning through life (Revelations 1:6; Romans 5:17).

33. I am the salt of the earth, a light of the world (Matthew 5: 13-14).

34. I am more than a conqueror (Romans 8:37).

35. I have the mind of Christ, being transformed by a renewed mind (1 Corinthians 2:16; Romans 12:1-2).

36. I know God's voice (John 10:3-5,14)

37. As I was saved by Grace, I now walk in His grace (Ephesians 2:8, Colossians 2:6).

38. I can do all things through Christ Jesus (Philippians 4:13)

39. I am firmly rooted, built up and established in the faith (Colossians 2:7)

40. I am strong in the lord and in the power of His might (Ephesians 6:10)

41. I am kept in safety wherever I go (Psalm 91).

42. I am provided for and all my needs are met (Philippians 4:19; 3 John; 2 Corinthians 8:9).

43. I am in peace, as I keep my mind on Christ (Isaiah 26:3; Romans 5:1; Philippians 4:7 Colossians 3:15).

44. I am the healed of the Lord. I am healed by Christ's stripes (Isaiah 53:4-5; 1 Peter 2:24).

45. I am blessed with all spiritual blessings. I am full of abundant life (Ephesians 1:3;14, John 10:10b; Deuteronomy 28: 1-14).

46. I walk by faith and not by sight. I am not moved by what I see (2 Corinthians 5:7; 2 Corinthians 4:18; Psalm 16:8).

47. I am a possessor of the Holy Spirit living within me (John 14: 16-17; Acts1:8, Ephesians 1:19-21; Romans 8:11).

48. I have received the power of the Holy Spirit to lay hands on the sick and see them recover (Mark 16:17; 2 Corinthians 5:20).

49. I am led by the Holy Spirit (Romans 8:14).

50. Thanks be unto God who causes me to triumph, I have the victory (1 Corinthians 15:57-58; 2 Corinthians2:14.)

APPENDIX 3:

My God Is.

1. Love: He shed His love abroad in my heart. I rejoice in His great love (1 John 4:16; Romans 5:5).

2. The Beginning and the End, the Alpha and Omega, the Author and Finisher of my faith in every situation I face. (Revelation 1:8; Hebrews 12:2)

3. He is all powerful, my God almighty (Jeremiah 32:17, 27; Exodus 6:3)

4. He is Kings of kings and Lords of Lords (Revelations 17:14)

5. He is my covenant-making, and keeping God (Hebrews 10:16, 17)

6. He is my everlasting Father of mercies and comfort (Isaiah 9:6; 2 Corinthians 1:3)

7. He is full of power and mighty to save (Romans 13:1; Isaiah 63:1; Ephesians 1:19; Hebrews 7:25)

8. He is my God who raises the dead (2 Corinthians 1:9; John 11:11, 43)

9. He is my God who meets my needs through Jesus (Philippians 4:19; 3 John 2)

10. He is the way the truth and the life (John 14:6)

11. He is Immanuel, God with us (Isaiah 7:14; Matthew 1:23; Hebrews 8:11)

12. He is the great shepherd of the sheep (Hebrews 13:20; Psalm 23)

13. He is the same yesterday today and forever (Hebrews 13:8; John 8:58)

14. He is my all sufficiency (2 Corinthians 3:5; 9:8)

15. He is faithful and true, My High priest (Revelation 19:11; Hebrews 9:11; 10:21)

16. He is the living Word (John 1:1-4)

17. He is the bread of life (John 6:48-58)

18. He is my sure foundation (Isaiah 28:16)

19. He is upholding all things by the word of His power (Hebrews 1:3)

20. He is watching over His word to perform it for me (Jeremiah 1:12; Psalm 138:8)

21. He is a rewarder of those who diligently seek Him (Hebrews 11:6)

22. He is no respecter of persons (Acts 10:34)

23. He is the true light (John1:9; 8:12)

24. He is my God and He is working in me (Philippians 2:13; Hebrews 13:21)

25. He is the Greater in me, than He who is in the world (1 John2:27; 4:4)

26. He is my wisdom, sanctification, righteousness and redemption (makes me wise, holy, accepted and free (1 Corinthians 1:30)

27. He is my never leaving, nor forsaking me God (John 14:18, Hebrews 13:5)

28. He causes me to triumph in Christ Jesus (2 Corinthians 2:14; 1 Corinthians 15:57)

29. He is my Savior and redeemer (Luke 2:11; Isaiah 48:17)

30. He is my healer (Isaiah 53:5; Jeremiah 32:27; 1 Peter 2:24; Matthew 15:13)

31. He is my deliverer (Romans 11:26; Colossians 1:13)

32. He is my resurrection power (John 11:25; Romans 8:11)

33. He is my justification (Romans 3:26;1Corinthians 6:11)

34. He is my strength (Philippians 4:13; Psalm 18:2; Isaiah 12:2; 40:29)

35. He is my peace (Ephesians 2:14; Isaiah 26:3; Philippians 4:6-9)

36. He is my Advocate (1 John 2:1)

37. He is my faithful High Priest (Hebrews 9:11; 10:21)

38. He is my Lord and my God (John 20:28)

39. He is the Hope of my glory (Colossians 1:27)

40. He is the giver of wisdom and spiritual understanding to me (Ephesians 1:17)

41. He is Christ my armor (Ephesians 6:10-18)

42. He is providing me with Angels for protection (Psalm 91; Hebrews 1:14b)

43. He is faithful to complete the work He started in me (Philippians 1:6)

44. He is rich in grace and mercy (Psalm 136; Hebrews 4:16)

45. He is leading me by His Spirit in the way I should go (Isaiah 48:17; Romans 8:14; Philippians 2:13)

46. He is the giver of all good things to enjoy (1 Timothy 6:17; Psalm 23).

47. He is worthy of all praise (Psalm 18:3)

48. He is worthy of all glory, honor, power and praise (Revelations 4:11).

49. He is worthy to receive power, and riches, and wisdom, and strength and honor and glory and blessing. (Revelation 5:12)

50. He is coming back again. "Surely I am coming quickly," says the Lord of hosts (Revelation 22:20)

BIBLIOGRAPHY

Chandler, Matt. 2014. *Recovering redemption: How Christ changes everything.* Nashville,TN: B&H Publishing Group.

Hagin, Kenneth, Jr. 1982. *The prison door is open: What are you still doing inside?* Tulsa,OK: Faith Library Publications.

Jones, Beth. 2004. *Why the gory, bloody details? An explanation of the passion & thecross.* Portage, MI: Valley Press Publishers.

Lake, John Graham. 1978. *Spiritual hunger, the God-men: and other sermons.* Dallas: Christ for the Nations.

Myers, Ruth, and Warren Myers. 1997. *Thirty-one days of prayer.* Colorado Springs, Colo:Multnomah Books.

Osteen, John. 1978. *How to demonstrate Satan's defeat.* Houston, TX: A John Osteen Publication.

Richards, James B. 2001. *Grace: the power to change.* New Kensington, PA: WhitakerHouse.

Spiropoulos, Rona. 2011. *The Blood: Entrance Into the Supernatural.* CSA Publishing.

Wommack, Andrew. 2008. *Grace, the power of the Gospel: It's not what you do, but whatJesus did.* Walsall: Andrew Wommack Ministries - Europe.

ABOUT THE AUTHOR

Patricia Maragh (pronounced: Mah-ra-ge) is a 2007 Rhema Bible College graduate. She spent three years in the Pastoral Ministry program. She then continued to serve Rhema Bible Church for five years in various ministries of Helps, before moving on to an Associate pastor position in the advancing of a young church for approximately three years.

On the instruction of the Lord, she took the time to write this book, with the great help of the Holy Spirit. The book is the product of a journey of much struggle to find her place "in Christ" and peace in closer relationship with Him. She is still on that journey developing intimacy and as you read, you're invited to come along, to find your path to the peace, and rest promised by your heavenly Father. May God grant your rest in Christ, as you let Christ be in your life, and as you yoke yourself to His love in relationship with Him. She is a retired business woman and is married to her loving and supportive husband Paul for thirty three years: with three adult children Kristen, Raven, and Jason-Paul.

Her calling and passion is teaching the Gospel of God's faith through grace and helping Christians to grow up in the things of God, as well as helping to fulfill the great commission to evangelize. Seeing people being born again and growing in Christ is her great delight!

CONTACT INFORMATION:
Patricia Maragh
8033 S. Mingo Rd. #119
Tulsa Oklahoma 74133
(918)-893-1714
patmaragh@gmail.com

This book available for purchase from
Amazon.com and Kindle.